ENDURING WOMEN

Enduring Women

TEXT AND PHOTOGRAPHS BY *Diane Koos Gentry*

TEXAS A&M UNIVERSITY PRESS : COLLEGE STATION

Copyright © 1988 by Diane Koos Gentry
Manufactured in the United States of America
All rights reserved
First Edition

The paper used in this book meets the minimum requirements
of the American National Standard for Permanence
of Paper for Printed Library Materials, Z39.48-1984.
Binding materials have been chosen for durability.

Library of Congress Cataloging-in-Publication Data

Gentry, Diane Koos, 1943–
    Enduring women.
    1. Rural women—United States—Biography.
    2. Women—Employment—United States—Case studies.
    3. Life style—Case studies. I. Title.
    ISBN 0-89096-362-2
    ISBN 0-89096-324-X (pbk.)

To Howard Chapnick, with thanks for caring so much

CONTENTS

ACKNOWLEDGMENTS

I was born in the middle of World War II, so I was always fascinated by my mother-in-law's stories of depression-era strangers who stopped at her farmhouse in Oklahoma while moving West. She always gave them a hot meal and a bed for the night. Those may have been the worst of times for a nation, but to me they seem to have been some of the best of times for humanity. Neighborliness was the American way, and people really trusted one another. Working on this book was an eye-opener for me because I quickly realized that my idealistic image of America was not history. As a stranger driving over twenty-three thousand miles across the country, I found 1930s-style trust and hospitality everywhere I went in the 1970s and 1980s.

Good neighbors, heroes, heroines, and ordinary-extraordinary people live around every corner in contemporary America. Above all, I thank the women in this book for their generosity in sharing their lives, homes, and families so freely with this stranger.

There are other special people who have made this book possible. My work flowed smoothly because of my tolerant husband Dick, who rarely complained about staying home in San Antonio working, babysitting our cats, and cooking for himself while I had all the excitement of traveling the country and meeting new people. Howard Chapnick kept this project afloat with his moral and financial support.

Along the way these many years, numerous people have been caught up in the book and given freely of themselves. My thanks to my parents, Richard and Bernice Koos of Kenosha, Wisconsin, for their help in so many ways. I owe a great deal to the supportive staff of Black Star in New York and to G & W Processing Lab, especially Jack Giacopelli, for processing and printing my pictures when I was on the road. Ernest Braun, David Bowers, Chuck Holmes, Maria Gonzales, Charles Busch, William Simpson, M.D., Kelly Chapman, Edison Laselute, and Norman Epping played major roles in helping me find the right women. Alice Slone, Vara and Erling Madsen, Mattie and Marvin Moore, and Hila Heffernan housed me, fed me, and gave me valuable insights. Lois Boyd cheered me on in the latter years. This book would not have materialized without the interest and enthusiasm of all these people. Thank you all for being there when I needed you.

INTRODUCTION

By the mid-1970s when I began working on this book, women were breaking into the male bastions of the work force, in everything from corporations to construction sites. As the media reported on women's changing roles, a stereotype of the successful woman emerged. She was urban, white collar, and often found climbing a corporate ladder in a tailored suit, an American Express card tucked in her briefcase.

It was important to focus on the success of corporate and professional women in the 1970s and report on their breakthroughs. Those were great stories, but they were not the whole story. There was a broad spectrum of equally strong, independent, determined women whose stories were not being told. These women do not fit the corporate image or any other mainstream trend. They are not interested in wealth or power. Devotion to family, home, hard work, a piece of land, and a community are their traditional values and the yardstick by which they measure their success. Many of them have fought poverty and injustice and endured numerous tragedies to achieve self-fulfillment on their own terms. Their struggles and courage are an important addition to an incisive portrait of American women in the 1970s and 1980s.

In an era when so many people equated women's success with a board room, I sought to broaden that narrow view by documenting in words and pictures the lives of a diverse cross section of American women who, by choice or by circumstance, did not mesh with the media stereotype of the modern, successful woman. The ten women I chose to profile in this book were no less hard-driving and no less talented; they just lived and worked in smaller arenas where only their families and communities saw them. Most of the women I spent time with worked very hard for small sums of money. Some were highly educated women who had already achieved careers in urban areas, then dropped out of the mainstream to start radically different lives in the country. Others were clawing their way out of poverty. At a time when family farms were going bankrupt, two of my subjects clung stubbornly to the soil. Other women sought fulfillment and financial stability with backbreaking work such as shrimping and coal mining.

Although six of the ten women I finally selected had once lived in cities, they were all living in small towns, rural areas, or on the fringe of a city by the mid-1970s. In their choice of life-styles, these women are not rejecting the advances made by women who focused on upwardly mobile careers. Instead, they are telling us that success and fulfillment are words with many nuances that are defined in different ways by different women.

I knew that the lives of these independent women would be as interesting as the urban success stories so often featured in the media. In the twenty-two years since I began my career as a photojournalist in Appalachia while getting my bachelor's and master's degrees at Ohio University, I've shunned media events and lugged my cameras and tape recorder down back roads, exploring the life-styles of ordinary people. So often they are extraordinary. There's so much quiet courage out there, such grit. I didn't search for the "average" woman for this book. I looked for women with special qualities: courage, tenacity, love, dedication, and faith.

The first question I'm asked is how I went about finding women all over the country with such different backgrounds and occupations. Unlike Charles Kuralt, I had no budget to drive around the country bumping into great subjects. Instead,

I developed a prototype list of the diverse cross section of women I was looking for, then wrote and called friends and strangers all over the country to help me turn my ideas into real women. It took me more than a year of research to find the ten women I settled on, who ranged in age from twenty-eight to seventy-five and lived in nine different states.

Fortunately, in my work on magazine assignments over the years, I traveled all over the country and met a variety of perceptive people, but I received just as much help from complete strangers. When I wanted to talk to a migrant worker, a caseworker at the Southwest Migrant Association in San Antonio, Maria Gonzales, dropped her work and drove me around South Texas to meet fourteen migrant mothers she admired. Chuck Holmes of Freeman-United Coal Mining Company in southern Illinois interviewed all his women miners on my behalf and called to tell me that Margie Cunha was by far the most interesting. Sometimes I was unusually lucky. During a three-day vacation in Vermont in 1973, I clipped a *Vermont Life* article on Ada and Will Urie and filed it, telling myself I'd like to meet them one day. Three years later, I pulled it out, called Ada, and ended up living with them for three weeks.

When a woman recommended to me sounded ideal, I wrote her a long, personal letter describing my project and the role she would have in it, if she were interested. I asked her to respond with questions in a letter or collect telephone call if she was willing to be interviewed and photographed. When an affirmative reply came in, I followed up with a long telephone call or two so that we could ask each other more questions and make a mutual decision on whether we'd be comfortable working closely together for weeks. In most cases, that was the only contact I had with each woman before I pulled into her driveway.

The only woman I had known before was Mahala Combs of Lotts Creek, Kentucky, whom I had met while doing an Appalachian story several years before the research for this book. I remembered her name and her spirit, but she had no telephone and I didn't know her address. I wanted her in the book so much that I drove fifteen hundred miles to find her, hoping she'd consent. She was up on her roof spreading tar when I drove up, but I could see that she recognized me. When I asked her to be in the book, she said, "I'm poor. I ain't got much, but I'll help you. If you're hungry, you're welcome to sit down and share anything I've got to eat." That warmth and acceptance followed me wherever I went.

When I finally found all the women, I grouped them into logical trips and drove alone across the country to each location, a total of 23,222 miles!

Each chapter of the book tells the story of one woman, based on hours of taped interviews and hundreds of photographs I made in the mid-1970s while living with or near her for up to three weeks. A decade later, I interviewed each woman again to see how her life had changed and whether her hopes and dreams were coming true. The mid-1980s epilogue at the end of each chapter shows how the woman has endured change, problems, and sadness as well as good fortune. Through the woman's words, we learn more about the inner strength that makes her a survivor.

There are few bucolic stories here, though most of them are positive. The women's happiness and satisfaction with their lives have been tempered by hard times, hard labor, and disappointment. At times it seems as if their recurring tragedies are set like hurdles on a track. The more they jump, the more resilient they become.

At 75, *Ada Urie* is still a full-time Vermont farmer, though her farm hasn't turned a profit in years. Her simple life of haying and sugaring with a horse and making renowned doughnuts on her wood stove satisfies her. The simple but tough rural life attracted two women with master's degrees. *Harriet Johnston* was heading a department at Radcliffe College in Boston when in her mid-fifties she met and fell in love with a Wyoming cowboy on a dude ranch. When they realized that they shared the dream of running a ranch in Montana's high country, they married, bought one, and started raising Herefords. Thirty-seven-year-old *Marsha Stone* can't tolerate injustice. She was in the forefront in the civil rights movement and Vietnam protests until constant turmoil threatened her marriage. With the support of her husband and sons, she started a new life as a weaver in a remote area of northern California.

Nora Warren left the financial security of her job as a book-keeper in San Antonio to follow her husband's dream of building a boat and shrimping the Texas coast. Fighting serious illness, she remained a shrimper for over a decade, deriving an almost spiritual satisfaction from the sea. *Mahala Combs* had known grinding poverty all her life in a remote hollow in Kentucky's Appalachia, but it never dampened her spirit. Though she was supporting a husband and several children on $216 a month, she saved to buy $50 worth of scrap lumber so that she could build her kids a "dream" house. Life-long migrant worker *Teresa Camarillo*, mother of eleven, had just stopped migrating and found her first full-time job when I met her. Teresa's story is one of a family pulling together to rise from poverty to the middle class, and helping their neighbors along the way. *Gladys Milton* was once poor, too, but she became a midwife and a licensed practical nurse, putting her son through medical school by delivering babies and cleaning houses. When her rural Florida community needed a safer way to handle the growing number of midwife deliveries, Gladys built her own midwifery clinic, giving both blacks and whites a personal, low-cost alternative to hospital births.

Dorothy Smith was one of a handful of Zuni Indian college graduates and the only Zuni teaching on the reservation. In a decade when drugs and alcohol were destroying many families there, Dorothy tried to save the children. *Nancy Smidle* fought to save the nation's family farms by lobbying on Capitol Hill while her own large Wisconsin dairy farm was deeply in debt. Finally, there is *Margie Cunha Irvin*. Few have faced a tougher struggle than this divorced mother of two small children who was abandoned by alcoholic parents and then by a husband. After five long years of looking for a decent job, she became one of the first woman coal miners in southern Illinois. Her job helped her regain self-confidence, and her life takes a turn for the better, with an interesting twist.

Although the ten women I chose have very different geographical locations, incomes, educations, and outlooks, they have a great deal in common. As many American women strive toward white-collar work, most of the women profiled here have moved in the opposite direction. With few exceptions, they enjoy hard, physical labor and working with their hands—digging in the soil, shoveling coal or gently bringing a baby into the world. They say they find hard work both refreshing and satisfying, especially when they work in the environment they love. Each woman possesses one of two kinds of modern pioneer spirit. Women like Margie, the coal miner, and Harriet, the professor-turned-rancher, are individualists who have no fear of entering new or unconventional occupations for women. Others, like Vermont farmer Ada Urie, cling stubbornly to the old-fashioned traditions they value in a changing world.

Most significantly, I found that each of these very different women has chosen a similar set of values to live by. Just what are these values? Above all, they have a strong bond to their family, and they work very hard in the best way they know how to provide for them. "We were poor, but we had each other," Texas shrimper Nora Warren says many times. That theme is repeated often, by others. Their devotion to family members doesn't end with their immediate family, but extends to several generations. Sociologists tell us the extended family is dead in a mobile society, but this isn't true with my women. For all but three of them, three generations of family live within a ten-minute drive. When children grow up, marry, and leave home, they tend to settle close to their parents. Two of the three women without extended families simply had no living relatives to form one.

These are women with roots—roots that connect them to family, to home, to a piece of land, and to a community. In an era when such roots aren't very fashionable, when homes or even families are often temporary if they exist at all, these women further show their independence.

Nearly all the women I worked with hold strong religious beliefs that have helped them through the crises and struggles in their lives. Most of them speak openly of God and their personal relationship with him, but for the most part they have rejected formal, organized religion. Only two of the women attend church services regularly. Their beliefs, like their wills, are strong and shaped in individual ways.

The values these women live by are solid and make them strong. The ten women often confront insecurity, problems, and tragedy, but they fight back. They are society's survivors. These women will endure.

It will be obvious in this writing that I admire these women. They are remarkable. Realizing my bias, I have striven to see them three-dimensionally, as real human beings capable of warmth, caring, and excellence but also of faults, mistakes, and failures.

Since 1965, when I began working professionally as a writer and photographer, I've been grappling with different techniques to document people's life-styles incisively. During this research, it all jelled. The formula that works for me is spending a great deal of time with a person or family, collecting field notes and lengthy taped interviews on a daily basis, and photographing day-to-day activities constantly until cameras are so routine that people ignore them after a while. I transcribe tapes every night on location so that I knew what I had, what I needed, and could have questions answered on the spot.

I've let each woman tell her story in her own words as much as possible, arranging her taped commentary into a logical form and editing lightly, if at all.

I found photographs far more effective than words in establishing each woman's environment—her land, her home, her workplace. I made hundreds of photographs of each woman, with cameras dangling around my neck most of the time. That way I could catch fleeting expressions such as Mahala's weary-eyed exhaustion in building a house by herself or Gladys's pride in slapping a newborn baby to life. Cameras are wonderful for capturing moods and real emotions such as Nora's spiritual feeling toward shrimping.

At night, I spent many hours alone looking at quotes and thinking about pictures. I was fortunate to have my friend Howard Chapnick, president of Black Star photographic agency in New York, working closely with me. After producing the first few chapters on my own, I'd send Howard boxes of raw film to process for me while I was on the road, with long accompanying letters about the women. He'd mail contact prints to me immediately, then talk to me about each shooting. His critiques and enthusiasm, based on forty years of blending pictures and words together, were invaluable to me.

I lived with or beside each family in the book for seven to twenty-one days. Every morning, sometimes as early as 4 A.M., I rolled out of bed to accompany each woman—to listen, observe, photograph, tape, or work beside her. Many times, to my great delight, I left my role as observer to provide an extra pair of hands. I stomped hay in an ancient wagon in Vermont with Ada and Will Urie, crewed on Nora Warren's shrimp boat, and dug postholes and strung barbed wire on Harriet's Montana ranch. I was never really a detached observer, preferring instead to be their friend, getting dirty and sweaty with them. I laughed when they laughed and sometimes cried when they cried, not because it was expected of me, but because I had gotten that close.

When I planned this work, I never intended to live with any of the women. I drove because I firmly believe that journalists can't feel the pulse of America by flying into international airports and commuting to the countryside from airport hotels. Besides, watching the changing landscape and listening to local accents along the way put me in a proper frame of mind for each visit. I enjoy long-distance driving, and fortunately I owned an ideal vehicle for the trips—a van camper equipped with a refrigerator, bed, portable toilet, and plenty of storage space for my equipment. My idea was to park on each woman's property and eat and sleep in my van. That way I'd save a great deal of money and be close enough to each woman to see how she lived without getting in her way. But when I arrived, most families insisted I stay with them and had already prepared a bedroom in their home for me. In Ada Urie's farmhouse, my bedroom was directly above her kitchen. Each morning I awoke to the aroma of homemade bread baking. In Montana, the Johnstons set me up with both a bedroom and an office. In return, I'm afraid I often awakened them at night laughing at the yarns Charlie spun for me on tapes I was transcribing.

I'm sure there are places in the United States where fright-ened women peer out of triple-locked doors, never meeting their neighbors, let alone strangers, but that's not the America I experienced. These women took me into their homes and into their lives, refusing payment beyond an occasional dinner out. That still amazes me. I'm always moved when I think back on the instant rapport I had at every home, the caring and enthusiasm each woman showed toward my project. Working with these ten women was the most valuable learning experience I've ever had. It forever changed the way I work and taught me more about America than I had learned in thirty years of living.

As a woman traveling alone for months at a time, I had to be cautious, but I was never fearful. Most of the time I felt like an excited explorer discovering America, even though my exploration wasn't on foot or in a canoe, but in a van with a porta-potty, armed with an arsenal of AAA maps. The surge of independence I felt warded away my loneliness. Survival and success were entirely up to me.

There were days I could have done without, such as crossing the Mojave desert in my van when it had more than 100,000 miles on it. Or being harassed by eight men in a van on a lonely highway in Wyoming where there was plenty of sagebrush, but few cars and no gas stations, stores, or towns. The men would drive alongside me to annoy me. I knew I couldn't outrun them in my old van, so I drove so slowly that they eventually grew bored enough to pass me. When they were out of sight ahead of me, I ducked into an old construction area and hid. My gamble worked. I never saw them again.

Those incidents were rare, compared with the warmth I found in CB radio conversations with other long-distance drivers, especially truckers. "Commodore" from New Hampshire in his red, white, and green spaghetti truck was the best of them. He picked me up on the CB in Vermont and guided me through radar traps, construction zones, and detours all the way to Ohio, where we parted to follow different interstates.

Another trucker called me on the CB to ask how tall I was. I'm careful about my CB communications, and that question seemed too intimate for conversation on an interstate. I snarled back, "5'1". Why do you want to know?" "I thought so," he laughed. "I just passed you. You have a long, black greasy stripe down the top of your otherwise clean van. I figured you couldn't reach it."

Cross-country drivers traveling alone must be prepared for anything. When my entire electrical system in the van shut down during a blinding thunderstorm in Texas, I pulled into a country gas station seeking help. I had neither headlights nor windshield wipers that worked. The man in charge said he had no idea how to fix it, so I asked him if I could borrow his garage. I lay down on the floorboard with my legs hanging out the door, checked all the connections on the wires under the dashboard, reconnected something, and had everything operating within ten minutes. It was one of my finer moments. I grinned widely and waved as I pulled out of his garage.

No one could spend years on a project like this without being fundamentally changed. These women made me immensely proud of America and Americans. I will be forever grateful to them for putting up with my cameras and unrelenting questions and for letting me into their lives. The good-byes were long and sad, and the hugs were genuine. I never left a woman without tears in my eyes.

ENDURING WOMEN

Ada Urie

"Dadcy, aren't his peas lovely?" asks Ada Urie, seventy-five, a farmer admiring another farmer's handiwork. Her voice is melodic, a precise but lilting northern Vermont Yankee accent. A curious woman, Ada seems fascinated by the smallest things. Her Husband Will, eighty-five, pokes his head up for a quick peek as he inches his brown 1971 Plymouth up and down miles of hilly dirt and gravel roads from the East Craftsbury United Presbyterian Church to Sunnyside, their farm near the village of Glover, Vermont, population 850. He drives slowly so that Ada can crane her neck out the window and continue her garden report. "It makes me hungry just looking at all that beautiful lettuce," she exclaims. "Walter Young is old and retired, so he can tend his garden all day. He's not farming anymore. . . ."

For the Uries, Sunday is a day reserved for God, and their only day of rest from full-time farming. It's a day when they can indulge in something as frivolous as a tour of the neigh-

Ada Urie in the doorway of her home.

bors' gardens without feeling guilty. Even if their hay were drying golden in the field and storm clouds rolled in, they wouldn't work on Sunday. One recent Sunday, however, when Will was dressed in his best suit and tie, a neighbor pounded on the door shouting, "Will, your heifers are out!" With reflexes that belied his eighty-five years, lanky Will sprinted down the road in his dark blue suit, tie blowing in the wind. Ada, in a pretty flowered dress, was at his heels. As Will chased Goldy and Sylvia, their frisky cows, Ada anticipated their direction, waiting to grab them as they charged past. Together they corraled the animals, put them back in the pasture, and mended the fence. Playful heifers don't respect Sundays, and two lifelong farmers don't ponder too much over age, their best clothes, or Sundays when their Holsteins are escaping down the road. Ada and Will just brushed themselves off, laughed a bit, and strolled back to the house.

The Northeast Kingdom of Vermont, just south of the Canadian border, is rugged mountain land legendary for chiseling out independent, self-reliant Yankee farmers. Like the granite outcroppings in their pastures, they are stubborn and immovable, planting and harvesting crops in thin, rocky soil that would make an Illinois farmer cringe. Both Ada and Will grew up on farms near Sunnyside. "I've been here all my life and I've really never had any desire to live anywhere else," Ada says. "Oh, I have loved all our yearly anniversary trips, camping, canoeing, and climbing mountains in New England and Canada, but it is always good to come home where I know everyone and everyone knows me. I'm proud that all five of our children decided to stay in Vermont. I worry about our two grandchildren who moved out West to work and raise their families. They must be awfully homesick. I'm glad they come back to visit and bring their babies to see me. I'm afraid I wouldn't go to Texas to see them."

The Urie farming tradition started in the Glover area in 1832 when Will's great-grandfather bought a farm about five miles from Sunnyside. "Most of the Uries were weavers of paisley shawls in Scotland," Will says. "My great-grandfather must have been in hard shape to leave his home and sail for sixteen weeks on that old ocean to get to the United States. His farm is still in our family, though it's a modern, mechanized dairy farm now. Our daughter Marion and her husband Albert run it. Two of our children, Marion and Alan, decided to be farmers."

"They used to laugh at me in school because I said I wanted to farm for a living," Ada says. "They thought it was a crazy occupation for a girl. I've always loved working outside with my hands. There's no honest work you can do with your hands that's degrading as long as you do the best you can. I still get excited every time I see a plowed field. As a farmer, I can look out the window on a sunny day and know I have the freedom to do anything I want."

Fifteen years ago when their son Alan married and left Cozy Bend, the 110-acre diversified farm Ada and Will had worked for forty years, they lost their best hand. At age seventy, Will could have easily justified retiring and moving to town. "Retirement?" Ada repeats the word with obvious distaste, as if it were a swear word she shouldn't be using. "We haven't even thought about that yet! Where would we go? To the old people's apartments in the village? We don't belong there. What would we do? I wouldn't be happy unless I had my hands in the soil. Will would probably be terribly homesick without his cows. When Alan left, the big farm was too much work for the two of us. We couldn't plow all those fields, milk twenty-three cows, and tap eleven hundred maples as we always had, so we sold the farm and drove our six favorite cows down the

Ada Urie and husband Will make hay with the help of their big Percheron Jack and some neighbor children. "It's nice to be alive any day on the farm working together outside, close to nature," Ada says.

road to Sunnyside, this little thirty-acre farm which is just perfect for two old people. Will hated giving up his dandy team, but Jack, our big white Percheron, is a pretty good hand for plowing, haying, and sugaring on Sunnyside. We'll stay right here on this little farm and keep busy like we've always done. Farming makes us happy. We enjoy our life."

Fortunately, Ada and Will had the foresight to buy Sunnyside in 1945, when they realized they needed more pasture for their growing herds of cattle and sheep. The purchase price for the thirty-acre farm, with its three-bedroom farmhouse and large barn, was only eight hundred dollars. "We thought that was quite a buy," Ada says grinning. "It was very run down. The house had stood idle for 39 years and was falling down. I wondered sometimes if I could make it livable, but we fixed the roof and repaired it little by little. We think it is about 150 years old. There's hand-hewn timber in both the barn and the house. Some of the timbers are thirty-two feet long and eight inches square, solid without a splice. We built on, put in new underpinnings, new plaster, and completely fixed the barn. After that, the old place looked a lot better. We planted a thousand pine trees when we bought the property. Waiting for trees to grow is a slow way of getting rich, but everything helps. We sold enough cottage lots off the property to quadruple our purchase price, so we did well. Best of all, the farm was there for us when we needed it."

Sunnyside sits on a quiet gravel road near Shadow Lake and in front of Daniel's Pond, with Uncle Jimmy's Mountain

Ada Urie rocks her great-grandson in her living room.

as a backdrop. Thanks to Ada, the white two-story frame home is beautiful now, surrounded by beds of iris, lilies, roses, columbine, sweet william, daisies, tulips, and hyacinth. Inside it looks like the traditional grandma's house of so many warm childhood memories—neat with white tie-back curtains, healthy plants and knickknacks on tables and windowsills. There's a comfortable rocking chair. Pictures of children, grandchildren, and great-grandchildren are everywhere. Pure New England architectural style, the home proudly faces the road, but attached behind are a storage room and then the barn. Even 150 years ago, Yankees shunned walking to the barn through waist-deep snowdrifts to milk their cows those many months of winter. On the Urie farm one can milk cows, gather eggs, and chop kindling wood without ever going outside. The connected barn, with its massive hand-hewn rafters and unpainted planks, has gracefully weathered a century and a half of Northeast Kingdom blizzards, displaying a rainbow of earth colors, from burnt umber to rusty tan to weather-beaten gray.

Ada and Will have the same stalwart New England presence that their home and barn do, but not the stern stare of Grant Wood's *American Gothic* farm couple. They laugh too much for that. Will still has the impish twinkle in his eyes that Ada says he had in his twenties, when he rode on his "snappy" Morgan horse, Dick, turning everyone's head. As he walks into his woods with an ax slung over his shoulder and wearing his favorite baggy patched pants and wide red suspenders, Will

Will and Ada Urie march from their house and barn through the fields on their way to the woods to cut firewood by hand.

looks like the indomitable old man of the mountains. Ada, with her ever-present sweet smile, appears soft in comparison. "But my Ada, she's rugged," Will says proudly. "She does just about everything here but draw manure." Whether Ada is haying, digging in her gardens, or collecting eggs from her chickens, she always wears nylon hose, a flowered polyester dress, and an apron. She feels uncomfortable in the pants and blue jeans most farm women wear, but over her neatly braided brown waist-length hair, which she pulls back tightly in an orderly ring, she often wears a dusty Blue Seal Feeds cap at a jaunty angle, as if to banish the image of formality.

Ada and Will work constantly on the farm, using every acre. "We're a good team," Ada says. "We've always gotten along. Sometimes Will is the boss and sometimes I am. The secret of a good marriage is working together, playing together, talking things over, and not getting angry over everything. Will and I have always been too busy working to fight."

Ada and Will's activities follow the seasons. In the winter Ada and Will sell Christmas trees. When spring breaks through the ice and the sap runs, they tap four hundred maples on the farm with Jack, the horse, their only "hired hand." Will and Jack gather while Ada boils at the sugarhouse. In the summer, the three of them hay to keep all the farm animals alive through the winter. Ada raises two big vegetable gardens,

Ada behind her booth at the big fair at Craftsbury Common, Vermont, where she sells her baked goods with daughter Marion. She spends weeks in preparation for the fair, which she loves. In 1976, she cleared $115 profit, her "mad money."

has a weekly egg route, and sells bread and other baked goods to at least twenty regular customers. Sometimes she caters whole dinners for summer people, who pick up her renowned homemade chicken pies, fresh garden vegetables, and fruit pies. Apple trees abound on the farm, producing five different kinds of apples. Gooseberries, raspberries, plums, and currants grow on the farm for Ada to preserve or make into jams, jellies, cobblers, or pies. At Sunnyside, no berry ever rots on the vine and no apples spoil. If their apple crop is too big for their own use, Ada and Will sell the surplus door to door. Ada is so thrifty that she saves the weeds from her garden to boil for her chickens and feeds them peels from fruits and vegetables, too. Beyond the chickens and the horse, Will always has a cow or two to milk and several to raise for beef.

"Small farmers in Vermont have to have a lot of sidelines," Will explains. "This land is plentiful if you prepare it and use it wisely. Everything is there waiting, just calling us to come get it. You have to be there to pluck everything when it is ready."

Unfortunately, Sunnyside ceased being a profitable venture years ago. With the inflated cost of taxes, insurance, feed, and fuel oil, the tiny farm barely breaks even. Its rewards are more subtle than money. "I guess you could say this farm keeps us young," Ada says. "We are so busy that we never feel bored like so many old people in town seem to. There's always something to do. Neighbor children come to see us nearly every day. They love to ride on Jack and follow us around. You don't grow

Ada picks gooseberries on the farm. The Uries' little farm is full of berries and apples, and they let nothing go to waste.

old as fast with children laughing around you. Working together has strengthened our marriage and kept us healthy. It doesn't seem as though we're ever sick. Will hasn't seen a doctor in years. The best therapy I know for tension is raising a garden. It's just nice to be alive any day on a farm in the changing seasons with the haying and gardens in summer, beautiful snowfalls of winter, and in the spring sugaring, just working together outside close to nature."

"But I'm afraid we're slippin'," says Will with a frown, interrupting Ada's dreamy euphoria. "If I knew how to run this farm at a profit, I would. If we didn't have the savings from the big farm, we'd be in a bad fix. We have to be thrifty. We used to sell our milk until three years ago, when someone decided it wasn't worth picking up milk from our six cows without a hauling fee. So now I just milk Rachel. She gives plenty of milk and cream for our use. She's an ornery one, though. She likes to whip her tail across my face when I'm milking her, especially after she wets on it. I'm going to teach her she can't maul me with that tail. I'm going to sit on it when I'm milking her whether she likes it or not. That'll fix her.

"I always sold my own butchered beef and lamb to people until the state closed me down because I didn't have a slaughterhouse. That hurt our income. It seems like everything is stacked against the little man. Sometimes I wonder who is running my farm. A few more restrictions and I won't have to go outside a'tall."

"I think a lot of people suffer from money problems," Ada

A neighbor boy breaks up Will.

adds. "So many couples divorce. I don't believe in that. I think it's terrible. One of our advantages is that we've never had enough money to squabble over. We've always had to be saving with our money, and I think it is a good thing. People spend money foolishly and unwisely. They want the finest of everything, like cars to improve their social standing. I say if a car runs, it's good enough for me. We've had two or three new cars, but we keep them ten years. We never believed in getting in debt. I appreciate the simple things in life most, like growing pretty flowers, making a good loaf of bread, and watching the garden grow. You don't need much money for that."

In no way are Ada and Will impoverished. They live frugally, but well, on their savings and a combined Social Security check of $240 a month. Their simple life suits them, though Will would much rather be selling his milk and meat than collecting Social Security. "I don't believe in the government handing out money," he says. "Welfare ruins people. They lose their independence and ambition. A man needs to work for a living. I don't even like this Social Security check, though we're living on it. It's wrong for young people in their productive years to work and slave to pay into Social Security to support old duffers like me. We didn't make that much money farming and we're not entitled to $240 a month. We don't need it. I planned for our future without any help from the federal government. Farmers fail every day around here because they are so in debt to machinery. I'd quit, too, if I were them. It scares me to death to even walk around all that modern farm equipment. If one bolt falls out, it costs you a thousand dollars."

The most expensive piece of equipment at Sunnyside is

Jack and Will.

Jack. Inflation boosted his purchase price to $250. Jim, his more able predecessor, cost only $125, a price Will finds just about right for a hard-working draft horse. "I bought all my farm equipment secondhand," Will says. "I paid $25 for the mower, $15 for the wagon, $12 for the plow, $4 for the cultivator, $5 for Jack's harnesses, and $4 for the hay rake. Everything we've got wouldn't even buy a tire for Albert's tractor. One of the reasons we don't want any help around here is that you have to pay a good man $20 a day plus room and board. There ain't nothing on this farm worth $20."

On a sunny day in June on Sunnyside, the brown 1971 Plymouth protruding from a stall next to the barn is the only evidence of the twentieth century. As the hay sways in the breeze below Uncle Jimmy's Mountain, Will's straw hat looms up occasionally, and as it comes closer, the gentle sound of the old McCormick mower rises above the jingle of Jack's harnesses as he stomps his massive, hairy feet. The mower's sharp blade levels the grass in four-foot swaths. Six times around the field. That's about enough. Jack gets tired, not Will. "I like to stop and breathe him often," Will explains. "I really think he appreciates being an old people's horse so he can rest a lot. I don't push him. I wouldn't like him to push me. I can go in the house and get something right in the middle of mowing or raking and he stands right there in the field exactly where I left him. He never runs away with me. Jack and I understand each other. He does things for me that he wouldn't do for anybody else."

Will smacks his lips to start Jack. His firm "Whoa!" stops him flat without reins, and only occasionally does Will have to discipline Jack with a verbal scolding. Jack senses Will's anger by the tone of his voice and greatly resents being corrected. He gives Will an unfeeling stare, lays his ears back, then sneers and snaps his lower lip.

"I'm afraid Will gets too used to talking to Jack, especially in the summer," says Ada. "Just the other day he was taking me out on my egg route and parked on a lady's steep driveway. He jumped out of the car without realizing he had put it in reverse instead of park. As it rolled down the driveway,

he yelled, 'Whoa!' Thank goodness I was still in the front seat and shifted it before it rolled out into the street and hit someone." Will slumps into a corner of the couch after Ada tells her story, obviously embarrassed.

"I hate machines," he finally says. "I can't even get the lawnmower to run. Ada cuts all our grass." It is comical to watch Will tackle the lawnmower. Ada can start it with one pull, but it resists all Will's tugs. "You icy-hearted thing," Will mumbles under his breath. He jabs the spark plugs with the prongs of his pitchfork. As the machine dies, it invariably shocks him. He doesn't do much better with the car. It belches and coughs whenever he tries to start it, then jerks two or three times as it chugs out the gravel driveway. The radio lies silent on a kitchen shelf. They rarely watch television because the electric fences snap so much interference on the screen that Will has to disconnect them, hoping the cows won't notice and take the opportunity to escape. He takes this chance for an hour every time his favorite program, "The Waltons," comes on.

"Will is so humorous in his own way," Ada says laughing. By comparison, she is shy and more serious than Will, lacking his quick wit and knack for finding himself in amusing situations. He obviously entertains and delights her with his antics. She frequently lets loose with a happy, soprano laugh that sounds something like a cardinal singing at dawn.

Will still cuts and splits eight cords of wood a year, but there isn't a chain saw on the place. "Chain saws are no better than lawnmowers," he says. "They have motors that won't start for me. They are so noisy that they give me a headache and they wear out. My ax and my bow saw never wear out and neither co I. I cut two cords of wood a year for Ada's cookstove and six cords for the sugarhouse. I like to clean up the woods, sawing up dead trees and limbs that have fallen. I don't cut down live trees. That's our future. I planted an acre of pine trees and sold a hundred of them as Christmas trees last year. We bunched up pine boughs into fifty-pound bundles to sell to people who make wreaths and roping. We made an extra seventy dollars on that."

Most neighbors are in awe of Ada and Will and envy their simple life. Some think they are foolish for working so hard at their ages. Nobody fails to find them remarkable. Children are enchanted by "Aunt Ada and Uncle Will's" farm. For the most part, their frequent visitors are local farm kids who find their own family farms "just plain boring." At home they are warned that tractors can run them down and hay balers chew up feet and legs. Their own modern milking parlors with stainless-steel milking machines and holding tanks seem to them as sterile as a dentist's office. Children time their visits to Will's milking schedule. He always invites them to sit on his milking stool (a pail with a board on top of it) in the dark old barn and "pull on Rachel's tits." When they finish, Ada is waiting for them with a plate of homemade cookies.

In haying season, when Jack is hitched up, Will and Ada rarely refuse children a ride on his broad back. Jack is gentle and appreciative as the children feed him hay and hug his neck. Station wagons line up in the driveway and in front of the farm when Jack clomps home with a load of hay. Farm wives gossip as they stand around waiting for their children to take fifteen or twenty flying leaps from the ancient hayloft into a

Neighborhood children from modern farms cannot resist the attraction of Will and Ada haying with Jack in the summertime.

six- or eight-foot-deep mound of freshly pitched hay. "This is the only farm that I know of in northern Vermont which still has loose hay," says one mother. "My kids are fortunate to have the Uries to show them what farming was like in their great-grandparents' time. I think every farm community ought to have an Aunt Ada and Uncle Will."

Hay grows high at Sunnyside because of Will's "top dressin'" of manure in late fall and spring. After mowing just

enough hay to yield two wagonloads, Will attaches the eight-foot-wide Yankee rake to Jack. It's a mean-looking implement with sharp, sickle-like teeth at the rear and two wooden spoked wheels in front that look as if they were borrowed from a covered wagon in a John Wayne movie. Will sits up high in an iron seat, but after sixty or seventy years of bruising his tailbone over woodchuck holes, he recently added a flowered pillow for comfort as a concession to age. He bumps along swatting voracious black flies that bite constantly, leaving his cheeks blood-smeared. He rakes the hay into long windrows across the field so they can pitch it easily when it dries out. Ada follows closely behind, picking up the scatterings with an awkward-looking bull rake, six feet wide with wooden teeth. About half of its teeth are broken off. It's hard to find replacement teeth for bull rakes these days.

When it comes time to pitch hay, Ada is out in the field in her polyester dress and hose, hoisting forkfuls of hay nearly as big as she is. She systematically drops each bunch in its appropriate place in the old wooden horse-drawn wagon Will souped up with automobile tires. Fifteen bunches make a layer and four layers can be loaded on if the hay is stomped down. Ada is the official hay stomper. "I can't stomp hay like I used to," she complains. "Once it seemed as though I never got tired, but this year I feel a little older, like I can't talk myself into doing quite as many things after dinner. I got a pain in my chest after sugaring this year that wouldn't go away. The doctor said it was angina, but I know it was just a muscle strain from do-

Ada pitches hay near her home.

ing Jack's work. There were fifty-two inches of snow on the ground. We had to go out in snowshoes and dig out the sugarhouse, then take the buckets on a hand sled. By noon you'd fall in, so you have to go very early in the morning when it's so cold the snow has a good crust. We usually gather with the horse by pouring pails of sap into a big gathering tub on the sled, but Jack couldn't get through that depth of snow. He just smiled back at us from the barn while I carried the pails of sap by hand through waist-deep snow to the sugarhouse. In time the pain went away and never came back."

Will watches Ada zoom around the field with forkfuls of hay. "Wife has angina, they say," he says in a pseudoserious tone, then they both burst into laughter. "That Ada, she's something," he says with respect and love. Sickness has never been in the script at the Urie farm. There's too much work to be done. Last year the two of them loaded twenty-seven tons of hay into the barn from the ten acres they mow. "When we finish there will be hay pitched in every corner of the barn to the window at the peak," Ada says. "We'll just leave enough room for the barn swallows' nests and so the angels can fly through."

If Ada sometimes feels tired, there's a very good reason. Nearly every morning she awakens at 5:30 A.M. to start baking bread, a routine she began more than twenty years ago when neighbors and summer people urged her to start selling them her homemade specialties. By 6 A.M. smoke curls out of the chimney as Ada fires up her black iron Archer wood range made in 1893. Will is still asleep, but every evening before Ada bakes he always splits wood to stove length and has it waiting for her in the wood box. Ada prefers the huge range with four

After haying all day, Ada falls asleep on her living-room couch, her cat beside her. On the wall is a painting of their farm, Sunnyside.

burners and two big ovens to her modern gas stove across the kitchen. "I suppose I should learn to be a modern cook, but I don't change too easily," she says. "I'd rather get a meal and fry doughnuts on a wood stove. I can put four or five kettles on it at once and not have to watch them every minute like I do with gas. I go to the homemakers' extension service out of curiosity because I love to cook. All I get are shortcuts preached to me there. Save time! Save time! My time's my own. If I want to spend all of it fooling around in my kitchen, that's my privilege!"

About 7 A.M., when Will stumbles sleepily through the kitchen on the way to milk Rachel, Ada has kneaded about six loaves' worth of bread dough, separated it into loaves, and covered it to rise. Hands white with flour, she rolls out enough doughnut dough for two or three dozen raised or sour-milk doughnuts. Lard bubbles on the wood stove on its way to 400 degrees in a cast-iron kettle that belonged to her mother. Many mornings she also bakes several different kinds of cookies or her famous apple, lemon, gooseberry, rhubarb, or mincemeat pies. These days, Ada's baking is the cash crop on the farm. She has never needed a sales pitch. Her reputation as a cook spread over northern Vermont decades ago. *Yankee* magazine has even featured her in a couple of articles.

On Fridays, Ada has a regular bread and egg route with twenty customers. Each week they buy thirty dozen of her extra large brown eggs, leaving her plenty for baking. Every night the telephone rings as the summer people on Shadow Lake place additional orders. Sometimes Ada bakes all day, running out to help Will with the haying, her timer tucked in her apron pocket. "When the timer rings, I slip back into the house for a minute to take the bread out of the oven. I haven't burned a loaf yet."

Ada is often out in the fields when customers come to pick up their orders, but she has arranged all the baked goods on the kitchen table, wrapped them, and labeled them with the customer's name. Beside them is her cashbox full of bills and change. "My kitchen door is always open," Ada says. "People just walk in and pick up their items, then make their own change. I never worry about the money. My customers are all honest. They're all good people. I don't keep very good books, but I'm sure I make a profit over expenses. I don't figure very much for my time by charging eighty-five cents for a loaf of bread, but the way I look at it, baking keeps me out of mischief."

By 7:30 or 8 A.M., when wonderful aromas waft over the kitchen, Will has finished milking Rachel and separating the milk from the cream. He comes to the table famished. Ada has his daily oatmeal waiting for him with plenty of cream and their own maple syrup. They always have orange juice, a bowl of fresh fruit, and hot blueberry muffins or doughnuts as well. Sometimes this feast is topped off with bacon and eggs. "Around here we believe in a good breakfast before a morning of hard work," Ada explains. Unfortunately, she is a diabetic who must savor her baked delicacies in small bites because dinner (at noon) is twice as heavy as breakfast. Ada always fixes a hot meat dish and potatoes while the wood range is fired up. While that's cooking, she picks fresh vegetables and salad greens from the garden. Often she throws in some young dandelion greens from the yard, a family favorite. Ada never serves dinner without dessert, usually a homemade pie fresh from the oven. In the summer, all Ada's cooking is carefully orchestrated between pitching and stomping hay whenever Will needs her.

"I'm glad women got the vote, but I don't see what all this fuss about women's lib is about," Ada said during one serious dinner conversation. "I feel liberated. Sometimes you have to

Will samples one of Ada's famous doughnuts hot off her Archer wood stove.

make choices that show consideration for other people. I'd like to take a week off and work in my gardens, but then who would get the meals?"

Ada's two large vegetable gardens are a thing of beauty, with perfectly straight rows and lush green plants. The Uries blend their own fertilizer, a mixture of chicken, cow, and horse manure; ashes from the wood stove; crushed leaves; and a bit of lime. "A garden is like a little animal," says Ada. "It needs

Ada's floury hands making doughnuts are very reminiscent of a potter's hands molding clay.

a lot of attention as it grows up." Ada grows four kinds of beans, three kinds of peas, two kinds of carrots, several types of lettuce, tomatoes, cucumbers, beets, turnips, potatoes, squash, three kinds of corn, and pumpkins, among other things. She plants on Memorial Day and usually harvests the last of it on Halloween. Ada rarely sells anything from her garden. What she doesn't can for their own use or eat fresh, she gives away.

Will doesn't believe in splurging on a freezer, so Ada cans frequently, making hundreds of trips down to the root cellar under the house.

"My farming at Sunnyside isn't very different than growing up on my family's small farm above Shadow Lake," Ada says. "That's where I learned how to make a garden, milk a cow, and hay with horses. My two sisters and I worked hard on the farm, but we thought nothing of it. That's where my love of farming began. It's sad to see our farm all grown up now. There's nothing there but woods. Nothing. Just memories.

"I was born in a lumber camp on top of Black Tom Mountain, where my father had hired a gang of men to cut wood for the winter. He was a lumberman at first, a farmer later. I was born on a cold winter's night—Vermont mountain cold—on January 31, 1901. The hired man hitched up one of Dad's nice white horses and drove six miles through the snow to tell the doctor. On the way back he picked up my grandmother at their farm to be nurse. The doctor came on his sleigh just in time. He only charged $3.50 to deliver me.

"My grandfather trapped and was a cooper—he made buckets—in addition to running his little four-cow farm. He got sick shortly after I was born, so Dad quit lumbering to take over the farm. I'm glad, because I had a lovely childhood there. I'm sure we were poor, because we had little money to spend, but we never felt poor. We had everything we could possibly eat on the farm, and mother was a wonderful cook.

"Our one big splurge as a family was going to the Barton Fair. It was a big country fair, a real occasion no farm child wanted to miss with show cattle, a midway, and a merry-go-round I remember one year when my sisters and I pulled the kale out of the beans and Dad gave us each fifty cents for the fair. It was a fortune to us. We cleaned the surrey from top to bottom and polished up the harness. We all wore our very best clothes. I can still see my white dress with all the pleats in it lying on the bed waiting for me to put on. I had starched white petticoats under it and wore shoes that pinched my feet. Of course my white dress got dirty at the fair, but so did everybody else's. Mother made the most wonderful lunch. She was one of the best cooks around Glover. After we pulled up in that shiny surrey with our two fine horses and all that home-baked food, relatives just flocked around us waiting to eat.

"Mother and Dad didn't have too much formal education, so they were determined that we would all graduate from high school. The first nine grades were easy because Center School was only a mile away. We walked, picking up friends all along the way. In the winter when it was real bad, Dad would take us in a sleigh. That little school had some great entertainment, especially on Memorial Day. We always had a Civil War veteran come in to tell us what a hard time he had in the war. It gave us shivers and made us proud. We were very impressed.

"High school at Barton Academy was five miles away. In those days, with the road conditions and weather we had, attending high school was difficult. You really had to want an education. We drove a horse to school until November, then we stayed with our cousins through the rest of the winter. Six of us girls shared the top floor of a house for a while. Mom

Ada loves to bake and is up at dawn to make cookies.

and Dad were so thoughtful. Every Friday night they'd drive the team in to bring us home for the weekend. Saturday we'd do all our washing on a scrub board. Sunday night they'd drive us back in a sleigh full of enough of my mother's home-cooked specialties to last until Wednesday. Father must have walked up two flights of stairs to our apartment ten times twice a week with his arms full of wood for our cooking and heating stoves. He was determined that we'd never get cold or starve. On Wednesday, when they decided that our food had run out, they'd come in again with the sleigh filled with a new supply to last until Friday when they picked us up to go back to the farm.

"I wasn't very socially inclined in high school, in fact I was just a plain old wallflower. I went to parties and dances because I thought I should, but I hated it so. All I'd do was sit in the corner all alone. I didn't have any dates and I didn't have much fun. I don't know what was wrong with me. Must have been something. I guess I was very shy in crowds. I still am. I concentrated on studying. The year before I graduated I was so impressed by the valedictorian of the class that I made up my mind that I would be one. It was hard work, but I made it. Math was my specialty."

"I didn't care much for school," Will says. "I went through the eighth grade in a one-room school. It was only the last two years that made me realize what I was there for. They made up for the other six I had wasted. When I was sixteen, I started working full-time on my father's farm, then hired out to help other farmers. I worked for my uncle James Young milking eleven cows a day and tapping fifteen hundred sugar maples in the

spring for $16 a month. Then it went up to $1 a day. You could get a whole meal of vittles and an evening of dancing for 35 cents back then, and important things like overalls only cost $1.25. In the fall of 1913, my brother and I bought our own farm with twelve milking cows and twenty young ones. We cooked for ourselves, made our own bread, and churned butter to sell to stores. Two years later, when I was still single, I bought Cozy Bend, the 110-acre farm up the hill from Sunnyside where we lived for forty years and raised our children."

"I had known Will for a long time from when he and his brother used to come threshing on our farm, but he didn't pay any attention to me until the last of high school," Ada says. "Will is nine and a half years older than I am. He was a tall, handsome boy with heavy black hair. Oh, I rather liked him, but I was too shy to show it until he made the first move. He was interesting and so much fun. We started going together in 1918. He was a real treat for me after all those years of having no dates. We did a lot of things together when we were courting. We galloped off together on horseback and climbed a lot of mountains. I love mountains. One Fourth of July we climbed up Owl's Head Mountain. We were tired, wet, and muddy, but I remember we went to a street dance as soon as we came home. There were a lot of things to do in Glover back then. On New Year's Eve there was always a ball with dance cards and everything. Most people in town came. All ages. We had quite a band, with piano, drums, violin, and bass fiddle playing waltzes, two-steps, and square dances. Sometimes they'd have an oyster

Ada and Will Urie stop work for a big noon meal every day.

supper at midnight. We danced all night and often didn't come home until 4 A.M. Will had a car. That was exciting because my family had never owned a car. His spirited horse was even better. We went to fairs and all sorts of outdoor events in a covered cart pulled by that snappy horse. We drew everyone's attention."

Will, somewhat amused at Ada's excited reminiscences of their three-year courtship, added in his typical dry humor, "All I remember is that I sure et up a lot of good food at your house on Sundays."

"For a year after high school I was the one-horse telephone operator of Barton, Vermont, the only one in town!" Ada says. "I had my own little room with the switchboard which I was supposed to watch twenty-four hours a day for sixty dollars a month. I had a cot in there. Fortunately, my younger sisters had the apartment upstairs. If Will and I wanted to go to a movie, it was only across the street. One of my sisters would watch the switchboard while she studied. It really wasn't as bad as it sounds. The switchboard was very busy from 7 to 9, then there were just intermittent calls. I had plenty of time for crocheting and hem stitching decorative sheets and pillowcases for my hope chest. Will and I married September 20, 1921."

The wedding was a simple family affair at Ada's home. Several of Will's friends made off with the honeymoon car and hid it in the horse barn. They were just chaining it to the wall when Will discovered them and saved his car for their honeymoon vacation.

Ada remembers every minute detail of the honeymoon. With Will, her life had become exciting and adventurous. "We traveled all through the White Mountains for two weeks in Will's old Chevy convertible with a mattress in it. When we got tired we parked any place we thought looked nice, dead-end roads or the playgrounds of old schoolhouses. We'd just pull the top up and draw curtains over the windows and lie on the mattress over the seats. We bought meat and vegetables along the way and cooked them on our little kerosene stove. In September when the fall foliage was at its peak, we climbed Mount Washington. Our honeymoon was intended as a camping trip, but neither of us had ever stayed in a hotel before, so we spent one night in a hotel room in Portland, Maine. I wanted to see how everything in the room worked, so I started pressing all the buttons. We were dumbfounded when a bellboy appeared at our door. I didn't know what to say to him. He just smiled. I guess he must have known we were from the country."

Ada and Will quickly settled into life at Cozy Bend. One day after they painted the house, Will decided to make the farm's name official by hanging letters spelling "Cozy Bend" on the barn's peak. He climbed precariously high on wobbly ladders, spacing out each letter and fastening it securely. When he descended to admire his handiwork, he realized he had hung the Z backward. It stayed that way through at least four decades. The barn with its backward Z finally burned down after they had sold the farm.

"Cozy Bend was a big farm for the two of us to run with all the animals we had, but as the children grew up, they helped," Ada says. "They were all interested in the farm. We had three horses, Will's dandy team, and a lighter driving horse. When we were haying, the team pulled the mower and the wagon and the light horse did the raking. It was my job to get the cows in the morning and bring them into the barn. Will and I milked all twenty-three of them by hand twice a day for years until we finally bought a milking machine. He'd let me milk the ten easiest ones, while he tackled the hard ones. I named every one of the cows and stenciled their names above their stalls. Oh, I wouldn't think of raising animals without naming them. Sometimes we named them after people we knew and sometimes after a personality trait they had. Every animal seems like an individual to us. We even named all the sheep. Not the chickens and turkeys, though.

"We sold milk and butter all those years. As my babies came, I carried their bassinets right into the stable where I milked. One winter Will built the children a wooden horse to swing on from the rafters of the barn. It hung on chains and moved by foot power. I pulled a stocking over its wooden head and sewed on button eyes and leather ears. Will made the mane and tail from hair borrowed from our cows' tails. The children swung on that horse for hours."

The dairy herd, which is a full-time job for most farmers, was only one aspect of Cozy Bend. Will sheared sheep, raised beef cattle and hogs, and butchered all the animals himself. Ada kept hens, sold eggs, and baked for people as she does now. "I raised geese and turkeys and dressed them to sell to people, too," Ada says. "Once I had fifty-nine turkeys. Many a day I was covered from head to toe in goose down. When you pull the feathers off, the littlest breeze spreads down all over the walls and practically buries you in fuzz. I'd finally collect it all and make pillows."

Maple syrup paid most of the Uries' bills. "Sugaring let us pay off the mortgage on the farm in six and a half years," Ada said proudly. "It was a good thing, too, because Will and I hate being in debt. We buy only what we can afford and owe no one for anything. All those years we tapped eleven hundred sugar maples in two or two and a half days unless the snow was so deep we had to wear snowshoes. Then it took a little longer. It was hard work, but it was fun back then when everyone sugared with horses. You never know about sugar. It can flow right fast. You just hope you can move fast enough to hang the last bucket on the trees before the first drop arrives and you have to start gathering. Sometimes we'd have to shovel a path through the snowdrifts so the horse could get through. Now they use bulldozers and tractors. The magic we experienced in the serenity of the snow with just the clomp of horse hooves is almost gone now, but it was always there for us.

"I'd usually have one of the children in a playpen in the sugarhouse when I'd boil the sap down on a wood-fired evaporator. It takes thirty-five to forty gallons of sap to make one gallon of maple syrup. I remember one year our children had to do their own sugaring as a project in their little rural school. We had an extra bull, so they hitched him to the sled for gathering. They boiled the sap themselves and made enough syrup to make about five pounds of sugar cakes, little two-ounce candies. They took them to Barton to sell and made twelve dollars one year. It really taught them the value of money.

"Sometimes it sounds like the farm was all work and no play, but it wasn't that way at all. One of the neighbors would always throw a sugar party. We'd spread thin strips of hot syrup from a pitcher into a trough of snow to make a gummy candy treat like taffy we call sugar on snow. You scoop it up on sticks to eat it. We'd always serve doughnuts with it and sour pickles in between bites of sugar to cut the sweetness so you could eat more. Everybody from babies to eighty-year-olds would come. We'd also have wonderful moonlight neighborhood sliding parties on sleds we called traverses, which six people could ride. All the families would go.

"There was a real sense of community back then. People seem so rushed now that we can't get together. We were always having neighborhood parties or parties at the schoolhouse. One year the neighbors put on a play in which all of our children had parts. They used our hill as an amphitheatre, then everyone came to our house for refreshments. One farmer fixed a dance hall in his barn loft. They always had big crowds— grandparents, parents, and children.

"I think something began to happen to neighborliness when they started scraping the roads back in 1934. Before that everyone traveled in sleighs and life was much slower. I remember when Will's sister was visiting from Nebraska, we hitched up a team, lined our sleigh with straw, and stuffed ten people into it, a real overload. We drove all the way to South Albany and had a wonderful party at Father Urie's. Once we hitched four horses to a bigger sleigh and carried four or five families to Will's brother's in Barton to have a big supper. Somebody gave us a gas lantern to keep warm, but mostly we huddled under blankets. It was a snappy cold night, 20 or 30 degrees below zero. The horses couldn't trot, the sleigh was so loaded.

It was 4 A.M. when we got home. Even when winter comes and our chores are lighter and snow tires on our cars have replaced horses and sleighs, people just don't go out anymore. They would rather sit home and watch TV. Something important has been lost when everybody is so busy some families can't even get together anymore.

"It saddens me that some people decide not to have children. They miss so much. We were never a demonstrative family, hugging and kissing all the time, but the children always knew we loved them. When they grew up, married, and moved away, they always came home to visit. They still do. Most Christmases all five of our children come with their families to eat Christmas dinner with us. We have eighteen grandchildren and four great-grandchildren. Why there's so many people, some of them have to eat on the floor!"

All the Urie children did well. Olive, fifty-three, is a nurse who helps in her husband's thriving dental office. Fifty-year-old Marion is a teacher who helps her husband run their modern farm, which was once owned by Will's great-grandfather. Beyond their dairying, they have a highly successful maple syrup operation on the farm. Joyce, forty-seven, married a funeral director with three funeral homes and a private plane. Their only son, Alan, forty-three, owns a modern dairy farm with an outstanding herd of registered Holsteins and Morgan horses. Fay, forty-two, has a good job in the business office of the telephone company where her husband is a service foreman. None of these five modern children could comfortably drop into Ada and Will's nineteenth-century life-style, but they come often and always find on the little farm a serenity that is hard to describe. There's a magnetic pull, an admiration for their parents and their gentle life-style that none of them can express. It is the kind of place that overloads the senses—smells and images of home that don't fit into words. It's the aroma of Ada's homemade bread and all the pine trees Will has planted and the steady chomping of grass in the back pasture when Jack and Rachel are turned out. It's the peace of Rachel lovingly licking Jack's face and the chickens cackling under the back porch as darkness sweeps over Uncle Jimmy's Mountain.

"I wouldn't like to see an outsider come and buy up our farm and divide it into lots for the summer people," Ada says. "I'd like to see our old house kept up. I wouldn't want the fields to go back to nature. A lot of hard work has gone into this farm. I hate to see a berry rot on the bush or a good maple go untapped. We'd be thrilled to death if someday a young person comes here to buy the land who wants to farm it the way we do and learns to be a good farmer, but right now we're doing just fine."

When the electric light pole in front of Sunnyside began to deteriorate recently, the power company replaced it. Will asked the servicemen if he could have the old pole. He and Ada dragged it off. Ada held it tight while Will sawed the twenty-four-foot-long pole in half. He then split it into eleven rails to make five lengths of rail fence. It was a tough job because the pole was long and cumbersome and the wood was knotty and hard to split. Ada sanded a smooth place on one rail while Will borrowed his grandson's wood burning pen to write a simple message: "1976 WILL URIE MADE RAILS AGE 85." Ada carefully varnished the spot to preserve it; then they built the fence together in front of Goldy and Sylvia's (the yearling heifers) pasture. It was, perhaps, one tough old Vermont couple's Bicentennial message, telling of their love of life on the farm in their simple, understated way.

JULY, 1986

Ada and Will continued farming Sunnyside for years, steadfastly refusing to succumb to the demon, retirement. Never for a moment did they consider moving to the senior citizens' apartments in town. Instead, they gradually decreased their farm chores for a variety of reasons, most beyond their control. They hayed throughout the summer of 1977, then later that year Jack died. "It was unexpected because he was quite a young horse," Ada says. "We just went out one morning and found him lying there in the field. He was gone. After that, neighbors did the haying for us."

The Uries had enjoyed unusual happiness and good health for more than sixty years. "We kept real well," says Ada. "Neither of us had ever been sick." Somehow the whole family had escaped most of the bumps, bruises, and traumas the majority of American families endure. Then in the late 1970s, tragedy hit. Cancer consumed Alan, the Uries' only son, when he was in his mid-forties. "They had to take his leg," Ada remembers sadly. "But he was brave. As soon as they fitted him for an artificial leg, he went back to farming until the cancer came back. We lost him March 27, 1979."

It was especially difficult for Will to justify Alan's death when he was so healthy himself in his late eighties and still farming. The Uries found that hard work eased some of their sadness. Ada baked constantly and kept her hens, the egg route, and the gardens. Will still had some cows. They even continued sugaring without Jack. "We tapped sixty trees in 1982," Ada says proudly. Her voice is still youthful whenever she discusses farming, which still excites her at age eighty-five. Her hair hasn't even turned gray yet. "We decided to tap only those trees closest to the sugarhouse because Will's legs were getting weak. He was falling a lot. I carried all the buckets of sap to the sugarhouse that year myself and did all the boiling because Will couldn't walk good enough in the snow.

"Will got quite sick after that and had to go to the hospital. When he came back home, he couldn't walk. I managed to handle him by myself for months with his help, but he was such a tall man that when he got weaker and completely gave out, I didn't have enough strength to get him out of bed and into a chair. Everybody advised me to put him in the nursing home at Glover. They thought it would be better. We both hated that, but there was nothing I could do. We took him there in February, 1983. Oh, my, Will was so healthy all his life that he hardly ever saw a doctor. He was quite patient with his sickness, but he didn't like the nursing home. I went to see him twice a week. His mind stayed clear. He always knew me. He got thinner, but he was still handsome with his thick white hair.

"I never thought I could live alone, but I could. I didn't like it, though. I missed Will terribly. The only way I could survive was to stay very active. I baked for the summer people, made jams and jellies, tended all my gardens, and kept my hens. Although I never learned to drive, I even managed to keep my egg route going. When the neighbors took me to church, I'd bring my eggs and hand them out to my customers. I ran my business from the house. People came to me. I continued working alone even after my Willie passed away on March 4, 1985, at age ninety-three. You just have to go on, whether you feel like it or not. The more active I became, the better I felt."

Ada's daughter Marion worried about her spending winters alone at Sunnyside in subzero temperatures, blizzards, and ice storms. In the winter of 1984, she finally coaxed Ada to leave Sunnyside during the worst months and live with them. Marion and Albert had retired from farming, leaving the old Urie farm in the capable hands of their son Bruce. Their new retirement home, just five miles from Sunnyside, had plenty of room for Ada. Ada stayed that winter and returned December 10, 1985, for a second winter. On December 19, 1985, her Christmas plans were dashed by an unexpected, serious heart attack. "I had never had an attack before," Ada says. "It came on so suddenly. I was talking to Albert and he told me I just stopped talking. That was it. I was in the hospital for two weeks, but I'm not sick anymore.

"I was in good enough shape to have a big eighty-fifth birthday party on January 31. Everybody came, even my daughter Joyce, who flew all the way from Beaumont, Texas, where she lives and works now. There were wonderful refreshments, but what I loved most was just being with all my daughters talking like old times."

Family was always important to Ada, but with Will gone and no more chores on the farm, they now fill a deep void. "I have eighteen grandchildren and twenty-one great-grandchildren—nine girls and twelve boys—and two more on the way," she says proudly. "I get to see them often, too. At least two-thirds of them are still in Vermont." When she talks about them, it is in that same lilting melodic voice punctuated with soprano laughs.

"I feel just fine now, though I guess I'm not quite as lively as I used to be, but I miss my baking . . . oh, I do," Ada says. "And my gardens. This is the first summer I haven't baked for people and raised vegetables. Sometimes I sneak out and hoe Marion's garden. It's good exercise for me. I don't know whether I'll get to go back home this summer or not. Marion doesn't want me to be there by myself. I tried to talk my youngest sister into coming to live with me at Sunnyside. She's eighty and has a car. We could have such a good time there baking, but she doesn't want to. She's lived in town quite a while now and she really likes it there. I guess she's not as anxious to go back to farm life as I am."

Ada isn't used to sitting. She misses work and looks for it wherever she goes. "She asks to do all our mending," says Marion laughing. "Three generations' worth. And Mom loves to iron. On a recent visit to Olive's, she insisted on ironing her curtains! She thinks that's fun."

"I get to go up to see Sunnyside quite a bit," Ada says. "I have someone cutting the lawn and doing the haying so it doesn't look run down. I couldn't stand to see Sunnyside grown up. It will be sad, but I'll probably have to put Sunnyside on the market soon because the children all have their own places and they don't want it. I hope someone will buy it that will like it as much as we did."

These days, the farm's future is much more on Ada's mind than it was ten years ago, but her desire to find a buyer who is a farmer remains the same. "I think it is an awfully good little farm for a retired couple. I'd like to sell it to someone who will use the land. I wish I could write that into the contract. It has so many possibilities. They could sell garden stuff and do baking for people at Shadow Lake. It's such a nice kitchen for baking. . . . They wouldn't have to milk cows. That's hard for some people. They could raise beef cattle. They wouldn't have to hay and sugar with a horse, but that would be nice. There's still two farms around here, bigger than ours, that use horses. Oh, wouldn't it be nice if a young person came and loved the farm as much as we did, even if he had to work in Orleans in a factory and farm on the side? Well, time will tell. I have so many happy memories of Sunnyside. I want them to go on."

Harriet Johnston

Harriet Clarke grew up wealthy and well bred in a sprawling brown-shingled home on the shore of Lake Erie, fifteen miles east of Cleveland. "I guess I had a storybook kind of country childhood," says Harriet, now a trim, muscular seventy-year-old with a lined face and sparkling eyes. "We had ten or fifteen acres, with a cow, chickens, horses, a goat, and a hired hand to care for them. Mother was the kind of warm, happy woman everybody loved. She'd been raised on a farm and knew all about animals. I rode horseback all my life. Many summers I'd go to my grandparents' farm in Michigan, where they'd let me milk cows and help with the haying. That's where I really learned to love the country.

"Father was a manufacturing chemist and an inventor who owned a factory which made epsom salts. He worked with hospitals producing nitrous oxide gas that anesthetizes people. He even mixed the gases that make fizzy drinks. He loved the coun-

try, too, and made sure my sister, brother, and I had all the things you'd like to have if you lived close to the earth. Dad loved to grow beautiful flowers and fruit trees. I'd always help him work. About 1910, when my sister Urana had a birthday, Daddy thought she should have a goat for a present. There we were outside in the backyard, a whole group of kids having a birthday picnic around the table, and the goat prances up, pulls the tablecloth off, and gobbles it up! He was a billy goat and a great catastrophe. A trolley-car line went by our house. He went up there one day following a man with a basket of grapes and got right in the car with him. After that, Dad surrendered and took him back."

At about the same time, across the country in the dusty sagebrush desert of southern Utah, little Charlie Johnston's father handed him his first saddle. Charlie was only five years old. "Later that day I went out on my first trail ride with my father," says Charlie, now seventy-two, with the weather-beaten look of a lifelong cowboy. "Dad was a cowboy from a long line of cowboys. We drove cattle a hundred miles through Arizona and Utah on that trip. We camped out together and cooked meat, beans, and fried potatoes over an open fire."

Harriet grew up loving sports and wanting to teach physical education and riding. "My parents were ambitious for us to go to the right colleges. We were wealthy to start with, but by the time I was ready to go to college, my father had lost all his money. He was more of an inventor than a businessman, and everyone took advantage of him. I wanted to go into sports, but I didn't think I should go to college when there wasn't much money. I could go to a school in New York, take only two years of courses, then start teaching and earning sooner. I thought that was sensible. The family talked me into taking college entrance exams anyway. I didn't care if I passed them or not, since I didn't plan to go. My sister Urana had most of the brains in the family, but she had such bad eyesight that she couldn't go to college. Instead, she engineered my future. She talked me into applying to Wellesley. While I was working as a counselor at a summer camp in the North Carolina mountains, the papers came through that I was accepted at Wellesley. Urana sent the acceptance back and filled out the courses I was going to take. When I returned home, I was surprised to find out I was going to college. Though I didn't plan it I enjoyed it very much. Wellesley was a wonderful place, small enough to know everyone. I stayed for five years, majored in phys ed, and got my teaching certificate."

Across the country, Charlie's mother died in the 1918 flu

Harriet Johnston emerges from milking in the barn on her Montana ranch near Livingston.

epidemic, leaving seven children. "My father was so brokenhearted that he gave up the ranch and gave us children to various aunts and uncles," Charlie says. "I made it through seventh grade, then I started wrangling horses for a cow outfit at twelve, rounding them up and driving them in. It was a hard job because there were no fences and we had to find all the horses and bring them in for men to ride. I earned fifteen dollars a month for that. I was completely out on my own at age fourteen, making thirty dollars a month. By that time I was a regular cowboy, camping out with the round-up wagon and sleeping out in tepees or under the wagon in all kinds of weather. I've pretty near rode the whole state of Wyoming on horseback."

After Harriet finished college, she went home to Ohio to teach in her old private school. Two years later, when she returned to Wellesley for a visit, they asked her to stay to teach crew, gymnastics, fencing, and riding. "I taught ten years and got my master's while I was teaching so I could stay on. They wanted me to do further research and get my Ph.D. I wasn't interested. It seemed senseless to me. Luckily, Radcliffe made me an offer. I became head of the department there right away and stayed twenty years. I never enjoyed living in Boston, but all the grand people on my staff made it worthwhile."

Meanwhile, Charlie Johnston started homesteading 640 acres of government land near Laramie, Wyoming, in 1924. He fenced it, put up a house, and began ranching. He married in 1924 and had one daughter, but the lonely ranch life, Charlie's cowboying, and his taste for liquor ended the marriage. Charlie later returned to full-time ranch work. He's an expert in calf roping and driving cattle, and he has even run wild mustangs for the government. "I guess you could just call me an all-around cowboy," he says. "I spent my whole life punchin' cows and breakin' horses."

"As soon as I got out of college, I started supporting my parents," Harriet says. "My sister was never very well, and she couldn't save much money living in New York. Although my brother became a chemical engineer, he got married and said he couldn't afford to help support Mother and Daddy. I just took over the whole responsibility. My father was twenty years older than my mother. He was very emotionally upset when he lost his factory. After he died, I brought Mother to live with me. We always lived simply in faculty housing. I invested in mutual funds. Beyond that, I never really considered my own life. I wanted to take care of my parents the way they took care of me. I couldn't imagine being married. I wasn't really free with Mother, but beyond that I didn't picture myself as the marrying kind. I enjoyed my work, had a lot of friends, and kept very busy. At both Wellesley and Radcliffe, most of the faculty I worked with were single, so there was never any pressure to marry.

"The summers were the best part of my life. I had found a job at the Half Moon Dude Ranch in Moose, Wyoming, through the Wellesley placement bureau. I was a counselor there for seventeen summers, organizing and leading pack trips for children into the Teton wilderness. They were wealthy eastern kids who were escaping places like Boston, just as I was. It became more and more depressing each year to leave the high country and wilderness to return to the city and sea level."

It seems unlikely that a Radcliffe professor would ever have a chance to spend much time with a cowboy, but in 1955 Charlie and Harriet worked together at the Half Moon. "Wranglin' dudes was something new to me," Charlie says. "I wanted to get off Pole Mountain, where I was punchin' cows. It was lonesome up there in camp. When a friend told me I had a big enough line to wrangle some dudes and make good money, I got in the car and headed for Jackson. I was assigned as Harriet's guide on pack trips. We'd take boys and girls nine to sixteen out on trips into the wilderness for a month at a time. I always loved kids and so does Harriet. We worked well together from the start."

"Charlie knew a lot more than any of the other western guides I had worked with," Harriet remembers. "He could really handle horses. I loved the kindness he showed toward animals. He was tops with the kids. He has an unbelievable sense of humor and lingo that everybody loves. Charlie was so easygoing that we really hit it off. We compared notes at the end of the summer and decided to get better acquainted, so we went to work at another ranch the next summer.

"We've led some pretty wild pack trips together. Dr. Gamble, one of the heirs to the Procter & Gamble soap fortune, wanted to take his family on a special pack trip in the Teton wilderness. He didn't have to practice because he didn't need the money, so he taught birth control to the Indians. We had to pack the poor horses with his typewriter, a flute, folding chairs, a typewriter table, and an arsenal of movie equipment. It took seven pack horses. All this in the Teton wilderness! We even had to bring a special tarp so he could sit under it to type. He said he was making a documentary of the trip."

"He had us all prancing around in front of the movie camera," Charlie says cynically. "Even the horses."

"Every night, even the evening we had a surprise ice storm, he made us make a big camp fire so we could sit around it while

Harriet fells a straight lodgepole pine.

he read poetry and played his flute," Harriet laughs. "It was a unique experience."

"What about them four old-maid professors you brought out from Wellesley?" Charlie asks Harriet. "They were real go-getters. Every night each of them would pour out half a tin cup of straight whiskey before supper and guzzle it down."

"Up in the Yellowstone meadows where the river started, Charlie was up ahead leading the horses," Harriet adds. "Along came six moose. You can't trust them. One ran straight along with us. He was so close you could see him blink his eyes. The ladies thought it was lovely; Charlie and I were dying a thousand deaths. One night bears spooked the horses and they all ran down the trail. The ladies slept in tents and never saw the bears. They loved the trip. We had them out for ten days, riding fifteen miles a day.

"Our relationship grew over several summers of pack trips. I wasn't surprised to fall in love with a cowboy. I didn't think too much about that. We were both older. We had similar interests. He shared the same feeling about people and animals that I did. It seemed like a nice idea to team up for your old age. That's about all we had left! We talked about the things we'd like to do and decided we could do them much better together than apart.

"My Radcliffe friends couldn't believe we were getting married. I had never talked too much to them about the West. Mildred Sherman, dean of Radcliffe at the time, was a big pumper and had a feeling what was happening. She knew I was crazy about the West and figured there was another reason beyond scenic beauty. I think she's the one who really talked me into

getting married . . . or gave me the courage. I was in my mid-fifties by that time and had had a very different life, but so had Charlie. It would be an adjustment for both of us, but we both said, 'Let's try it.' That was seventeen years ago.

"I'm sure if I had taken the aptitude tests they give to students now, I would never have gone into college work. I'm much more peasant than intellectual. I enjoyed the people and made my way for thirty years, but it isn't where I belonged. I should have been a ranch wife from the beginning. I'm strong. I like to do hard, physical work and the variety of jobs a ranch provides. I don't regret the Wellesley and Radcliffe years, but I would have regretted marrying young. I would have never done anything as wild as this back then. I'd have married a Cleveland businessman, and I don't think I would have enjoyed it half as much as this."

The 1959 wedding trip was Charlie's first (and he says his last) trip to the East and his first plane ride. He arrived several days ahead of their scheduled wedding at Urana's home in Barrington, Rhode Island. "I left early right after calving two year-old heifers on a ranch. If I had stayed longer, they'd have had me diggin' them dang postholes. I just come on to Salt Lake and sent her a telegram that I was a-comin'. I'll never forget that airplane ride.

"When we got on at Salt Lake, there was a fellow who had heart trouble. They tried to get him to a hospital, but he wouldn't get off. He got straightened up and set back on his seat, but before we got to Chicago he was layin' on the floor just about dead, so they took him off there. They made us all stay and witness that they tried to get him off at Salt Lake and he wouldn't git. When we started to take off in Chicago, I guess they forgot to take that ramp they run up to the door off, and it tore the door right off. We were hung up there for four hours. I finally got to New York. An Italian lady sat next to me on the next flight. The plane just bucked terrible across there. Every time the plane would drop, she'd grab me around the neck and squeal like a pig. The aviator stopped me when we were getting off and said, 'Well, cowboy, what do you think of the ride?' I told him, 'Bring it to Wyoming and we'll break it to ride!'"

Charlie was like a pied piper in every small Massachusetts and Rhode Island town he entered. Children followed him everywhere; they had never seen a real cowboy before. He had purchased special "silver wedding boots" for the occasion, black dress cowboy boots with silver eagles on them.

"I wasn't through teaching at Radcliffe he came so early, so he stayed with one of my married friends and had dinner with Mildred Sherman, dean at Radcliffe, while I broke the news to my Wellesley friends at a scheduled bridge party. They were so happy, they gave us a big wedding present with which we bought two horses, Wellesley and Papoose. My class of 1934 sent us twelve Wellesley Wedgwood plates in addition. Charlie hit it off so well with Mildred Sherman that night that he later named his prize heifer 'Little Mildred' after her!

"Our wedding had a wonderful cross section of people. My entire staff at Radcliffe came, and so did many other close eastern friends. The minister was an ex-Canadian Mountie, and the best man was a banker from Boston. Charlie enjoyed the people, but he couldn't wait to get home. For our honeymoon we drove day and night to get to Wyoming to work on a ranch."

"Damn, I wouldn't live in that country," Charlie says, showing his distaste for the East. "It's too thick with people. Wasn't no grass. I got so tired of puckerin' up my lips and kissin' all those old maids. God, those lobsters they fed me almost sickened me. It was like eatin' a spider. I really didn't settle down until we reached Nebraska. Finally I could see cattle and some range."

After the summer, Charlie went to work on a ranch in Deeth, Nevada, and Harriet returned to Radcliffe to teach one more year so she could get her annuity. "I'm basically more conservative with money than Charlie. He was used to having nothing. I wanted something to live on. I went out to Nevada to visit him at midyear because I knew he would never come back to the East to see me. I flew to Salt Lake, then took a bus into Nevada. When I told the driver I wanted to get off at Deeth, he looked at me strangely and asked if I was sure someone would meet me there. We drove and drove. Finally, he stopped and said, 'This is Deeth.' All it was was a road and a snowbank. Fortunately, Charlie was there. Oh, it was cold. We loaded huge sleighs with hay in the early morning to feed the cows. I was the only woman. When I finished Radcliffe in June, I stayed in the West for good."

Harriet admits her naively romantic view of marriage was sometimes shattered. "There are a lot of adjustments in marrying so late and marrying a very different kind of person, but you don't think of them when you go off to the wedding. You think everything's going to be romantic and exciting in the West.

"I remember well the first branding I went to with Charlie. Branding is a very dirty job—wrestling calves, throwing them

Harriet talks to her horses, and they seem to talk back.

around in the dust, castrating, dehorning, all the blood. It's just dirty. This one started at 4 A.M. Everyone went from ranch to ranch to help, and we had three Thanksgiving-type dinners by noon [as "payment" for the work]. At branding time, the whole community pitches in. Charlie was usually called on to do the roping. That's a great honor; it shows that all the other cowboys think you are the best. The dehorning is the worst. You can almost see the brains. The dehorning hurts, the brand-

ing hurts, and the castrating hurts. The poor calves don't know what to yell about most. The wife has to cook a big dinner and serve plenty of beer. Fortunately, all I had to do was the inoculating and help with the cooking. One rancher had married a very attractive little girl from California. This was her first experience fixing a meal for cowboys after branding. She put out all her most beautiful linen tablecloths and napkins and her good silver. Nobody cued the poor kid in. I felt so sorry for her when all those dirty people strolled in to eat. She'd do better the next year."

What Harriet and Charlie wanted more than anything was a ranch of their own that they could work together. In 1960 they found it. "I've dreamed of living in the wilderness since I worked thirteen summers as a camp counselor in the North Carolina mountains," Harriet says. "The woman who ran the camp was an idealist. She was an inspiration to me to lead the good life, work hard, and live in the wilderness. I've saved all my life for this and finally got it. It was a real plus that it involved marriage, too. Marrying Charlie and owning a ranch in Montana began a whole new life for me. Another era."

Their Lazy S Bar K ranch setting is beautiful, 320 acres at the 6,200-foot elevation in the Absaroka Range of the Gallatin Mountains, twelve miles southeast of Livingston, Montana. Framed in the living-room window was dramatic Shell Mountain, 9,346 feet high, a light show of patterns and colors that

Harriet hikes over her upper eighty acres with Gabby, an Australian shepherd. She often hikes ten miles a day in the mountains.

Harriet cooks up a big batch of chokecherries she's just picked to make her famous chokecherry syrup. She uses a large wood range for all her cooking, ignoring the "modern" stove.

change constantly—in different seasons, at different times of day, or when storms are approaching. Harriet and Charlie bought an additional, much higher 80-acre meadow, surrounded by majestic snow-capped peaks, for grazing land. Away from highways and civilization, the ranch is off on a long, lonely back road surrounded on three sides by mountains covered with pine, spruce, douglas fir, and balsam. Above timberline the

mountains are snow-capped. In the summer blankets of wild flowers spread over mountain meadows and the chokecherries, wild raspberries, and serviceberries are ripe for picking. In autumn the aspen trees in the wetlands turn golden. Fortunately, the ranch is too high for poison ivy, rattlesnakes, and mosquitoes. It abounds with mule deer, elk, bear, moose, bobcats, mountain lions, and coyotes. Bald eagles and golden eagles soar over the mountains.

A great deal of vision and hard work on Harriet and Charlie's part made the Lazy S Bar K what it is today. "This was a mess of a place when we bought it," Harriet says. "Beer cans and piles of junk were everywhere. The people who owned this land took all the lumber out and put nothing back in. The loggers left a mess of treetops and brush everywhere they went. When we came here I had never owned any land before. To me that's the tops in responsibility. If you can own land and improve it, I think it is one of the greatest things you can do in this life. It is the peak of joy to me to clear the land and make it beautiful. Charlie has worked very hard to seed all the land and get it back into production. He's owned three ranches, but he says he never had to work harder getting one into shape than this one. When we weren't running cattle, farming, or haying the land, we were clearing, piling, and burning."

The ranch house was, and still is, just a small, rustic three-bedroom, one-bath frame home almost completely hidden by pine trees. A fifty-year-old Cole potbelly stove heats the whole place with its crackling wood fire. Harriet, more than Charlie, prefers the simple life. She's shoved her large electric stove into a corner of the kitchen, preferring to cook on the big, yellow

Monarch wood stove. Nothing is fancy. The chairs and couches are slip-covered, the beds sag a bit, the floors are old-fashioned linoleum, and the bathtub has feet. Dogs and cats run in and out freely, flopping down to rest wherever they choose. It is the kind of warm, comfortable place where you can work all day on the ranch, then come in with muddy boots and dusty jeans and sink into a chair. No one cares. There's not the slightest bit of pretense in Harriet, Charlie, or their home. The only clues to Harriet's scholarly past are the classics on the bookshelf. When Charlie and Harriet fall into bed about 8:30 P.M., it is Charlie who devours *U.S. News and World Report* from cover to cover and Harriet whose head is buried in detective novels.

Although Charlie wanted to raise Herefords and horses from the beginning, the real-estate man told them it would be too hard to raise cattle the first year. "He talked us into raising his sheep on shares," Harriet says. "We'd get the lambs and the wool. We took forty ewes and two bucks. The bucks ran off, but we had about sixty some lambs. We weren't properly fenced for sheep, so we spent most of our time chasing them. Charlie was impatient because he felt no self-respecting cowboy should spend so much time off his horse chasing sheep on foot. He never liked sheep much anyway. In the spring the bears moved in on us and we lost four big ewes. I got started raising bum lambs. Those are the ones that are rejected twins or triplets, lambs without mothers. Sheep men just kill them off because they are so hard to raise. You have to feed them a bottle every four hours. They are very hard to keep alive because they don't have the will to live like a calf. You have to give that to them. They get sick and die easily, so there's a lot of heartbreaks.

Harriet and Charlie relax in the living room of their simple ranch house.

Charlie got awfully mad at me because I wept when every little lamb died. I went around to other sheep ranchers and collected their bum lambs to raise. I always had my little flock of sheep. The bum lambs were born about February or March, so I used to bring them inside and keep them in a box or an old cradle beside the stove all winter. They were the cutest things. They'd bah whenever they were hungry. Of course they got very dependent when I bottle-fed them. At night they'd jump in bed with us. Charlie was thrilled. I used to follow them around with old tuna cans to catch their droppings. I never managed to housebreak one. When spring came they went

Dirty Face, Tuffy, and Gabby wait patiently for Harriet and Charlie to finish eating, knowing that Harriet will always fix them each a plate of leftovers.

out. One night coyotes came and killed every one of my lambs. That broke my heart. I never raised another lamb."

Montana is friendly country, so Charlie and Harriet were quickly welcomed into the community. "The neighbors were awfully nice to us, though at first I detected some suspicion about me, being both eastern and a schoolteacher. That's an

awful combination for a Montana ranch wife. I soon learned that if you liked them, they liked you. After one of our early sheep-chasing expeditions we came home all hot and sweaty. Just as I was washing dishes, the family from over the hill came in. The wife started picking up things around the house. Then she warned me the neighbors were all coming up the road to give us a surprise house-warming party. I rushed and found a dress to put on and told Charlie to change quickly. He raced into the bathroom and put on the first clean pair of jeans he saw. They happened to be mine. They were so tight around the waist he almost died before the evening was over. All the neighbors brought food. The men played cards while the women served dessert and coffee. Then they gave us money for a present. I bought some tools to make my first garden. Neighborliness is strong in this country in an old-fashioned way. Somebody is always there to help. The West is more open. The people may be friendlier. In the East there are so many people that you are herded around. In the West you live the way you want to live."

Looking back, Harriet decided that the greatest obstacles in their adjustment to marriage were their differing tastes in food. "In the East I had been considered a wonderful cook. Charlie quickly let me know that everything I cooked was wrong. That hurt my pride terribly. He's strictly a meat, potatoes, and beans man conditioned to chowing down off a chuck wagon. He wanted fried potatoes three times a day. The only way he'd eat vegetables was cooked in grease for hours until all the nutrients had vanished. I finally got used to the deal of cooking hot cereal every morning and hotcakes, eggs, and bacon, too. When I first started baking homemade biscuits for him, they were much different than the sourdough ones he was used to. He looked at them as they came out of the oven and said, 'Your biscuits squatted to raise and baked on the squat.' That was his way of saying they were flat and hard! We've both given a lot since then."

When Charlie started raising horses, Harriet found herself sitting on their heads instead of riding into the sunset. "I'd always castrate my own studs," Charlie explains. "I'd have hell with her then. I had to hog tie 'em and she had to sit on their heads while I cut 'em so they wouldn't rare up. She could hardly stand to do that. One really threw her."

"The first year we were here, Charlie helped run a nearby hunting camp, sometimes staying overnight. A skunk got in the chickenhouse one night before he left, and skunks kill chickens. Charlie decided I had better know how to use his rifle. I've never shot a gun in my life. He got his rifle and went through the routine of opening it and showing me where to put the shells. He touched the trigger, and *whammo*—it went off! Luckily, he had it pointed toward the floor. It went right through and down into the cellar. The cat jumped about a mile and so did I. Charlie didn't care about me or the cat. He ran down the cellar to see if he had hit the deep freeze. That was the end of my shooting lesson. I never did learn how to fire a gun."

More often, the combination of Charlie's experience and Harriet's enthusiasm and determination was what transformed

Now that Charlie's emphysema has worsened, Harriet splits all the wood, which she uses for heating and cooking.

the once neglected ranch. Together they'd go into the woods to cut the perfectly straight lodgepole pines, drag them home behind a team of horses (later replaced by a Ford tractor), and peel off the bark. Charlie built exquisite rail fences with high, majestic pine gates. "His gates are a real work of art, a lost craft," Harriet boasts proudly. "Most ranchers just string barbed wire over crooked, unmatched fence posts."

When they bought the Lazy S Bar K, it had few outbuildings, and those were dilapidated. Charlie taught Harriet to build log structures from the same straight lodgepole pines, notching the corners of the logs so they'd fit together perfectly. Harriet's experience in teaching crew and gymnastics gave her powerful arms to hoist logs and chop wood like a man. They'd manage to build a log building every year, including guesthouses; storage for tractors, tools, and cows; a tack room; a huge hay shed; and even a chickenhouse. "Building is satisfying because you can see what the labor of your hands has created," Harriet says. "Though I loved what I was teaching in the East, teaching is just teaching. I never felt that I was really creating.

"Working together was an important part of our adjustment to marriage. It was hard at first because I always wanted to use my head. I'd consider all the angles and measure everything. Charlie builds everything by eye. I wasn't supposed to think, just follow the boss. I learned that you must never question a western man. Whatever he's decided to do is it. You have to be quiet and work around him. I might add that things have changed a bit since then.

"Another thing I learned about building with a western man is that he'll never tell you what he's going to do. You're supposed to watch him all the time. If Charlie wanted to move a log, he'd just move it, whether or not I had a proper hold on the other end. I've gotten a lot of broken ribs because of that. He'd swing a log real fast and knock me backwards over a pile of logs. He really did a job on me several times. I learned. I also bought a tight elastic bandage to hold my ribs in place while they healed each time."

Once the fences and outbuildings were in place, Charlie began building up a herd of fifty or sixty Herefords, which he claims they bred until they were the best cattle around. Like every other animal on the ranch, each cow had a name and a distinct personality. There was Little Bobbie (her tail froze off one cold winter when she was a calf), Sugar Pop and Raisin Bran (named after cereals), Blondie, and Little Mildred, among others. It was a cow-calf operation in which the calves would be born in spring and sold in the fall. They kept most of the old stock and heifer calves until they eventually had an entire herd of their own stock. "It's important to breed local stock because they never eat the delphinium, the blue wild flower all around here that brings sudden death to a cow," Harriet says. "It's poison which makes the cow's blood thicken and stop flowing." The Johnstons' herd was always gentle and manageable because as Harriet puts it, "We were always good to them."

Charlie and Harriet are among the few ranchers in the area who always herd their cattle on horseback with a dog, the old-fashioned cowboy way. That, for Charlie, is the only way. He'd never drive a pickup across the ranch like a modern cow-

Gabby, Charlie, and Harriet herd cattle for one of their neighbors.

boy or check cattle on foot "like a damn sheep man." Tuffy, a mixed-breed dog, and Gabby, an Australian shepherd, are always beside them. Charlie has trained them to be excellent cow dogs; Tuffy and Gabby tear after stray Herefords and bite their heels until they rejoin the herd.

"I taught Harriet to work cattle," Charlie says proudly, then adds, "but I had a hell of a time with her. She'd be way behind me like a squaw. I'd squall at her, 'Whip up! Get up here!'"

Harriet tells her own version of the story. "I learned to work cattle by going along with Charlie, but the trouble with a western man is that he never tells you what to do. He waited for me to make a mistake, then laughed at me. That's the way I learned."

She learned well. The supreme test of her ability came only a few years ago when the two of them had to slowly and carefully drive their entire herd of cattle, including young calves, down to a winter pasture on the Yellowstone River about fifteen miles from the ranch. "It took two days because of the calves," Harriet says. "It would be no great task in open country, but we had to herd the cattle over Interstate 90 and a river bridge. Everyone told us we'd never get them over the bridge, but Charlie has yet to find a place he can't drive his cows. The highway patrol didn't show up like they were supposed to, so we had to get people on the scene to help us stop traffic so we could move the cattle across the bridge that went over the highway. The cattle made it without a bit of trouble. Snowball, my horse, was a different story. She had never seen a truck before and all those cars and trucks were whizzing under us at seventy miles an hour. If there had been a place for her to jump,

she would have. All she could do was jump in the air. I held on tight. I wasn't scared. That's exactly what I like about ranching —all the variety and challenge. Every day is different. There's something new to tackle all the time. Ranching is living and teaching is just teaching. For me, ranching is much more satisfying and twice as creative.

"I think a lot of the reason our marriage worked with all our differences is that Charlie is unusually kind to animals for a western man. I love that about him. We both have basically the same idea about growing old and working hard on a ranch as long as we can. Not giving up too soon.

"Dying is the only thing I could never adjust to on the ranch. It's hard to raise an animal, work with it and get close to it, then see it die. It's just nature. Some things live and some things die, but it's always sad. You miss them and you feel bad. We always try to make life as comfortable and happy for our animals as we can while they are alive so they don't die from any carelessness on our part. We try to watch for symptoms and take care of them. The pleasure of having animals is worth the sad times.

"Sissy was as good a milk cow as we ever had. She was half Hereford, half Guernsey. We milked her one year, then let her out on the range because she always raised such good calves. Whenever I turned her out, she'd head straight for the mountain. She was a natural born leader of the herd. She was about twelve years old when she died. We found her very sick with a half-starved calf. We got the calf and put it on an old milk cow, but I saw that Sissy had brisket disease, heart disease where the brisket swells up. I knew she didn't have long to live. She was still alive when we turned the cattle out on the forest. She followed, as sick as she was. She made it back to her favorite place on the mountain and then she died. I found her on a big rock on top of Shell Mountain. She'd made it. It was a fitting tribute, I thought.

"Another cow we had was down in the barn with her head on my lap. She gave me a sorry look and a tear rolled out of her eye. She died right there in my lap. It was terrible. I cried. I always do. There's a lot of dying no matter what you do."

"We had a perfectly matched team of buckskin horses when we first came to the ranch," Charlie adds. "When we went after the horses in the spring, we couldn't find old Judy. I rode and rode and pretty quick I seen her. She was layin' right astraddle of the electric fence, deader than the dickens. God, it like to broke my heart. There was a bad electrical storm, and she was a horse who was always nibbling. She must have nibbled on the other side of the fence just as lightning struck."

The Lazy S Bar K has serious problems as a winter cattle ranch. It is so high that snow, which falls as early as September, doesn't melt until June, making it necessary to feed the cattle for a very long season. "I was afraid we'd starve to death on the ranch," Harriet remembers. "It seemed horrible not to have a monthly paycheck and to watch all the money go out on animals, equipment, and hay. I'm glad I had saved quite a bit in mutual funds. There weren't enough fields on the ranch to produce all the hay we needed. Buying so many extra bales a year became an increasingly expensive proposition. Some years we'd barely break even. In the winter Charlie and I would often go out together on the tractor through ten-foot snowdrifts to

Harriet, Tuffy, and Gabby wait in the pickup while Charlie fulfills his promise of catching a trout for breakfast.

feed the cattle twice a day. The temperature sometimes plummeted to 37 degrees below zero. We spent four hours a day feeding in that weather."

In order to meet the high cost of ranching and turn a small profit, Harriet and Charlie decided to turn the Lazy S Bar K into a summer dude ranch for children eleven to sixteen. "We both loved working with the children at the Half Moon and wanted to create a special kind of ranch experience for them that they couldn't get in other places," Harriet says. "At most

Harriet saddles the horses for her almost daily ride around the upper eighty acres of the ranch.

dude ranches kids ride and go swimming in a creek, but they never do any work. How can eastern children ever learn what the West is all about if they never work with cattle? We wanted to run a working ranch where children would learn what goes into making a beefsteak.

"My sister was a good friend of Norman Cousins, who ran *Saturday Review.* For my birthday present, she took out an ad in the magazine advertising our working ranch. We got all kinds of response and just the kinds of children we wanted, from New York, Massachusetts, Michigan, California, Connecticut, and Texas. They were from wealthy families who could afford to pay six hundred dollars for eight weeks on the ranch, children who would really benefit from a wilderness experience. We took ten to twelve children every summer for ten years.

"Charlie and I built log bunkhouses for boys and girls and added a big dining room addition to our house. I served all their meals on my Wellesley Wedgwood with the silver I inherited from my mother. In ten years, the children never broke a plate.

"We had thirty well-broken quarter horses for the children to ride twice a day. They could swim in the clear mountain stream that runs through the ranch and fish in that or five trout ponds we stocked for them. They helped us with all of our haying and fence mending and did whatever other chores they enjoyed most—milking the cows, gathering eggs, feeding chickens, or tending the garden. When the haying was finished, we always took the kids on a ten-day pack trip into the boulder country as a reward. They loved that. We also took them to Yellowstone, Virginia City, and all the other points of interest.

"I did all the cooking. I raised huge vegetable gardens. I made my own butter, bread, and homemade ice cream. We usually butchered one beef, a couple of lambs, and some pigs. We had our own chickens, eggs, and milk. All we had to buy was sugar, flour, and some canned staples. It was almost all profit for us. The kids kept our ranch going and had a valuable experience. They were really interested. We hear from them every Christmas. Many still come back to visit even after they've grown up. A number have moved to the West to live.

"The children became so attached to the ranch animals that tearful good-byes to cows and horses were common. Our prolific cat Dirty Face, who is now sixteen, provided about 150 kittens over those years. Every child who wanted one always had a kitten to sleep with. At the end of the summer, if their parents approved, I'd let the kids take a kitten home on the plane. Dirty Face's offspring are spread all over the country. I'm sure all the stewardesses who flew east out of Bozeman knew exactly when the Lazy S Bar K broke up every summer. One girl couldn't part with her pet chicken. She managed to take it on the airplane to New York on her lap! Crackles enjoyed a bed in the bathtub of a plush Manhattan hotel and exercising up and down the carpeted halls. It's the only Montana chicken I know that lived the good life in Boston and summered at Martha's Vineyard."

The pace of life on the ranch wound down a bit after the last year of children. The Johnstons sold off all the quarter horses but three: Pally, Snowball, and Wellesley. Four years ago Charlie had a series of bad colds that turned into pneumonia and sapped his energy. He's had emphysema for decades, but now it is a depressing, debilitating disease he can no longer ignore. A walk to the barn, the smallest amount of work with the cows, and even smoke from the chain saw send him into coughing fits or gasping for breath. A breathing machine placed next to the bed sends medicine down his lungs three times a day. There's an oxygen tank for emergencies. A great deal of Charlie's love for the ranch has been sacrificed to emphysema in the last year. He's an all-or-nothing man, an old-fashioned

Charlie gets a nuzzle on the belly from his favorite horse, Pally.

cowboy who cannot bear to see his wife do all the ranch work while he sits breathless in his chair. "You'll work until you fall down dead if I let you," he often warns Harriet. He pressed her hard to sell out. She rejected the idea, saying she could still do the work herself or hire a man to help.

The cattle went first. Although Charlie insisted on selling most of the herd, it hurt him deeply. "I hated that more

Harriet Johnston

45

than anything," he says. "We worked so hard to breed them into the best herd in this country." He drives his maroon pickup to other area ranches and calls the cows by name, and they still come running. Only a few remain with them on the ranch. Neighbors ask Charlie and Harriet to help them drive cattle with their dogs. No one can do it quite as well. Even with seventy-two years and emphysema, Charlie still has the swagger and squint of a cowboy. When he rides Pally, the old rhythms return. He tolerates the labored breathing when he's back in the saddle cutting cattle again.

In the winter the Lazy S Bar K is often snowed in for months at a time. When Charlie came down with pneumonia again, the doctor had to make three house calls in a snowmobile. Finally, Harriet bought a snowmobile for emergency use. "Charlie got better, but it was still very snowy," Harriet says. "We had our truck parked down at another ranch where we could get out more easily. Charlie got cabin fever and wanted to go to a sale of building material in Big Timber, so we got all dressed up and jumped on the snowmobile to get to our truck. The snowmobile slid off the bridge over Mission Creek. I dumped Charlie into the icy creek fresh from having pneumonia! We got him right out, and fortunately, he didn't get sick again. I left the snowmobile in the creek until a friend could pull it out with another snowmobile. That ended my short love affair with snowmobiles. Charlie refused to stay on the ranch in the winter after that." The Johnstons bought a small house in Livingston, rent a pasture there, and make several fall trips

Harriet talks to Pally on her Montana ranch.

from the ranch bearing the dogs, cats, cows, and chickens to their winter home. They return to the ranch when the last snow melts.

Finally, after three or four years of Charlie's constant hounding, Harriet reluctantly agreed to sell the original 320-acre ranch, but only with the stipulation that they lease back for five years the house and surrounding 20 acres where the barn corrals, and outbuildings are. That way she can keep several cows, the three horses, and chickens. Harriet refuses to sell the upper 30, some of the most wildly beautiful high country in Montana. She pastures the horses there and in good weather rides every day on the mountain ridges.

Except for the loss of the cattle, ranch life hasn't changed drastically for Harriet. She still rises every morning at 6 A.M. to do chores, making the rounds of feeding the chickens, gathering eggs, milking the cow, and separating the cream as she always has. Charlie fires up the wood stove for breakfast, but Harriet chops and splits all the wood. By about 9 A.M. she's up on the tractor heading for the eighty acres to mend fences, build a shed, or cut some posts. "I love work," she says. "It is relaxing to me to get out and do physical labor. Chopping wood gets rid of my frustrations. I just whack them out. I've seen so many people retire and just go to pot physically and in every other way. I'm not about to give in. Selling was the worst mistake I ever made. I intend to do things my way from now on. I love animals, and I think the routine of being needed by them helps me. I suppose that's why I insist upon keeping milk cows, calves, and chickens besides the dogs, cats, and horses. I'm convinced milking a cow cures arthritis. I could

Harriet brings a horse home from the upper eighty acres, faithful Gabby following close behind.

hardly write. Medicine gave me no relief. Since I've resumed milking, I've had no more trouble."

Harriet assumed the new, rather amusing role of adopted earth mother to several clusters of hippies who live nearby. The longhaired neighbors who are trying to live off the land come to the ranch to watch Harriet work. "I realize I'm interested in a lot of things those far-out people like. I have books that tell me how to cure meat. I've always milked my cows by hand and separated my own cream to make butter, cottage cheese, and homemade ice cream. I've learned a lot I can tell

Harriet descends from the upper eighty on the old Ford tractor.

them about raising animals. In gardening, I make a compost pile instead of buying fertilizer. I guess I don't have to share their ideas about morals and so forth. Maybe I would if I were their ages. Basically they are very nice people when you get to know them. They boost my morale. It's great to be treated as an equal by a young person. They like me for what I do and pay no attention to the fact that I'm an old wrinkled person. Charlie hates the way they look and disappears every time they come. He shouldn't. He has so much to offer young people with his stories and lifelong experiences in ranching and cowboying. I hope he doesn't give up too soon.

"I'm afraid I don't look to the future, nor do I reminisce on the past. I just live from day to day. Otherwise I'd just worry myself to death. I'd like to build a cabin and live up on the eighty acres if it weren't for battling Charlie. He'd think it was pretty foolish at our ages. If something ever happened to Charlie, I'd never be without a place in the country where I can be free. I'll always stay in Montana, though I might like to make one more trip to see my friends in the East. On second thought, I'm not sure I'd do that. They can come here."

DECEMBER, 1985

It took plenty of coaxing, but in 1984 members of the class of 1934 at Wellesley finally convinced Harriet to make her first visit East since marrying Charlie in 1959. June, 1984, marked the class's fiftieth reunion, and Harriet was their guest of honor. "There's a lot of rah-rah spirit at Wellesley," Harriet said in a strong voice that sounds more like a Wellesley coed's than that of a woman about to turn eighty. "I graduated from Wellesley in 1927, but I came back to teach in 1930, so the class of 1934 and I grew up together. They made me an honorary member. When they first invited me to the reunion, I told them I couldn't possibly get away, but they insisted and sent me a ticket. How could I refuse? What a lovely time I had with 125 of them and many of their husbands. I was the featured guest, but I was awfully surprised by their special gift to me. Wellesley is building a big new sports complex. The class had a room in it named in my honor. I coached crew at Wellesley, so I got to know a lot of people. We got a crew together at the reunion and went out in the lake rowing for old time's sake. We even got in and out of the boat without turning over, which is pretty good for a bunch of old ladies who hadn't rowed together in fifty years!

"They had a class supper where they wanted to show clothing styles of fifty years ago. Leave it to my sister Urana. . . . She had saved the green velvet dress I wore to the class's senior prom in 1934. Believe it or not, it was perfectly whole and still fit me. Well, I had to suck my gut in a little bit, but. . . ."

Since 1976, life has not always been as enchanting for Harriet as those fun-filled days at Wellesley. It was a very sad day in 1980 when their five-year lease for the ranch house and twenty acres ran out and Harriet and Charlie made their final trek off the ranch that together they had worked, greatly improved, and loved. They moved the few cows and chickens they kept to a rented barn and pasture in Livingston, a few miles from the small frame house they had bought in town after Charlie refused to winter on the ranch. Charlie secretly hoped Harriet would splurge on a new brick ranch-style home instead of saving her money. Harriet valued the simple life she had found on the ranch too much for that nonsense. She even hauled the old wood range to the house in Livingston and carved out a big garden spot in the backyard. She built Gabby a log doghouse, still hoping they might build a small cabin on the upper eighty acres she kept. It wasn't to be.

Charlie's emphysema worsened each year until he finally just stopped breathing in March of 1982, dying in the hospital of emphysema-induced heart failure. "He had to be on oxygen all the time that last year, so life wasn't much fun for him anymore," Harriet remembers. "He didn't go out much because we couldn't cart all the oxygen tanks and stuff around. He hated that because he loved being around people, telling his stories and laughing. He was in and out of the hospital three or four times the year before he died, but they were good to him there.

"Several years before that, I decided to become a Mormon. When the missionaries came to our home to teach me lessons, Charlie answered all of their questions about the Bible. I was flabbergasted. Charlie had never showed any interest in religion or acted like any Mormons I had ever met. Back in Utah, when he was small, his mother had taken him to the Mormon church and he remembered all that! Still, he was against joining the church. 'What will all your friends think?' he often asked me. I answered, 'The hell with my friends if I want to join the church!' That quieted him. Urana is still horrified. She's convinced I've joined some kind of cult.

"The Mormons keep me busy. I go to church every Sunday and teach a class in cultural refinement every month that I really have to study for. I respect the way the Mormons take care of people. We do meals on wheels and visit shut-ins. I'm on their state board now, so I go to Bozeman for meetings and always meet a lot of interesting people. Charlie would never go to church with me, but I noticed that when he was admitted to the hospital that last time, he told them he was Mormon. Before that, he had never admitted a religious affiliation. I guess he knew he wouldn't be coming home again. The members of the church were awfully good about coming to see him often. They got a kick out of him. Everyone loved Charlie. I think Charlie had a good life. He outlived most of his old cronies and even his only child. He did almost everything he ever

Harriet milks her cow, Abby, taking time out to feed the waiting cats a can of fresh warm milk.

wanted to do. We were married twenty-three years—good, worthwhile years. That's more than a lot of couples have together.

"Charlie wanted to be cremated. The place he loved most was the upper hayfield on the ranch because he did so much to improve that land. We worked up there constantly, reseeding it, making it smooth, making everything just right. Charlie had a wonderful knowledge of farming and a way with the land, so I scattered his ashes up there on the highest knoll. I had a simple marker made from the local travertine marble. It just says "Charlie." Our good friend, Bry Cox, the present

owner of the ranch, was good to let me have Charlie's favorite spot. He's a Mormon high priest, so he came with me to bless the land. In the last two years I've gone up there, it was covered with forget-me-nots. I thought it was so lovely. I never expected to find them there."

Harriet snapped back from that emotionally draining year. "I feel great now," she says enthusiastically, two months before turning eighty. Every day, even in below-zero temperatures and Livingston's howling winds, she walks five miles to her rented pasture to "do chores." Today that has wound down to milking a single cow by hand and feeding her. "I can still throw bales of hay around," Harriet boasts. "I do my best thinking while milking—my hands warm on the poor cow's teats, my head against her belly feeling the throbs of life. When she was about to have her calf, I came prepared with my sleeping bag and a flashlight just in case she needed some help. I didn't want to lose my one calf. She was most considerate about saving me a sleepless night. She had a handsome black bull calf at 7:30 P.M. with no complications. I love cows, their calves, and the rhythmic music of streams of milk hitting my pail. I don't want to give that up."

Harriet has never given up ranching. She still keeps her old Ford tractor and helps others with haying and harvesting of grain. "With the tractor to rake and haul hay, the work is not heavy. It's a challenge. I had almost forgotten how much I love that part of Montana life, working in the fields and looking up at snow-capped mountains. That's the way to live."

Harriet also works a minimum of five hours a day at the local sawmill, running a cut-off saw and stacking lath they make.

"It's good for me," she says. "I'm in as good shape now as I was when I was ranching every day. I can keep up with any of them. It's a joy to work with Matt Cox, the young man in his twenties who owns the mill. He's such a good worker, so careful. I love being around young people like that."

Matt Cox is the son of the Bryant Coxes who have owned the majority of Harriet and Charlie's ranch since 1979. This warm Mormon family with three grown children became close friends of the Johnstons immediately. "I'm sort of one of the family," Harriet says proudly. "They invite me to all their family things and parties. They are so nice to me. They offered to build me a summer cabin on the upper eighty above the ranch but I haven't taken them up on it because there's no water there. I'm surprised that I haven't returned to the ranch as much as I thought I would. All the horses are dead now and Gabby, too. It's different when you don't have animals out there on the land with you. Now I just enjoy other people's animals, like the dogs and kittens at the sawmill."

Harriet came to Matt Cox's rescue at the mill after he had hard luck and could no longer afford to hire a full-time mill hand 'Matt and his wife were to have twins, but one was born dead and the other was brain damaged. They had a lot of expenses and disappointments. I wanted to help them. It's loads of fun working at the mill every day. I love being there.

'This is one of the happiest times of my life. I have my health, great friends who constantly enrich my life, and no spare time to become lonely or depressed. I can't ask for much more."

Harriet rides the high mountain ridges of her upper eighty acres, land she'll never sell.

Marsha Stone

OCTOBER, 1976

Deep in the Sierra Nevada of Northern California, three miles from a tiny gold-rush town called North Columbia, Marsha Stone spins wool under a canopy of towering ponderosa pines. Sun filters through the needles like light slanting through a cathedral window, creating a majestic, almost spiritual natural beauty. It draws Marsha out of her shop to work under the trees on every pretty day. Even without makeup, Marsha is an attractive woman, 5'5" and slim. Her face has a serene, contented look about it.

Tucked in the woods behind Marsha is the small, sturdy log home that her husband Jerry Tecklin, thirty-eight, built for Marsha and their two sons with his own hands. It took him nearly two years. They are justly proud of the first home they've ever owned, on twenty acres of wooded land that has been inhabited by deer and bear but never built on by men. In the first eight years of their twelve years of marriage they bounced around to at least fifteen rented apartments and houses throughout the South, Midwest, and Southwest. They were both ready to settle down permanently in a place they could call home. Marsha hasn't enjoyed this kind of stability since she was a child growing up in the turn-of-the-century white frame home her great-grandfather built on the main street of Gurnee, Illinois.

Marsha and Jerry live on a wild, remote, and nameless ridge at the thirty-two-hundred-foot elevation, cut off from surrounding communities by rivers. Nevada City, the nearest town of real size, is twenty-five miles and an hour's drive away over red clay washboard roads, switchbacks, and steep grades. Most

Marsha Stone, a well-known and respected weaver in California, works outside in their twenty-acre woods whenever she can. Her log workshop is on the left and the house is on the right.

ridge residents like it that way, keeping an eye and ear out for bulldozers, which might signal development and woodsy second homes for harassed city dwellers. They've deliberately chosen rural isolation over city life, 9-to-5 jobs, and fitting into mainstream America.

There's an interesting blend of people on the ridge, most of them under forty, except for a few aging hippies, poets, and urban activists from the 1960s. Some farm. Others slice deeper into the woods to raise a cash crop of marijuana. Artists and artisans gravitate toward the serenity of the woods to work but enjoy the proximity of excellent urban markets within driving distance. There are many young people in skilled trades—loggers, carpenters, and stonemasons—who have built interesting contemporary homes on ridge acreages and commute to their jobs. In California there are always the nomadic kids who try living in a commune or building their own cabins in the woods until the money runs out. They come and go on the ridge.

"There's a restlessness here with the transients," Marsha says. "I would prefer the strength of permanent residents so there would be more continuity in dealing with large issues like zoning and the school system, but there's always a richness added by these visitors who bring us news of the outside world—new books, new adventures. We have unity in this community because we are so remote. We help each other in an old-fashioned way, trading skills. You can find someone up here who knows something about most anything. Everyone is needed and precious. I don't like everything my neighbors do, but they are still very important to me. I knew there would be a lot of longhairs up here, but that pleased me. With them comes a toler-

ance I never found in the Midwest. I was tired of always being the only different one. There's such a great variety of people here, I don't stick out. Everyone is pretty much accepted for what he is."

Marsha loves spinning the long, carefully sheared wool supplied by her favorite Basque sheep rancher. She collects the wool personally during spring shearing time on ranches, looking for long, clean wool with interesting colors. She's talked some of the sheep breeders into raising wool for spinners, paying them more for it than they would get on the commercial market. She dyes some of her hand-spun in brews she concocts over a fire. "I dye with natural things in the immediate area that are plentiful and handy. Ponderosa pine bark gives me yellows and greens. Red clay makes a peach color. Lichens offer purples, pinks, yellows, and oranges. Black walnuts give nice browns, and manzanita leaves grays. In the spring I gather wild flowers for natural dyeing. If you watch the plant life in various seasons, you get an intimate view of your surroundings, a real sense of place." That's the biologist in Marsha speaking. She earned a degree in biology from Grinnell College in Iowa, followed by a master's in linguistics from the University of New Mexico. She did not learn to weave until she was in her thirties, but hard work and dedication have earned her a respected reputation as a weaver and weaving teacher in just a few years.

Sometimes Marsha, in her hand-me-down long printed skirts and Vibram-soled thrift-shop hiking boots, looks transported from another era, spinning alone in the woods on an old-fashioned wooden spinning wheel. "Sometimes when I'm spinning, I feel centuries old," Marsha says. "I'm fascinated by the way primitive people solved their problems of food, clothing, shelter, and personal relationships. In my mind I travel back to a Neolithic farmer having to produce clothing, the first clothing that replaced the skins that were worn. I find history fascinating when I'm dealing with fibers or weaving. I feel that I could be sitting here spinning next to a Neolithic woman and feel perfectly comfortable."

It is fitting that Marsha and six of her friends in the area secured a grant from the California Arts Council to create the Primitive Arts Institute. "We run summer institutes with emphasis on the primitive," Marsha says. "We have a poet, a folklore specialist who does drama, a basketmaker, a potter, a man who sculpts in stone and wood, and me teaching weaving. All kinds of people come from all over California and other western states to camp out with us at weekend sessions at a state park. People range from age six to the sixties. That's what makes it so exciting. We try to integrate what we craftsmen do in our own lives—living simply in beautiful surroundings, working outdoors in the sunlight, eating good homegrown foods. Each of us teaches the skills we make our living from and share poetry, storytelling, and music around the fire at night."

Dwarfed by the pines, Marsha may look very small and isolated, but she isn't. To date, Marsha has taught more than a hundred people to spin wool. She is constantly sharing her skills with students and apprentices, some of whom move in and work with her on a one-to-one basis for a week. "This is

Under the ponderosa pines Marsha works with her warping wheel and swift, converting skeins of wool into balls and bobbins.

good work," Marsha frequently says. "Work that doesn't eat me up. People around here are looking for that. Many jobs in the outside world are not supportive to a person. They demand so many hours, you don't have the time you need for your family, personal relationships, and individual growth. Weaving is an alone occupation, but it suits my temperament. I don't do a lot of jumping around and traveling. I'm a conservative person, a product of the rural Midwest. A sense of place is important to me. And hard work. I never feel lonely because I'm happy and comfortable working alone. I love the quiet."

Marsha and Jerry came to California seeking tranquillity, looking for a permanent place to be a family. "We both wanted to stop moving and settle into a quiet, rural place where we could keep having our gardens. We thought we'd visit a few friends to look around, but after a few days here we went no farther. We walked two hundred feet on this land and we knew we wanted it. The price was outrageous at eight hundred dollars an acre for forty acres. We knew we couldn't afford it and would probably lose it, even though we had been very frugal and had saved quite a bit of money. I had a great-aunt who died and left me some money, which helped. Jerry and I came out here one rainy day and walked the boundaries literally soaking wet. We loved it. We sat down in the mud and looked at each other and said, 'This is the place.'"

Fortunately, Lenny Brackett, a young man from Minnesota who had spent years studying house building in Japan,

Jerry Tecklin sits on a stump with son Davy. He is a patient man who works well with the children.

was walking the same land with his Japanese wife. When they met, they realized they had an identical love for the land and the same desire to keep it natural. The two families became business partners, splitting the cost of the land fifty-fifty, building a common water system, and working every night for months on a detailed land agreement that they then had notarized. "Each of us has our own house site on the land and fifty yards around it where we can do anything we want to," Marsha explains. "Outside that area, the land is held in common and anything done there must be mutually agreed upon. We work at keeping our noise level down, especially chain saws. No chain saws at suppertime or when there's a fresh snow or rain when you just want to enjoy the quiet. We have strict rules about visitors, so we don't get overloaded with them. When one of us wants visitors for over a month, it has to be with the consent of the partner."

Jerry is not a carpenter. He has a bachelor's degree in biology and a keen interest in insects, and he has set up scores of beehives for people in the area. His own sixteen hives produce forty to one hundred pounds of honey a year. He lacks only the dissertation for a Ph.D. in American studies and is a specialist in ethnic literature, but fortunately, Jerry is a scholar with ample doses of common sense and a blue-collar background. As Marsha puts it, Jerry is too folksy for the academic community and prefers the working class. Their decision to move up into the Sierra Nevada to pursue "work that doesn't eat you up" requires the skills of a Renaissance man. He even looks the part in his baggy pants and S. I. Hayakawa tam.

"People are trapped by our society," Marsha says. "I feel really sad that people have to go on year after year in jobs they don't like. It's frightening. It's dangerous to give up your job for fear that you might not get another one. How will you pay the bills? How will you live? Fortunately, Jerry and I have always been able to get part-time jobs when we've needed them." In California, Jerry has already held part-time jobs as a baker, a beekeeper, a landscaper, and a house painter. Building the house was difficult, and not particularly enjoyable for him, but by studying building manuals and not being afraid to ask more experienced people when he had questions, he completed the construction step by step. It was a matter of necessity. Jerry needed a place for his family to live, and he couldn't afford to have anyone else build it. "Buying the land and building materials took every cent we had," Marsha says.

"I really feel good about this house," Marsha says. "We used the simplest native materials, like ponderosa pines that needed to be thinned out of our woods, and put them into the simplest design of house that would satisfy our needs. Even the tools Jerry used were simple. Most were given to him. Others he paid a quarter for at the salvage yard. Jerry peeled the bark off the trees he cut down with a draw knife and a spud, then let them dry out for six months while he poured the cement slab foundation and did concrete block work around the lower parts. The lumber was rejected by a local miller, all third grade. Jerry found the windows in junkyards. After Jerry notched the corners of the logs crudely with a chain saw, our eight-year-old son Johnny did most of the chisel work while his six-year-old brother Davy played in the sandpile. We chinked the house with a mixture of sand, our red earth, and cement. The whole

house only cost four thousand dollars, including the poured cement slab. My motto is More With Less. It's the opposite of Think Big or The Bigger the Better. It means living as simply as possible with a minimum amount of money."

During the two-year construction period, the family lived in a yellow school bus loaned to them by a young couple who had struggled to start a flourishing apple orchard. They knew about hard times. In return Marsha made them a rug, and every fall the whole family picked and sorted apples for them for free. The bus arrived well equipped with built-in bunks, propane lights, a stove, a refrigerator, cabinets, and a sink. Because Marsha has a damaged disk in her back, tires easily, and cannot lift much weight, she could do little construction work on the house. Instead, she went to work to support the family during those years.

Marsha's "cash income work," as she likes to call it, consisted of teaching extension courses in all types of weaving, spinning, and natural dyeing at a community college. She also taught night classes in weaving at a local high school. Marsha earned about $300 a month teaching and an additional $150 a month selling the rugs and tapestries she made in her spare time.

Before Jerry started the house, he built Marsha a workshop, where she could weave on her forty-inch, four-harness floor loom. There she makes ponchos, stoles, pillows, tapestries, saddle blankets, placemats, and personalized book bags for poets. Though much of her work is sold through a coop-

Davy colors at the open back door of the log cabin.

erative gallery in Nevada City, she does a great deal of weaving for close friends who work with her in selecting designs and colors for the pieces they want. "I have a few faithful customers who order things regularly. I cherish each one. They are all willing to pay the price for something handmade especially for them which will last forever and have the personal touch. I'm not a great artist, just an ordinary person, but I can't make junk. If something I weave isn't strong and doesn't look good, I throw it away. I won't even give it away.

"We were doing very well then," Marsha says of the two years of teaching for "cash income." "I think four hundred dollars a month is a good minimum income for us to live on. Six hundred dollars means saving and vacations. The simple life is no new thing to us. We've always lived that way. We've always been poor, but we've never failed to save money. Our tastes are not extravagant. I feel perfectly satisfied with my free shirt and twenty-five-cent slacks. I'm always ten years behind the current fashion because my clothes come as cast-offs from neighbors or from thrift shops. One time one of my students saw me at a weaving convention in a nice pair of slacks, a vest, and a frilly blouse and gaped at me. Then he said, 'I never thought you could look that good!' Some compliment! I love long, romantic dresses and good perfume, but I'm not going to work at a crummy job to get them. I don't care that much. We use things that other people throw away."

"To put it more simply," Jerry added, "we're cheap!"

Even if Jerry frequented junkyards for building materials and used discarded lumber, the result is far from cheap looking. The home is beautiful in its simplicity. Logs inside and out add a warm country glow. It's a house that reveals a great deal about the personality of its owners through design features and decoration. Marsha's home is sparsely furnished, but her hand-woven Navajo-style rugs and wall hangings are destined to be heirloom pieces. The first floor is one big, open room with the living room on one side and the kitchen on the other. An Ashley wood stove heats the entire home.

The kitchen floor is a work of art, a mosaic of native stones Jerry hauled home in a pickup and carefully fitted around a central drain he installed for easy cleanup. Everyone in the family bathes in the kitchen in an old-fashioned galvanized washtub after heating water in teakettles, and they simply dump the bath water down the drain when they are finished. A few swipes of the mop and the floor is clean again. The kitchen has an exquisite oak countertop that a friend built for Jerry in return for his help on some carpentry projects. The shabby-looking sink Jerry mounted on it is a neighborhood joke, however. One friend found it so amusing he wrote a poem about it. Jerry had spotted the old sink at a garage sale, but it wasn't for sale. The owner's chickens were drinking out of it. Jerry pleaded for the sink and politely handed the woman two dollars for it. She would gladly have given him the disgusting, stained thing for free.

The large kitchen table is a series of six tongue-and-groove boards left over from floor construction and lying across sawhorses. The bench beside it is a Girl Scout camp reject. Marsha cooks on a lovely forty-year-old Home Comfort wood range supplemented by a two-burner propane cooktop. A small propane refrigerator is just outside the kitchen door, where they

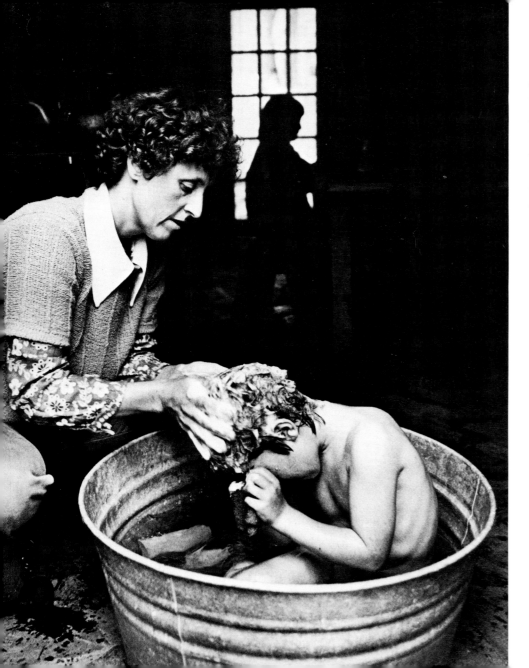

plan to build a covered porch. There is no electricity in the home now and no plans for any in the future. "When I had electricity, my appliances were breaking down all the time," Marsha says. "It just isn't worth the trouble." The rooms are illuminated at night by the yellow glow of kerosene lanterns.

"Power lines attract people," Jerry explains. "They suggest that life is easy. We don't want the land eaten up by roads. Rapid change is undesirable in any area. Slow growth is the only answer. When you offer all the services, life looks so comfortable that people stream out of the cities looking for homes in the wilderness. You suddenly find your woods in the middle of a subdivision. More permanent residents come in. The school triples in size. These kinds of changes are devastating to a community."

Life isn't all that easy for the family. There's no hot water, no telephone, no television. Marsha and Jerry are among a handful of Americans who have never owned a TV set. They keep informed through newspapers, magazines passed down to them, books from libraries, and the radio, when it has batteries. When Marsha splurged for a set of long-life batteries, she and the boys were so excited about hearing music again that they danced around the living room for a half hour. Davy grabbed a harmonica while his brother Johnny made a make-believe fiddle from two branches he found in the yard. They pulled old hats down over their eyes. Marsha clapped her hands and whirled to the soft rock beat, enchanted by the smallest plea-

Marsha washes Davy's hair in the kitchen of their log home. Eight-year-old John is silhouetted in the background.

sures everyone else takes for granted. Marsha is even excited about their homemade outhouse in the woods. "I want to be as simple as I can be and not disturb anything," she always says. "Once in a while it's a treat to go to a motel and lie in bed and watch TV and take a shower, but I can't do that very often. I feel uncomfortable. I prefer being in the woods with the animals and birds."

Eating at Marsha's home is like living full-time in a health-food restaurant. Everything she serves is "good for you," emphasizing California's endless array of fresh fruits, vegetables, and nuts. The family eats meat once a week, and then not very much of it. Cheese, eggs, and whole grains are substitutes. Marsha is well known for her delicious vegetable casseroles. She buys her food wisely, in bulk, much of it from a religious community of young people in the area who grow the food themselves. It is not uncommon for her to buy four hundred pounds of peaches when they are in season, for instance, canning many and drying most of the rest in the sun on wire racks for future snacks. She also frequents a community market aptly named Mother Truckers, which trucks in dairy products and produce from local farmers and sells them with little markup. The family eats better than the majority of Americans for a fraction of the cost. Even Johnny and Davy are great fruit and nut fans who rarely eat ice cream or candy and who never drink soft drinks. They are content to reach for a glass of water instead.

Jerry is proudest of the efficient common water system he and partner Lenny designed, built, and financed together. It's a ram pump whose energy source is a natural spring. The force of the flow through the ram directs water up the hill four hun-

Marsha pauses for a moment in the large, open kitchen of her log house.

dred feet into the two homes for use and into two fifteen-hundred-gallon storage tanks. The ram works constantly. If the spring ever gets so low that it won't operate the pump, water flows from the storage tanks down the hill by gravity into the two homes. Overflow from the storage tanks runs into a res-

With new batteries for their portable radio, Marsha and her sons enjoy the sound of music in the house.

"One of the things I love about weaving in the Navajo way is that the parts of a loom are so simple that I could go anywhere and start from scratch with my knife, my saw, and my ax and build one, then make all the tools I need. Part of Navajo weaving is to make your own loom. I like the posture of Navajo weaving. You are sitting down, stable and grounded. Some people call it being centered. The design grows up on the loom like a living thing and becomes very real." The beginnings of a large rug are developing, a line of geometric diamond patterns in shades of gray and white wool, then a line of black lizards, one of Marsha's trademarks. She weaves in the Navajo tradition, but uses no Indian designs. "I won't rip the Indians off again," she says. She's learned to work on the loom in the morning when sunlight strikes it and paints the whole living room with a yellow glow. "The loom only has life on it when you are weaving something. A rug is far more than a product to me. It's a part of me. Into it I've incorporated a lot of my life, my feelings, and my ideas. Even after I sell it, it is still a precious thing to me."

Near the loom there's a beautiful wood open staircase that turns the corner and leads upstairs. It couldn't have been built by a novice carpenter like Jerry. Marsha traded an elaborate long poncho to a friend in return for his building the staircase. Together they designed both the poncho and the staircase, then they paid for their own materials. They traded labor. The barter system is a way of life for people on the ridge who depend on their friends and neighbors to live. "Cash is hard to come by, so around here we trade energy," Marsha explains. One of her most interesting trades was with a doctor when her

ervoir they dug near the garden, so water is never wasted. "I don't like to see waste in any form," Marsha says. "I threw three beans out of the boys' bowls last night and really felt bad for not eating them because we never waste food."

The focal point of the family's living room is a wall-size Navajo loom Marsha built herself. She learned weaving from Navajo women during the two years she and Jerry taught on the reservation, two years which changed her life dramatically.

back condition became unbearably painful. He gave her a "year's worth of energy" with acupuncture treatments and in return Jerry set up a very nice apiary for him. The doctor's wife taught Marsha t'ai chi, ancient Chinese exercises for posture and relaxation, which have helped Marsha's back tremendously. Every morning she faithfully goes outside to practice her routine of t'ai chi movements, which look like a cross between modern dance and pantomime.

The second story of the home is unfinished inside. It was more important to Jerry to get the family inside before winter's deep snows and biting cold blasts than to labor over room partitions. The upstairs is one big room with three mattresses on the floor. Marsha and Jerry's mattress is separated from those of the boys by a white curtain and a low wall of boxes of disassembled New Zealand spinning wheels that she sells as a sideline. Their clothes are hung on nails or packed in boxes. Amenities like closets and interior walls are number one on the spring building schedule, followed by a covered porch, a deck, and a sauna. Eventually, they plan to add a study and workshop.

They moved into their home on Passover in 1976. "It was a very special night," Marsha remembers. "We were so happy to finally move into the house. We invited a dozen people over —people who had helped us with the building, people we felt especially close to, and other Jews we thought would enjoy celebrating Passover with us. My Basque sheep rancher friend gave us a lamb and killed and skinned it for me. I sawed and cut it up and roasted it on the outdoor grill. It smelled so good. I prepared honey-apple mixture and boiled eggs and herbs they

Marsha weaves a Navajo rug in her living room. She finds this weaving extremely relaxing.

use in the ceremony. The walls glowed orange with all the candles we put out. I brought out all my best rugs for people to sit on. We burned incense and drank a lot of wine.

"Jerry grew up in a strict Orthodox Jewish home in an immigrant ghetto in St. Louis, where his father was a baker. Both of his parents escaped Jewish persecution in Russia and came to the United States as teenagers. Jerry no longer goes to temple or practices Orthodox rituals, but his Jewish heri-

Marsha does her daily routine of t'ai chi exercises behind the log house.

tage is important to him. I'm a converted Jew and a practicing Zen Buddhist. Being Jewish is important to me because it is so important to Jerry. We wanted to raise the boys Jewish. It's Zen, however, that helps me to unclutter my mind and see things a little clearer. I meditate as often as possible.

"We don't celebrate Jewish holidays in the traditional way by the book. We use Jerry's inventions. He tells the children the traditional meaning of the holiday through stories they can relate to. At Passover he talks about the evils of slavery. He's teaching the boys religion and history and relating them to

contemporary issues. There were so many children there that night to hear his stories and listen to him sing Passover songs from his childhood in St. Louis. Others launched into stories about how they celebrated Passover when they were growing up. It went on into the morning. We had a wonderful time. I thought it was a beautiful way to dedicate our home."

It has been a long and often difficult journey for Marsha from Gurnee, Illinois, to singing Passover songs in her California living room. As a child, Marsha remembers sitting in the back pew of the community Protestant church in Gurnee coloring in her coloring book and chiming in occasionally when she recognized a hymn. "My mother was an atheist or at least an agnostic, so some of the old ladies in town felt compelled to take me to church," Marsha says. "Back then Gurnee was just a little village in northern Illinois with about three hundred people. It was a railroad stop and a place where farmers brought their grain. There was one main street with six or eight shops. We lived in a very big, great old house on the main street that my great-grandfather built in 1900 for two thousand dollars. It had a long, inviting front porch and a wonderful attic full of old clothes I used to love to dress up in. We were surrounded by pastures, fields, and hickory nut trees and even had a barn with a hayloft where the family once kept their horses. My father was a photographer, but I hardly knew him. He died when I was five, leaving us with very little money. I have one brother, four years younger. My mother was the tax collector of our township and also did the books for a radio station and an insurance agent to earn extra money. Later she landed jobs in the export business and did very well.

"I grew up very sheltered, living a quiet and very lonely life. Chicago was only fifty miles away, so it was possible to be more involved in the outside world, but I wasn't. I had music and dancing lessons and went to Chicago once or twice a year with my family to see a play or visit a museum. I found the city frightening. I still do. I feel ill at ease and uncomfortable the moment I enter a city. All the noise and hustle is just too much for me. I always forget what's on my shopping list and where I'm supposed to meet Jerry for lunch.

"College was decided for me by my mother and those people in town who looked out for me. They chose Grinnell in Iowa. Mother could afford it by then. I majored in biology because I was very interested in plant pathology and diseases in agriculture." Jerry was a biology major, too, a year ahead of Marsha. They met during her sophomore year.

"I thought Jerry was a very sexy-looking fellow," Marsha remembers. "I wanted to meet him, but I was so shy I didn't know how to do it. He used to come into my lab to borrow cigarettes. I didn't smoke, but I decided I had better learn how. That's how I first got to talk with him. I never grew up popular or even knew how to be comfortable with other people. I never expected to get married. Jerry and I never formally dated at school, but we wrote letters back and forth after we graduated. Jerry went for his master's, while I moved to St. Louis to teach high-school biology. I didn't like it. I felt too young for what I was doing, too inexperienced. I needed to push myself out into something different to get out more. The Peace Corps was starting up, and it looked interesting. I was one of the first ones accepted."

Suddenly, shy, sheltered Marsha found herself in a small town in Ethiopia teaching high-school biology to natives who could barely speak English. She was the only woman in the eight-member team. "It took me out of Gurnee in a hurry and into a very challenging environment. It changed my whole life. At Grinnell I was too shy to meet people and hardly had any friends. When I was thrown into a strange place with only seven other people who could speak English fluently, I suddenly stopped being shy. People became very precious to me from that point on. I became outgoing. The Ethiopians I taught were charming and wonderful, so eager to learn something about the outside world. They were very sharp, even with the language barrier."

At first Marsha lived in a dirt-floored hut. She contracted malaria and a wide variety of intestinal diseases. Getting clean food became a real problem. "At one point I was so weak I didn't think I'd make it. I ended up eating mostly rice and Kenya butter, cheese, and sardines in cans and something that resembled tortillas. It was scary to be sick with no Peace Corps doctor in the village, and it was always hard to deal with the poverty in the area. We were ripped off of everything we had. The only foreigners these people had seen were the Italians who occupied the country during the war. At first they thought we were Italian. It was a twelve-hour bus ride to a doctor in Addis Ababa. When I had diarrhea, it was out of the question."

Marsha's health improved when she moved into a cleaner duplex. As her students' command of English grew, so did her morale. "During those two years, I learned how stubborn I was and how much fight I had in me. I realized that I could do much more than I ever thought I could."

In that spirit Marsha finished her Peace Corps stint and moved directly to Atlanta, where Jerry was working with the Student Non-violent Coordinating Committee (SNCC) and making ten dollars a week. "I had to know right then if my feelings were real and if I really wanted to marry Jerry. I couldn't get him out of my mind. He'd grown on me until I wanted to be with him all the time. It surprised me."

When Jerry proposed to Marsha in 1964, she was working as a lab technician in the Coca-Cola plant in Atlanta. "We did chemical testing and taste testing. I've always hated soft drinks, so it was hard for me. I didn't like the work, and I didn't feel comfortable with the people. The one lady I related to was black. She was the only one with a biology background similar to mine. At that time blacks and whites weren't supposed to be friends. After three months, they told me to stop eating lunch with this woman. I told them I wouldn't because it was against my principles. They went on to accuse me of eating lunch with the black stock boys merely because I was the only white person who was decent to them and didn't treat them as inferiors. Then they asked me to leave. Frankly, it was a relief.

"Just before that, Jerry and I had set a date to be married, and I had arranged to get the afternoon off. Jerry called that morning and told me he had to postpone the event for a few days because he had to do a very important, symbolic thing. He sat down to eat with a black man in Lester Maddox's restaurant. Someone had been kicked out, so he had to respond with immediate positive action. I understood."

A few days later they were married by a justice of the peace. "We had to have witnesses, so we got two white men from SNCC and my black friend from Coca-Cola, who was about to have a baby. We all looked scruffy. The man who married us looked terribly uncomfortable. After it was all over we wanted to go have a wedding celebration, but there was nowhere we could all go because of the state of race relations in 1964. We wouldn't be served on the white side of town because of the black lady. If we went to a black place the whole establishment would be uptight because four whites walked in. We decided that we shouldn't make anybody feel uncomfortable on our wedding day, so we didn't go black or white. We went to our apartment and had our own party."

After losing her job at Coca-Cola, Marsha joined Jerry at SNCC. Both did office work, research, payroll, and a lot of telephone answering. "After we were married, we got a small raise, but we could hardly live on it," Marsha remembers. "We moved to a very cheap apartment building on the black side of town. I wasn't frightened because I worked from 8 A.M. until midnight most days, but it felt very strange."

Soon Marsha and Jerry were transferred to Little Rock, Arkansas, to help launch the "Summer of 1965" in Arkansas. It was patterned after the "Summer of 1964" in Mississippi, when northern college students came down to register blacks to vote. "We went down to do office work, not fieldwork or organizing, but we really got into it until it became a total way of life," Marsha says. "That was the problem. The tension and emotional strain was almost too much for me. There were times of real fright. I was working on their newspaper. To get the best south light, I moved to the windowsill to do my layouts. Black people came right in off the street and said, 'Don't work there, lady. They're going to shoot you.' I was living in constant fear. I never thought of myself as a radical, but the whites down there regarded us as communists, radicals, troublemakers, and northern rich kids coming down for fun. We lived in a black housing project in Little Rock, so the whites suspected us of a sexual interest in black people. The blacks tolerated us because they knew we were trying to help, but I don't think the majority ever totally accepted us. There was a fear that whites were running too much of the operation. After a while I just couldn't spend every second of my day on that kind of work. I felt good that I had spent a year and a half doing what I could for them. We realized we couldn't settle down there and do that for the rest of our lives under that kind of strain. It wasn't a viable way of life for us. We went to Albuquerque, New Mexico, where Jerry worked on his Ph.D. in American studies. I spent the first year trying out various jobs. I worked for the Gallup Poll for a while and found that very interesting. Then I worked for the Heart Fund."

At that time, even in New Mexico, Marsha couldn't escape violence. The Vietnam bombings had begun, and with them, protests had started in other states. Although Marsha was working on a master's in reading and linguistics at the University of New Mexico and writing a thesis on the speech of black children, she shifted from civil rights protests to Vietnam protests with little breathing room between them. "I was really concerned," she says. "I felt we were on a terrible course politically and that some kind of political protest must start.

There was no anti-war group at the university, so I started organizing one. In New Mexico, if you said you were against the war, they immediately labeled you a communist. At first we set up a literature table at the university to inform people and talk to them about the war. Then we started a silent vigil in the Quaker tradition for an hour a day, standing in complete silence with a little sign saying the war was wrong and had to be stopped. Sometimes people would join in, but many harassed us. They'd step on our toes, threaten us with fists and make violent remarks. It was hard to take. People I knew became very angry at me for being there. We demonstrated whenever there was a pro-war speaker. We were totally nonviolent, but I found myself tense before each demonstration, fearing some kind of retaliation. The FBI had photographers taking our pictures. I found out the university had a file on me. Once a TV cameraman zoomed in for a close-up, then asked me if I was a communist. I just looked at him. It was a big, important moment in my life. It took me about two minutes to even get out a no. I had had enough. Two years of this, studying for a master's, and working was too much. I finished my master's and started working at a school for the retarded in Albuquerque. I had begun to settle down. By the time we left New Mexico, it was safe to say you were against the war without being branded a communist."

Marsha became pregnant with Johnny in 1967. Fortunately, Jerry had been hired to teach full-time at the University of Wisconsin at Stevens Point. In the quiet period during her pregnancy Marsha began reading women's literature, formulating opinions, and writing down her thoughts on the in-

Jerry holds son Davy at night in the living room of their log home.

equality of women. "When I was in Albuquerque, it grated on me that I was called a 'graduate student wife' when I was my own person, getting my own master's. Then in Wisconsin, I was immediately labeled 'faculty wife.' That made me feel like a real peon. People were constantly asking me things pertaining to Jerry's work. I had no expertise in Jerry's field and no interest in it at the time. I found it devastating to exist just to be Jerry's wife. I wanted to be a whole human being. That's when I legally changed my name to Stone. It's a crutch, a constant reminder that I am my own person. I wanted a good Jewish name that I could feel comfortable with. Jerry didn't care until all the people began calling him, 'Mr. Stone.' He didn't like that at all!

"The women's movement was beginning underground, and I had word of it. I felt so strongly about it that I tried to start a women's movement in Stevens Point. Sadly, it was always a one-woman women's movement. No one shared my ideas. Even young women faculty members were put off by it. I got no sympathy or support from anybody. In fact, everybody hated me. It was a very painful period when I developed many negative feelings. Emotionally, I was in a very bad state because I was getting zilch response from everyone. I did radio programs, TV, and wrote newspaper articles on women's issues. I held a meeting on abortion which will go down in history as the worst thing that ever happened to 65 percent Catholic, provincial Stevens Point. Jerry wasn't rehired after the third year. They told him it was because he hadn't finished his Ph.D., but I always suspected it was because of my rabble-rousing."

Holding their marriage together through the tense years was a struggle for Marsha and Jerry. "We've had recurring, great, serious difficulties in our marriage," Marsha admits. "I think our mutual belief in the importance and strength of the family has held us together. Loyalty has, too. I'm interested in a strong, permanent, growing relationship with one person. It seems as though there aren't many people interested in getting involved in long-term relationships right now. Sometimes I feel like the odd person working so hard on one marriage."

Marsha is quick to praise Jerry, rarely criticizing him except about something quite unimportant, like his torn T-shirt or the baggy pants that almost slide off his slender hips. "Jerry is a good man. A very tolerant, solid person. That makes life a lot easier. He never worries about anything. Sometimes I wonder what I'd do without Jerry. I'm so dependent on him. We've been together so long our lives are intertwined.

"Maybe I finally have this women's lib thing settled now, even though I really don't feel liberated. I decided to strive to be the best human being I can be. I'm always struggling not to let myself slide into a pattern of thinking something is too difficult for me because I am a woman. It's a daily struggle for me to expect enough of myself and not put myself down. I'm still disturbed when I see little girls brought up by families to be cute and lovable. I'm afraid they will grow up sweet and adorable instead of being strong human beings reaching out and trying new things."

In 1970, after their exit from Stevens Point, Marsha and Jerry saw a *New York Times* article about a new community college starting on the Navajo reservation. They applied to teach there. Because of his specialty in ethnic literature, Jerry was hired immediately. Later, Marsha began teaching adult Navajos to read, a job she loved. "We were with the Navajos two years and got very close to them," Marsha says. "These were the first quiet years we had together without political strife. A student of Jerry's even offered us a medicine man ceremony as a gift. We stayed

Marsha weaves on her large floor loom in the shop Jerry built for her.

with him for several days while his uncle, the medicine man, introduced us to Navajo traditions and wisdom. He'd walk with us, pointing out natural phenomena and teaching us. I felt my way had been made beautiful. The phrase, 'Beauty before me,' jumped off the pages of books and became real to me. I did a lot of walking and quiet observing. I spent much more time with the boys, growing closer.

"I was fascinated by the way the Navajos did things. Navajo women are exceptionally strong. I liked the way they worked—very quietly, very efficiently, and very hard. I saw ordinary women weaving. I thought only artists did those things. At that point, I didn't know how they got from the sheep to the blankets, but I knew if ordinary women could weave such incredibly beautiful things, I could learn to do it, too. I found a Navajo woman willing to teach me privately. Everything she taught me was by me watching her, then copying. I found that kind of education very satisfying. I think it got me out of the book world. In college people are trained to be among the elite—lawyers, doctors, politicians, business managers. I came away with the idea that I should be one of the best because that's all that counted. I'm beginning to see a need for a whole middle level of artists and craftsmen. I'm not a great artist. I've never even had a college art course. I'm more interested in what the ordinary person can make, especially at a time when craftsmen may be a vanishing species, outmoded by machines. There's a place for my level of work. I don't have to have a graduate degree in art to produce a good rug. That's one of the many things the Navajos taught me. During those years on the reservation, I came to the end of most of my internal struggles. I was ready for a permanent place to settle down where I could be the best human being and craftsman I could learn to be."

Marsha works diligently at all aspects of her weaving, including the selling. "I like my life as simple as possible, but when you are running a business, you have to be bold and daring. Aggressive. A hustler. You have to take chances to succeed. I'll try anything with my weaving that a customer requests, even if I've never done it before. You have to try new things." Consumed with what she calls "that old midwestern work ethic," she has to lecture herself about taking time out for play. "I love my work and I never get bored with it. The nice part of working independently is that I can rotate off of one thing and on to another before I get tired. I weave on the big loom for a while, switch to spinning, tease, card, and dye wool, then relax with Navajo weaving. Good work . . . it's so fundamental, but play, there's my problem. The boys draw me out."

Marsha and her two sons are now best friends who do many things together. They love taking long walks in the woods down to the spring to climb rocks and splash in the clear water. The boys straddle tree limbs and pretend they're on horseback. Marsha tells them stories about the trolls that live in damp, leafy places like that. Every night Marsha pulls two or three kerosene lamps up to the Navajo rug where she and the boys lie, and she reads them the Hardy Boys, Alfred Hitchcock mysteries, or Pearl Buck for hours. Johnny and Davy catch her right after school, too. They love having her read to them. On warm days, they all sit on a pile of logs behind the house, Mar-

Marsha reads to her two sons by the light of a kerosene lantern.

sha with an open book on her knees and the boys with open mouths and dreamy eyes. If, as she says, she neglected them during her own personal struggles, those times are behind them.

"I don't think I'm the world's best mother by any means," Marsha says. "I sure do enjoy the boys, though. They're great. They've taught me a lot about spontaneity and a lot about love. And about forgiveness. I love to see their joy with new things. I love to hear them laughing."

Only dynamite breaks the tranquillity of Marsha's woodsy environment. When earthmoving "cats" growl in the distance, Marsha gives Jerry a birdlike call. They are immediately up on the road following the sound. Logging is one of the few industries left in that part of the Sierra Nevada, but Marsha and Jerry always fear land clearing might indicate development. Jerry keeps abreast of every land sale in the area. Sometimes he acts like a real-estate broker, encouraging his friends who are permanent residents to buy more land to preserve the quality of life they enjoy. They live in fear of subdivisions, shopping centers, and even five-, ten-, or fifteen-acre plots for second homes.

"I feel more like a political animal than ever here," Marsha says. "I have a string of running battles going on at any given time—chemical spraying on our borders, zoning to avoid chopping the land into small parcels, cattle grazing on our land. When we were at SNCC, politics wasn't integrated into my personal life; it took over and didn't allow for any personal life. If politics is full-time, it consumes you and destroys you. The real challenge is to be political, yet survive, and have time for

Marsha reads to Davy and Johnny in back of their log cabin.

eating, sleeping, children, sharing work, playing, and making love. It's important to be part of the world—to live a whole life.

"I couldn't have gone directly from Gurnee to here. I learned so much from my interactions and struggles with other people over the years. I learned by trying other ways of being. I had to keep on trying until I found what was right for me. Now I have a lovely house to live in, as minimal as it is, a wonderful husband, good children. That's what I need. Life seems awfully good to me right now."

JANUARY, 1986

When two highly educated people like Marsha and Jerry leave full-time teaching jobs for a subsistence life in the woods without electricity, bathrooms, and television, most people think it's a passing phase. They picture a disillusioned family limping back to the real world of 9-to-5 jobs and suburban tract homes a few years later, intellectually starved and financially busted. Marsha and Jerry don't fit the picture.

Ten years have elapsed. "Here I am in the same log house, with my husband of twenty-two years and two almost grown boys," Marsha, now forty-six, says. "Our inward lives, family hopes, and operating ideas remain the same, though a few outward things have changed. Jerry and the boys built two nice porches on the house, then Jerry terraced the banks with rock ledges right down to the porch and planted them. He's always been interested in plants, so landscaping is a natural outlet for him. He works with two architects part of the year now as a

Marsha and Davy laugh and talk together after a long hike in their woods down a deep ravine where their spring is.

handyman/landscaper on their projects. He made a lovely semicircular garden at the back of our house and built an arbor with an archway you walk through. It's beautiful."

Marsha
Stone
73

Early on, Jerry built three bedrooms upstairs, though he's just getting to the bathhouse/sauna he planned. "One good friend moved away to go back to college and gave us his shower," Marsha says. "Jerry built a temporary lean-to for that outside, and we now have a well dug for the dry months when there isn't enough water in the creek." Some things have not changed. There's still no electricity, but neither is there any of the second-home development Marsha and Jerry once feared. They both admit they'd sometimes enjoy electricity, but they don't expect power lines ever to reach them. "We have two wonderful propane lights, one over the kitchen sink and one in the living room in addition to the kerosene lamps," Marsha says. "And a phone." Their homemade outhouse still serves as the only bathroom, but the lack of electricity, indoor bathrooms, and television doesn't imply the family has withdrawn from society to live like hermits in the woods. Quite the contrary. Marsha and Jerry have always worked, sometimes part-time, sometimes full-time, maintained a wide circle of friends, and have been politically active in the community. Marsha's weaving ability led to her receiving two substantial year-long arts grants to develop folk arts programs in schools, teach, and hire other artists. In her opinion, however, the most exciting thing that's happened to the family was going to Israel in 1981 to live and work for a year.

"We've always wanted to spend some time in Israel, but we couldn't afford it," Marsha says. "We had enough money for airfare for the four of us, but that was all. We couldn't be tourists; we had to work. I called the Israeli Consulate to see if it was possible to visit for a year. They led us to an office in San Francisco which specializes in families who want to come to Israel. They really wanted us to emigrate, but I insisted we only wanted to visit. We started working on the arrangements in November and didn't finish until August! There were so many steps—personal interviews, countless phone calls and letters. Each of us had to write an essay on our backgrounds, what we wanted to do in Israel and what our intentions were. Finally, at the last minute, they found a kibbutz that would take the whole family. That's very unusual. They take single people or married couples, but rarely children. In kibbutzes children grow up in houses with their own age groups and don't live with their parents. They are reluctant to introduce strange children into a close group like this, especially if there is a language barrier. John and David had been taking Hebrew lessons for two years, so they could read, write, and speak at an intermediate level. Jerry started teaching them, then one of our neighbors who had been in Israel for a year taught them Hebrew in return for my making her a Navajo rug. The boys went to an all-Hebrew school in the kibbutz, lived with their age mates, and became fluent in the language. Jerry and I saw them every afternoon, but we lived in our own tiny apartment and worked in the orange groves, laundry, and landscaping alongside other members of the kibbutz. It was a wonderful adventure! We got home the night before John started high school.

"John is almost eighteen now, a cross-country runner and a fine student. After three years in public high school in Nevada City, he's taking his last year at a local private Quaker boarding school, the John Woolman School. He loves it. The school is set up like a cooperative farm. Everybody has a job to do to make it run. Like most kids his age, he's working on college applications now, though he isn't sure what he wants to study. He's awfully good at languages. David is fifteen and a sophomore in high school in Nevada City. He's a runner, too, and works on the school paper. He lives in a rented room in town with a friend in a congenial house where one of the high-school teachers lives. We had our problems getting the boys to high school. We all had to be up by 5 A.M. to get them to the school bus, but they couldn't be in sports and catch the bus right after school. I tried carpooling for over a year, but it is a long drive each way. Finally, we gave up and found good places for them to board in town during the week. They are here on weekends and vacations and we're in town quite often, so it isn't so bad. Their moving out in the world seems appropriate, just right for them."

Marsha was ready to make some life-style changes of her own. "I'm glad I wasn't a finished product when we married," she says. "I appreciate Jerry's full commitment to me over the years that's always given me a sense of freedom to move and learn what I can be. When I was a child in Gurnee with my nose in a book, I remember my mother saying, 'Real life is stranger than fiction.' At that time, life seemed very dull to me. Now change is like vitamins. Life zips along very fast and gets more intriguing every day. I realized I just didn't want to manage people on another arts grant or continue weaving eight hours a day. I did a number of large tapestries in the late 1970s that I liked very much. They were full of bears, mystical people, trees, suns, deer, and birds. Lately, I've made several stoles as gifts for people. I had to phase out spinning because it was too hard on my back, but I contracted out with other spinners to make yarn for me with textures I like. I made seven or eight rugs on special orders that way, and still owe the orthodontist one big rug. As much as I enjoy weaving, I decided that my natural bent is teaching. When we came back from Israel, I started subbing in schools.

"This is my first full-time year of teaching kindergarten and first grade in a five-room, seven-teacher school in Camptonville, a small town the next ridge over from us. I love it! The school is special. Parents take a real interest in it and help, and the staff is great. It is a beautiful thirty-five-minute drive to work for me. Mist filters through the canyon in the mornings, and there are a lot more dogwoods and maples as you drive that way. Best of all, teaching there is a way I can use all the things I've learned over the years. With that age group, I use my art constantly. Environmental studies are very big, so my biology training fits in. My graduate work in language and reading is invaluable. There are so many exciting things happening in education that I hope this will work into a lifetime career. I'm worn out at the end of the day, but I feel real good. I'm much healthier now, thanks to the yoga I've been doing for the last two years. Full-time teaching and weaving in my spare time and vacations is perfect for me."

Jerry has not entirely forsaken all his years of education for blue-collar work. With a scholarship he spent the summer of 1985 at Columbia University participating in a Yiddish program. He has, in addition to his landscaping jobs, a grant to do some translating. His flexible schedule also leaves him time to do community work. "Jerry spent eighteen months leading the effort against a gold mine that planned to locate half a mile away from us. It was a massive community effort with hundreds of people involved. We raised fifteen thousand dollars to pay attorney and expert fees. The local political action group watches out for anything with a negative impact on the land or the people. Things should be planned carefully to avoid sudden population growth, excess traffic, water and air pollution, and noise. The mine was going to be like a strip mine. After a long process, the company was given a use permit to mine, but the conditions for proctecting the area were so stringent they never started mining. Others are interested. We have to continually watch out for threats to the quality of life we have here.

"I treasure our area. I've had a lot of different experiences in my life, some good, some not so good. Everything started to fall into place since we came to California. It feels just right."

Nora Dott Warren

FALL, 1975

Clouds blackened the sky as the wind cut through the water, bouncing the *St. Jo* on a trampoline of waves. The Warrens' dog-eared old thirty-eight-foot shrimp boat barreled through Suicide Cut and Sam's Gut in Corpus Christi Bay. Each time the stern dipped dangerously low in the salt water, the heavy wooden doors on the net above crashed together like cymbals. Texans call this unseasonable storm a "wet norther." Old-timers say shrimping is best right after a norther, but the storm would not end.

Forty-eight-year-old Nora Warren rose above the gloom. The wind and water tore through her reddish-brown hair so roughly that she took cover in a hooded gray sweatshirt. With

After Nora Warren came close to dying, she savors each trip on the St. Jo, saying that shrimping brings her closer to God. Behind her are the massive "doors" of the net, which hang on the back of shrimp boats when they are not dragging the bottom for shrimp.

Nora stands on the stern of the St. Jo *as it pulls out of Ingleside, Texas.*

her round figure, rosy cheeks, and fogged glasses, she looked like a chubby midwestern teenager bracing for the first snow on the farm. She stood on deck quietly watching the fog wrap around offshore oil rigs, making them disappear. She studied the noisy seagulls swooping down for fish. These are commonplace sights for shrimpers, but Nora stared hard as if to let her mind photograph life on their shrimp boat. She hadn't shrimped in three long weeks, which was unheard of for her.

Nora and her husband Buddy, fifty-two, have awakened at 3 A.M. and shrimped the bays together nearly every day of the season for eleven years. Shrimping is a boom-and-bust occupation, but it is one they chose over their longtime, secure occupations in San Antonio. Nora had been a bookkeeper and Buddy a millwright for one company for twenty-four years. As soon as they had raised their three children, they sold their home and five acres south of the city, and followed their dream of an independent life-style—fishing and shrimping on the Texas coast. Often that dream has been cruelly tempered by reality. Gone are the magical years of 1970–73 when the brute force of Hurricane Celia stirred up the ocean floor, making a fertile field for shrimp and a gold mine for many Texas shrimpers. Hopefully, Buddy braced himself on deck, holding the feeler string of his five-foot "try net" taut over his index finger testing the waters for shrimp while Nora steered the boat. Buddy can feel the bump of shrimp entering his small net. When he pulled it up, his fears were confirmed. Inside there were only a few undersize shrimp, a couple of useless ribbonfish, and an aggressive little crab. It was time to head home for Ingleside. Nora and Bud knew it would be a waste of time and diesel fuel to drop their fifty-five-foot net and drag the shrimpless bottom for two hours. The net can hold twenty-five hundred pounds of shrimp, but it never has. This was a year when the Warrens would feel honored to pull up three hundred pounds of shrimp a day. Even a stormy retreat couldn't depress Nora. After weeks of being cooped up inside, she ached to be back on the water, even in a vicious storm.

"You feel so close to God out here," Nora says. "At times

the swells are so high that all you see is foam. The boat pitches like a wild horse. You wonder if the Lord will bring you back this time. You know how people felt crossing the Red Sea when the waters were parted. You just hang on and ride out the swells. You respect the water because it is powerful. More than that, you respect the Creator because he is even more powerful. That makes for a different kind of human being. We were lucky to find the one thing that satisfies us. Most people never do."

Nora had turned philosophical. She has been thinking constantly about God, life, and death for three weeks now, since a sudden illness almost ended her life.

It happened just outside Nora and Bud's 10×50-foot two-tone green trailer on their acreage near Ingleside, Texas. "My vision was so blurry that morning that I decided to let Bud go shrimping without me," Nora remembers as she stares pensively out her kitchen window. I offered to stay home and take care of Melissa and Sara Jo, two of our seven grandchildren. We were in a hurry to go out to the grocery store, so I ran to feed the chickens and let them out of their pen. With a big heave, I threw the chicken feed out and flew right with it. When I woke up, I was lying face down in the chicken pen covered with mud and chicken feed. Chickens pecked at my legs. I brushed them off frantically, still in a daze. It was the second time I had blacked out.

"I sat up and saw a blurry image of Melissa staring down at me. She yelled, 'Grandma, Grandma, why are you making mud pies with my chickens? I thought we were going to town. You went and got chicken poop all over your hair!' Somehow I managed to stumble to the bathroom. I don't think Melissa

Bud and Nora on the deck of their shrimp boat, the St. Jo. Bud is holding a string connected to a small "try" net, hoping for the encouraging "bump" of shrimp.

ever knew I was sick, but I thought anybody dumb enough to black out in a chicken pen better call the doctor."

It irritated Nora to ask her daughter Margarette to drive her to the doctor's office in nearby Corpus Christi. She had always been the strongest one, the earth mother who held the family together through tragedies—first the death of six-year-old grandson Felton, who was born with three holes in his heart,

then Buddy's three heart attacks, which nearly killed him.

"My head was bumping as I watched the doctor pace. He had taken my blood pressure five times and it just kept rising. I remember 196, then 198. I was scared stiff when he admitted I could have a stroke or heart attack at any time. A urinalysis brought more good news—severe diabetes, something I'd never been tested for. I thought he'd give me a pill and I'd be fine. I didn't want to go to the hospital. I had three dollars' worth of sirloin on the counter getting hot, and that's a lot of money. I had already cooked the potatoes. The only thing I wanted was to be on the boat with Bud. I'm very spoiled. Finally, I was so exhausted, I didn't care anymore. They did tests for a week. I lost track after number twenty-seven.

"I knew when they humored me by bringing me meat for lunch something was bad wrong. I'd eaten only dried toast and tea all the other days. The doctor told me I'd have to live in a controlled atmosphere and not get too mad or too happy and not do anything but vegetate to ward off a heart attack. He don't know me too well. He told me to lose 50 pounds by Christmas [she weighed 263 pounds], then he said I really wouldn't have to worry about it. I'd never make it until Christmas. He's got a weird sense of humor, but he challenged me. With a six-hundred-calorie diet, I'm losing weight fast. I've got to face this thing. I want to be here this Christmas and for all the rest of the Christmases. I want to see my grandsons play football and

Nora has pensive, sad moments when she talks about life and death and thinks out loud about her life and what it has meant. She often stares out the kitchen window like this, lost in thought.

my little granddaughters married in white dresses." Even hidden behind her huge tortoiseshell glasses, Nora's eyes looked unbelievably sad. She sat at the kitchen table staring out the window at the jungle of gnarled scrub oaks, boats, motors, and the tire swing swaying in the wind. Tears rolled down her cheeks. "I don't know why I'm crying," she apologized. "I think I cried then, too."

One sees Nora and Buddy's devotion to family on the living room walls. There are thirty-eight framed pictures of grandchildren—all blond, happy-looking kids, smiling impishly. There must be a picture for every year of every child's life. The screen door bangs constantly as small children run in, diving for Grandma's or Grandpa's lap and hugs. "If you are lucky enough to love kids, whether they are your kids, grandkids, or even the neighbor's kids, you get a lot more back than you give. Keep your heart soft, not hard. I wish I had a fifteen- or sixteen-foot-long table so I could sit everyone down in the family and just look at them."

The doctor agreed to let Nora go shrimping, realizing it would be more beneficial to her mental outlook than a continuing saga of daytime soap operas. He cautioned her not to get too excited and never to lift the nets to fling hundreds of pounds of shrimp around as she had done in the past. Bud hired Willie McCormack, a toothless fifty-nine-year-old war hero, as deckhand. He had been shrimping between wars since he was nine years old until his boat had run aground on a pipe and sunk a month earlier. Willie had clung to the mast for hours

Bud holds grandchildren Sara Jo and Melissa.

before a crew on a passing boat spotted him and pulled him to safety. Willie reduced Nora's labor to occasionally steering the boat and culling the shrimp from the trash fish on deck after he or Bud had dumped the contents of the heavy net.

"I feel so much more content on the water," Nora says. "Bud and I have been together so long. When I can't see him in the boat, in the yard, or asleep in his chair, I just don't . . . It's a weird feeling, the same feeling I got when my last child left home. It's like losing someone you love, someone who is a part of you. I have to be with him."

Nora and Bud's closeness is quickly evident. On the boat their motions are so synchronized that they react instantly, anticipating each other's needs and helping. At home they call each other "Mama" and "Daddy" and usually know what the other is going to say before a word is uttered. They mesh, like a well-oiled set of gears.

It was, as the storybooks say, "love at first sight." Bud's best friend lived in the small farming community twenty-five miles south of San Antonio where Nora grew up. They met on one of his visits, when Nora was fifteen. Two and a half months later, when Nora was still fifteen and Bud had turned twenty, they married in her mother's farmhouse. "Mother wanted us to be married in a church, but it was wartime and no one had much gasoline. I was an hour late to the wedding because my aunt starched my uncle's shorts and he wouldn't

Nora calls "trash fish" like this ribbonfish from the net load dropped on deck. They sort all marketable shrimp and fish and throw everything else off the boat for the waiting sea gulls.

put on his pants to take me. I finally shocked him out of his wits by walking into the bedroom and telling him to get his pants on—quick! Mama's old country house didn't have a living room, only bedrooms and a kitchen. We were married in my mother's bedroom, standing by the side of the bed while half the county looked on, all a-snickering and a-giggling."

The Warrens' short courtship was almost as comic as their wedding. "We went out by ourselves twice, once to a picture show and once to one of my school programs. Bud had arranged for me to rent a room in the house next to his family's home in San Antonio, where I was working to buy clothes and pay tuition to go to high school. Bud had a car, but it didn't have any tires. It just sat out in the street in front of his house. Most of our dates consisted of him walking next door to get me to come and sit for an hour or two in his car that didn't go anywhere. Then he'd walk me back home."

At that time Bud worked for his mother's second husband, making tractors out of old cars and doing machine shop and welding work. "We didn't go too far after we married," Nora says. "Bud rented an apartment four or five blocks down from his mother's. Actually it was a big old screened porch on the back of a lady's house. She rented other rooms out, too, and everybody had to use the same bathroom. What she neglected to tell us is that most of the tenants had to go through our room to get to it. On the first morning of our honeymoon two sailors came prancing through our bedroom to go to the bathroom. Bud nearly had a fit. He nailed the door shut. That same morning we started looking for a lot so we could build a place of our own."

Nora and Bud had several strikes against them when they married. They were very young, very poor, and starting a life together when the country was embroiled in World War II. Life wasn't always easy, but Nora is quick to explain why the marriage has endured for thirty-three years. "We both had this tremendous need to love someone who loved us back. Both my parents and Bud's divorced when we were very young children. We had love in our families, but our love was never completely fulfilled until we met each other. That's the object in life, I guess, to find someone who will love you even when you are mean and ugly, hateful, snotty, worn out, sick, or contrary. Somebody who cares enough to overlook your momentary weaknesses and will be able to love and forgive you no matter what. Bud and I really grew up together. We learned about love and mutual respect together."

Bud was only four or five when his parents divorced and his father won custody of him and his sister. "You don't know how hard it is to be torn away from your mother at that age," he confided, turning his head in silence. Bud's softness is one of his most compelling traits. Somehow one doesn't expect to see tears running down the cheeks of a very masculine millwright in the AFL-CIO. It doesn't fit the burly, blue-collar image of a man who built houses, filling stations, a plant, and offices for a San Antonio firm for twenty-four years. Bud finds it very difficult to discuss his childhood. "My father followed the pipeline, so most of our growing up was done in a walled

Bud and Nora relax momentarily on the deck of the St. Jo *looking around while helper Willie McCormack steers the boat.*

tent he broke down quickly to move to the next location. I caught school whenever I could, but it probably didn't amount to more than three grades. When my father finally married a woman with a daughter, she rejected me. I was alone, so I set out across the West for a few years, roaming from farm to farm doing odd jobs and manual labor. Fortunately, I wound up coming back to San Antonio to work and met Nora soon after that."

"I suppose I had a hard childhood, too, in most people's view," Nora says, "but it was the only one I had so I look happily on it. My daddy was thirty-two years older than my mother, and that's a lot of years. They came from different worlds. My mother was a barefoot country girl who grew up in a two- or three-room house with eight brothers and sisters and lots of hard work. Daddy was a rich man's son who got a degree in geology from Harvard, then became a Texas oil wildcatter. He was three times a millionaire and four times broke. They divorced when I was six years old.

"After that, Mother had it hard. She worked ten hours a day ironing clothes on a mangle at the state hospital in San Antonio. In the summer, the heat and steam from those machines would almost be unbearable, but it didn't seem to bother her as much as it bothers most people today when their air conditioner goes out for a few hours. Mother worked six days a week and made only thirty-seven dollars a month. We were poor, but we didn't realize it or think about it. One winter Mother made us all coats out of a blanket. They didn't look too pretty, but they sure felt warm.

"I worked all my childhood on my grandparents' or mother's farms twenty-five miles south of San Antonio with my twin brother and sister, who were three years younger. When the morning star crossed over our bedroom window about 4 A.M. we had to get up and start milking the cows and pumping water by hand for all the animals. After that we'd run back to the house, make our beds, clean our room, and get dressed to go to school.

"We walked two miles to our country school every day and two miles back through rain, hot sun, and cold. We went every day unless we had to pick a crop. Some of the roads were paved and baked in the sun all day until they were sizzling hot. We knew where all the weeds grew out of the cracks so we could run barefoot from weed to weed to rest our hot feet. We had eight grades in our three-room school and no indoor plumbing, just outhouses and an old hand pump for water. One year the school had a windfall and put a windmill in and a trough with fountains on it where we could get a drink without getting soaked. The school was about 96 percent Latin, but that never stopped us from learning. The teachers would take extra time with everyone, including the kids who could hardly speak English. As far as I know only two of us girls went on to high school. I quit high school to marry Bud, but twenty years later I went to San Antonio College and got my GED [high-school equivalency diploma]. I wanted to show our kids how important it is to finish school.

"Grandpa owned only thirty acres, but he used to sharecrop a lot of land around us. He raised beans, tomatoes, okra, squash, watermelon, cantaloupe, corn, peas, peanuts, and pumpkins. He was a good farmer, but then he had to be. If he wanted to eat, he had to raise it.

Nora sits outside her trailer hugging her grandchildren as often as possible. "If you are lucky enough to love kids, whether they are your kids, grandkids, or even the neighbor's kids, you get a whole lot more back than you give," she says.

"There were many days on the farm we children worked from sunup past sundown. In the fall we picked dry corn in the shuck. Our old mule pulled the wagon down the rows. He'd usually stop to eat every fifteen or twenty stalks, which would give us just enough time to shuck the corn and throw the ears in the wagon. Sometimes we'd shell two or three tow sacks of corn and Grandpa would haul them up to Pioneer Flour Mill in San Antonio and bring back ground cornmeal. Grandma cooked us the most delicious hoecakes—cornbread fried in the skillet on top of the stove like pancakes. That way you could get by with only one or two sticks of wood in the stove and not heat the whole kitchen up.

"Grandma used to tell us never to waste anything. Keep and use what the Lord provided. We used to pick the crops very carefully to save our own seeds because it was cheaper. We always had chinaberry trees. If you stick some chinaberries in with the seeds, no bugs will bother them. Juicyfruit or spearmint chewing gum does the same thing. Put a few sticks in with the seeds and the weevils and bugs will stay out.

"Grandma saved corncobs, too. I'll never forget the old corncob doll she made me. It had a sock head and arms and legs that were made out of corncobs hung together with a cloth body. She sewed bloomers, a slip, and a dress and a little bonnet for it. She took the thread from unraveling feed sacks and tatted pineapples on the doll clothes. Everything we had, even my drawers, had pineapples on them! We didn't have a lot of fancy things, but we had each other. Christmases at our house were never a big thing with presents as we know them today. It was simply a day for an exceptionally good meal which family and friends came from all over to share with us. I like to think of it as getting back to love of family. Simple things meant a lot to us back then.

"I remember what a big thrill it was to us when our little farming community got electricity. We all got wired up with a piece of wire running across the wall. The light was just a naked light bulb hanging there with a pull chain, but it was wonderful! Everyone ran out in the road to look up and down at their neighbors' lights the first time they turned it on."

When Nora was twelve or thirteen, she had an opportunity to leave the farm and live in luxury for the rest of her life. "My granddaddy's sister, Ella, married well and lived in a big, pillared mansion near Covington, Kentucky. She sent detectives to find us because she had lost track of us when Mother and Daddy divorced and we moved to the country. I never met her, but I remember her most for the silk underwear she used to send me, which was always too small. She had a very unhappy marriage and hated men with a passion. She never had children, so she begged Mother to give me to her to adopt as her daughter. Because she was rich, she could send me to finishing schools. I had to promise I wouldn't marry as long as she lived. Aunt Ella was blind by then and had no one to leave her fancy pillared house and three thousand acres to. The pictures were pretty. I had nothing against the lady, but I didn't know her or particularly want to know her. I didn't want to leave my family. That was the only world I knew, and I didn't want to give it up for something strange. When I refused to go, she willed her home and all her property to the state of Kentucky to be an everlasting home for the blind. She sent me the money to buy a typewriter. That seemed to me the greatest thing in the world at the time."

Nora has never veered from the simple life she knew as a child. 'Big brick houses don't mean anything to me. Until we bought this trailer, Bud built all our houses. Soon after the

Bud and a crew member try to untangle the heavy wooden doors of the shrimp net in a vicious storm while Nora takes the wheel. "You feel so close to God out there," she says. "The boat pitches like a wild horse. You wonder if the Lord will bring you back this time. You know how people felt crossing the Red Sea when the waters were parted."

sailors paraded through our room on our honeymoon, we found a country lot and paid fifteen dollars a month on it. It was wartime and you couldn't buy any lumber even if you had money, which we didn't. We were finally able to get some rough oak two-by-fours meant for a fence and some old black paper and

Nora
Dott
Warren
87

tacks. We went to Kelly Field and bought some wooden packing crates airplane engines came in. Bud built us a one-room house. It had so many cracks in it you could see daylight everywhere, but it was ours. Except for the bed Bud's mother gave him, we made all our own furniture out of apple boxes. Our bank was a gallon jug stuck down between the walls with a rope around the mouth. We saved for a car by putting every bit of change we got into it. We accumulated $155 worth of change, so when we heard about a Model A for sale at $150, we jumped at it. It took the man over two hours to count his money. We were so proud of our car, even if it had lousy tires. On a round-trip of thirty-five miles to visit Bud's mother, we had ten or twelve flats. It didn't have any floorboard in it, so if you ran over a mud puddle, it would splash all over you. We used to wrap up in a fur coat Bud bought me the first Christmas when he realized I had no coat. It was just amazing what we did with that old fur coat. Years later I horse-traded it to a Mexican woman as part of the deal to buy the land which became the little truck farm south of San Antonio where we raised our family."

James, the Warrens' first child, was born in their packing crate home exactly nine months and twenty-one days after they were married. "Some of my nasty aunts counted the days," Nora remembers. James was followed four years later by Margarette, then John. "We wanted ten children, but God only gave us three," Nora says. "We never had much money for a big, fine house, but we had each other. That was always more important to us. Our kids always knew that it didn't matter what happened to them, they could come home and tell us. They always did. We loved all the children. We'd pack fifteen kids in our nine-passenger station wagon and take them to every school football game.

"Our little truck farm was only five acres, but we raised a lot of vegetables to sell. Wonderful tomatoes and sweet peppers. We also had turkeys, chickens, and hogs. John won a third-place ribbon for one of his hogs at the San Antonio stock show when he was a boy. I suppose you could say our area had been by-passed by progress. We lived quite a ways south of San Antonio just off Highway 281 in an area that was about 99 percent Mexican-American. We were one of the few Anglo families around.

"I was a bookkeeper and a truck farmer, but I'm proud to say that I never missed a football game or a PTA meeting all those years our children were in school. Our elementary school and high school had no cafeterias, so I fought to get one. I figured out exactly what equipment was needed and how to get money from the state and federal government. Bud designed and built the building. Who do you suppose they chose to run it? Me and Bud's mother. We ran it for two years until they could afford to hire someone. In the first year of operation those little kids gained over seven pounds per child. Attendance jumped to nearly 100 percent. No one wanted to miss the meals."

Nora is a natural leader and an excellent organizer. When painters wanted fifteen hundred dollars to paint the elementary school, she organized community members to volunteer their time to wash down all the walls, repaint each room, and repair all the screens at a fraction of the painters' bid. Then they leveled the school grounds, cut down the prickly-pear cactus and grasses full of burs, made two ball diamonds, seesaws, and finally even put in indoor plumbing. When it comes to children, hers or anybody else's, Nora has a deep concern and a special rapport.

It was no surprise that when Nora and Bud decided to move to the Texas coast in 1964, all three of their children dug in and decided to make it their home, too. They all found jobs, married, and built homes within a two-mile radius of their parents. James, now thirty-one, has a wife and three children. He runs a prosperous fish house, where Margarette, divorced with two little girls, now works. Twenty-five-year-old John is a welder in a shipyard and wishes he could risk supporting his wife and two children on a shrimper's fluctuating income.

"It was Buddy's lifelong dream to become a fisherman," Nora remembers. "He lived near here with his daddy for a time and fell in love with the seacoast. He always said to me, 'Honey, when we get the kids raised and have some money of our own, let's build us a boat and fish together for the rest of our lives.' Fishing to me was catching pollywogs, perch, and catfish in the San Antonio River, but if that was Bud's dream, it was good enough for me. A man who puts up with a crackpot like me for thirty-three years deserves his dream. If he wants to go to Pismo Beach, wherever that is, to dig clams, that's what we'd do."

In 1964 Buddy designed his dream boat and started buying the materials to build it. He named it the *Dott*, after Nora, using the middle name she prefers. It would be a sleek thirty-foot wooden bay shrimp boat, just the perfect size for the two of them.

"Buddy is such a perfectionist when he builds something," Nora says proudly. "The *Dott* could have nothing less than the finest materials. Bud made every joint perfect, sanded every plank satin smooth. He even used brass screws—forty-eight hundred of them—at a cost of $2.60 a dozen! The materials were going to cost nearly $11,000, so Bud had to work nine hours a day building boats for a company in Rockport to pay for our boat. It took him five long years to build the *Dott*. It was too much for him. He'd work all day, then drive home and spend five or six more hours on the *Dott*. At night he'd stumble into the trailer and collapse in his chair, asleep for the night. On top of that, our grandson Felton was dying. Bud felt helpless because there was nothing he could do to help him. Felton's little arms and legs would turn blue because of his heart condition. Buddy was sick with worry."

"If there was any way to measure pain when I lost that grandson, I wouldn't be here now," Buddy says, turning his head toward the window. "That was one of the worst things that ever happened to me in my life." Tears streamed down his cheeks.

The exhaustion and stress finally conquered Buddy. In 1968, he suffered three serious heart attacks, which completely immobilized him for a year. Nora went back to work as a bookkeeper at the propeller works to support them, leaving Buddy alone, staring wistfully out the window at his unfinished dream. The doctor did not expect him to live. Fortunately, Buddy is a hardy, muscular man toned by a life of physical labor. When he felt bursts of strength, he began to tinker with the boat. It made him feel better. At last he finished her. Five years of labor sparkled with three coats of marine paint.

"She was beautiful, a shrimper's dream," Nora remembers fondly. "We launched her ceremoniously, just in time to catch the last of the 1970 spring shrimping season. Everything worked perfectly. We tied her up so she'd be ready for the big fall season which opens on August 15."

Memories of the *Dott* made Nora contemplate how fragile an existence shrimping can be. "Shrimpers are a vanishing breed," she says. "With all the rules and regulations that strangle us, the long hours and endless expenses, shrimping can become almost a nonprofit business. Whenever there's an important shrimping law in debate in the Texas senate or house, we go up to Austin to lobby. James, Margarette, and I are especially active. We testify and make speeches from the shrimpers' point of view, letting legislators know what life is like for fishermen. Sometimes we win. More often we lose, but we keep trying. Most shrimpers like us just get along financially. One year we cleared twenty-five thousand dollars, but some years are so lean, we wonder if we'll make it to the next. But shrimping fulfills a need in us that nothing else in the world satisfies. It's like being real thirsty and taking that long, cool drink of water that satisfies you. We never got that feeling from our 9-to-5 jobs in San Antonio. I think we feel a closeness to God every time we get out on the water.

"It's so quiet in the early morning darkness out there. The night seems so soft. The stars are out and the waves are hardly moving. All you hear are the birds singing. It is so still and peaceful, but any moment may be your last one. When you are out in the water, you are just one breath away. . . .

"Then the sun breaks, that rise. Fingers of light on the horizon after all the darkness. The water is slick, just like a mirror. You just want to start singing or shout, 'Glory Hallelujah!'

"After a while when it gets light you see all the other little shrimp boats around you and you know you are not alone. In the darkness you feel all by your lonesome, in a vacuum almost. It's a closeness I have never gotten anywhere else."

Nora and Buddy never made the big fall shrimping season with the *Dott*. Hurricane Celia blew in August 3, 1970, with 190-mile-per-hour winds. The eye of the storm hit the yacht basin.

"Just before the storm hit, we were at home going crazy," Nora says. "With the advance warning we had, we could have driven all the way to San Antonio to complete safety had it not been for James and Lynn [their eldest son and his wife] who had been out in the Gulf shrimping in their boat for two or three days. Out there they were experiencing the calm before the storm. Early weather reports said the storm would hit Galveston, almost two hundred miles up the coast. Buddy finally got through to them on the radio, warning them to come in immediately because the storm had changed course. We worried because the mile-long rock jetties in Port Aransas channel are treacherous. The least little miss can pile your boat up on the rocks. Dozens of boats have been lost there. The wind picked up fiercely as they came through there. James's boat developed an oil leak. The engine lost compression. Lynn took the wheel and steered the boat through the jetties while James held the oil line together with his hands, his fingers burning under the extreme heat. I don't know how they made it, but they did. Lynn is a good skipper. Finally, we got the whole family together, except John.

"I was terrified about John, our youngest son. He had been drafted and was in Charlie Company in Vietnam. He had just written us a letter saying he had been slightly wounded, stepping on one of those booby traps they set on the trails. Sharp bamboo pierced through his boot and into his foot. He should have been home by now. All our letters started coming back to us. I thought the worst. I just couldn't get him out of my mind, but we had to move to a safer place.

"We sure couldn't stay in our trailer because it would probably be blown away, but it was too late to drive very far out of town. We considered camping in the hospital lobby because of Daddy's [Bud's] and Felton's heart conditions. Sometimes Felton would black out. If you didn't get oxygen to him within two or three minutes, he could have brain damage. So we packed up all the oxygen bottles and drove to the International Motel in Aransas Pass, the newest and safest building we could think of. We rented a corner room. Buddy put all the children in the bathtub on a mattress with their mothers. The power was off and it was ungodly hot. When the winds picked up, we were terrified, but we couldn't show our fear because of Felton. Some of us started playing canasta to ease our nerves, but before we finished the first round, pea gravel from the roof hit the window and smashed it out. The cards went flying and so did we.

The St. Jo slides through calm waters.

"Walls peeled off the top floor, then the floor just lifted and flew away in hunks. There were two colored ladies with twelve or fourteen children above us. Just before that part blew away, Daddy, James, and the manager of the motel went out in that storm and got all those colored people down hand-in-hand, saving their lives."

"There were people screaming and hollering all over the place," Buddy remembers. "Gravel hit us like buckshot. Windshields in cars kept exploding. We didn't dare get too far out from the motel with the winds and all the flying objects. You are as helpless as a newborn baby out there. The manager got two broken ribs, but none of the rest of us were hurt."

When the storm ended, the Warrens had the only room left with four walls. Remarkably, everyone was safe.

"John and I are very close, almost like twins," Margarette says. "I knew he was safe, too. He had hit stateside the day Celia came. John was going nuts in Camp Pendleton, California, because his commanding officers wouldn't sign his release papers until they heard from one of us. I guess this place looked like a real disaster area on TV. It looked like everyone was dead. He couldn't call us and we couldn't call him. Finally, several days after the storm they hooked up four phones in Aransas. We waited in line to call his girlfriend, Eileen, in New Jersey. When I said hello to her all she could do is shout, 'John is home! John is home!' I started crying and so did Mother. The Red Cross lady rushed in with smelling salts. I told her not to worry about us. It was good news for a change. A few days later John flew to San Antonio and got relatives to drive him to us. We were so happy!"

"We drove back to our trailer in our windowless car expecting the worst," Nora says. "We were very lucky. Most people only had wheels left. All we had was wind damage to the roof, nothing Bud couldn't fix. The majority of the eighty-five trees on our lots had blown away. The ones that were left looked like skeletons. There wasn't a leaf on them.

"On the morning of August 4, as soon as we could drive through the rubble, all of us shrimpers converged on the yacht basin to search for our boats, our livelihood. There was little left. We picked through the fallen palm trees, coconuts, lumber, and piles of smashed shrimp boats. The *Dott* had vanished. We couldn't find a piece of it. It's a sinking feeling to lose your dream.

"The storm was the great equalizer. Everybody, rich and poor, was wiped out. It was unbelieveable how people came together after it was all over. No one had water, electricity, or phones for weeks. We lived like old-timey people. Every day people would come to check on us. Some came all the way from San Antonio to bring us ice. When Bud's doctor saw him two or three days after the hurricane, he just hugged him. Tears poured out of his eyes. He had only given Bud six months to live, and that was four months before Celia. He couldn't believe Daddy survived the stress of the storm, Felton's illness, and John in Vietnam. You really see how many friends you have when tragedy hits.

"I think people waste too much time accumulating things —the latest model icebox, fast cars, fine homes, expensive clothes, whatever. Things aren't important. What's really important is people caring about one another. The greatest treasures on earth are your husband or wife, children, and grand-children. When you live on the coast with all these bad storms and hurricanes that can wipe you out of everything you have in minutes, you don't bother to keep up with the Joneses. Life here brings you back to the point where it says in the Bible to store up your wealth in heaven, not on earth where rust and rot and thieves can take it away—and storms.

"We all cleaned up the worst of the destruction and tried to get back to our lives. I went back to work at the propeller shop while Buddy mourned the *Dott*. One day a man burst into my office yelling, 'Mrs. Warren, Mrs. Warren . . . your husband. You'd better sit down.' I was sure Bud had had another heart attack. 'Bud's at the yacht basin,' the man said. 'He dove right into the water!' I jumped in my car. When I drove up, they were pulling him out. He just sat there on the dock, dripping with water and caked with mud, yelling, 'That's my boat! That's my boat!' He had seen a piece of our mast in all that muck and mire and mud and crud floating beside all the other pieces of broken boats. There he was, in his shape, diving down to find the rest of it. He could have been buried alive down there.

"It was several weeks after the storm before they finally got to pulling up our boat. There were six boats piled on top of her, including a heavy tugboat. The hull was fractured, all broken up. It was so filled with mud that when the crane finally pulled it up, it dropped, smashing even more. We just stood on the deck with tears in our eyes. At least we got the engine out and sold it for salvage. Otherwise, it was a total loss, with nothing covered by insurance. We just kissed the whole $10,600

Content being at home together, Nora and granddaughters Melissa and Sara Jo tickle each other with blades of grass.

good-bye and waved good-bye to five years of work and forty-eight hundred brass screws.

"It never occurred to us to go backwards and quit. We had to move forward and buy another boat. I didn't want Daddy to go through the trauma of building another boat and losing it. There were very few boats to be had, but we all kept our eyes open. The government would loan you the value of the boat you lost to buy another one. Finally, we got a crack at buying the *Miss Kathy*, one of the last boats to sink. Daddy told the salvage company he'd pay them on the spot the min-

ute he saw her float and knew she was not beyond repair. Our whole family picnicked on the deck watching. She floated! We had to flush out the diesel engine immediately. It took Bud nine more months of work night and day to fix the hull, tear off the cabin, and completely redesign, rebuild, and paint it. By the time he did all that and stocked her with new equipment, we had only eight hundred or nine hundred dollars left, but it was worth it. We had a beautiful fifty-six-foot shrimp boat. We were so proud of her!"

Since the *Miss Kathy* was too large for two to handle alone, Margarette joined her parents as its congenial crew. Her two preschool daughters, Melissa and Sara Jo, grew up on the boat. "Daddy designed the cabin around the grandchildren," Nora says, laughing. "The *Miss Kathy* was originally a Gulf boat, so she had a big cabin with bunk beds, a kitchen, loads of storage space, and a head. Daddy built Sara Jo a playpen with padded sides so she could lie contentedly drinking her bottle. That was her territory, and she knew it. Melissa was a bird lover from birth, so Bud fixed her a baby swing on the mast so she could watch the sea gulls dive in as we culled shrimp on the deck. They had a big toy box jammed with toys. The girls loved life on the boat so much, they hated to come home at night.

"James and Lynn had a new boat, the *Sir John*, and would often work the bays beside us. In the middle of the day, the

Nora hefts five-year-old granddaughter Melissa (Margarette's daughter) in her front yard. Melissa and her sister Sara Jo are especially close to Nora and Bud because they virtually grew up on the shrimp boat Miss Kathy.

water usually flattened out like a mirror. It is too calm to drag for shrimp then, so we'd tie the two boats together. I'd fry shrimp, cook beans, and boil roasting ears—they all loved that. We had a big family banquet most every day in the middle of Corpus Christi Bay! Smells really carry over the water. When I'd go cooking a big pot of chili, the other boats around us would holler over the radio, 'Mrs. Warren, what's ya cookin'? Grandma, can I have a bowl?' We always found a little something for them.

"I think shrimpers are special people. When you are out on the water one step from your Maker, you live a little better, a little cleaner, and a whole lot slower. If you have money problems, sickness in your family, or any kind of trouble, someone is always there to help you. There was such an outpouring of love when our baby Felton died. Down here on the coast, towns are small enough that everyone knows you and cares about you.

"Shrimpers are great conservationists, too. They never injure the small or destroy nursery grounds. Those are our tomorrows. I like to think of shrimpers as farmers of the sea. When we drag a shrimp net, we turn the bottom of the bay over, just like plowing a field. That gets rid of sediment, the congestion that stifles plant life. Without the plankton and the grasses and other plant life, there would be no shrimp, fish, or crabs. So it is necessary to work the land, even if it is at the bottom of the water. It is essential to turn it over and stir it up, especially in these days of pollution from oil, chemicals, and people. People are the worst polluters. They throw every filth in the water, from beer cans to the most unbelievable garbage. It is removed by fishermen. We've caught pieces of airplanes, battery boxes, Christmas trees, telephone poles, a car hood, and even a four-hundred-pound piece of granite in our nets. We drug that granite two miles into the flats. It tore the bottom out of our five-hundred-dollar net, but we were able to remove it so it wouldn't be an obstacle to anybody else. The water worked by shrimpers on the Texas coast is alive and full of clean marine life, good fish to eat, good shrimp, and good oysters."

Bud and Nora eventually realized that the *Miss Kathy* was too big a boat to work the bays efficiently. Fuel prices were climbing. The extra fuel she guzzled was eating into their profits. In 1974, when a man offered them twenty-five thousand dollars in cash to buy her, they reluctantly agreed. "He was a stranger, a hippie type with long hair," Nora remembers. "He told us he planned to work the *Miss Kathy* off the coast of Alaska, but we noticed he didn't know much about boats. When he handed us twenty-five thousand dollars in cash in a brown paper bag, we went to the bank with him to make sure the currency was genuine before we completed the deal. It was. Bud and I had never seen so much money before. It was enough to buy a fine smaller shrimp boat tailor-made for our needs. Months later we were heartsick to learn that the *Miss Kathy* had been sunk off the coast of Mexico. She had been used for running drugs to the United States."

The Warrens mourned the *Miss Kathy* for years. Instead of splurging on a brand-new boat, they saved much of their twenty-five thousand dollars and bought the old, disheveled *St. Jo*, another boat Bud could tinker with and customize. Since 1964 he'd always had a boat in the yard to work on, and he wouldn't feel satisfied without one. At thirty-eight feet, the *St. Jo* is a good size for two to shrimp. When the shrimping season

Sea gulls are ready to dive for fish and shrimp as the Warrens' net comes up.

ends, the Warrens fish. "We thought about taking the whole family to Disneyland once, but we never got around to it," Nora says. "We don't even go to San Antonio. There's always something to do here with the boats, something that interests us more. I never want to leave here. It will soon be time to take the small skiff floundering at night by the light of Coleman lanterns. Fishing in the winter is a science we've come to understand after many years of working the bays. After a few north-

ers the fish huddle up in groups. The flounder start moving out of the bays and head for the Gulf. If you can correlate the weather with the way the fish pass, you can catch two hundred to three hundred pounds of flounder on a good night.

"We love to fish. It satisfies your mind and heals your soul. It's the best medicine I know. You get closer to God when you begin to understand the force of the water, the waves and the tides. You develop a respect for the tremendous being he must be and how small we are in comparison.

"Bud had an old Indian grandmother who lived to be 118. She was very wise. She told me not to worry if I burnt the meat. Just throw it away and forget it. God would give me another piece of meat, maybe not that day, but eventually. I think she was trying to tell me not to worry about things I can't do anything about. Just put them aside and let God tend to them.

"Everybody needs a little faith because when you get down to the nitty-gritty things in life like birth and death, faith in God is the only thing that can help you. I need it every day. I'm not going to let this sickness thing beat me. It would be easy to give up and die, but I don't believe I will. Sure, I'll die someday, but not that easily. Not now. There's too much in my life to love and look forward to."

SPRING, 1986

Nora did not die. She has stubbornly, defiantly fought ill health since her blackout spells of the mid-1970s. As she had hoped, she's seen her little grandsons play football. No grand-daughters have married in white dresses yet, but one is already eighteen. Nora has celebrated ten family Christmases since her doctor predicted she would never see another Christmas. She knows now that he was only trying to scare her into taking care of herself instead of ignoring her own health to take care of everybody else in the family. "Now I understand," she says. "I listen because I know what can happen. I'm still alive, and they didn't expect me to be, so I guess I've made some progress."

Though she was sick, Nora stayed on the shrimp boat for a number of years helping Bud as much as she could. But shrimping was poor on the Texas coast. There was a point when she decided her shrimping wasn't helping their income or her health, so she began a brand-new career based on her love of children. "I was a substitute teacher in the Ingleside schools for six years. It is a sedentary occupation compared to shrimping, but I liked it. I'd substitute at the grade school or the high school, wherever they needed me, but my real love was teaching fifth and sixth grades. Those kids had more manners and were more interested in their subjects than the high-school kids I taught."

In the late 1970s, Nora and Bud also got some unwelcome new neighbors. A trio of offshore oil wells sprang up close by, and a large oil refinery loomed up next door. Nora had predicted the surge in coastal development back in 1975. She was worried then, but she thought their four lots in the country would provide a buffer zone. "Trees breathe and plants breathe as every living thing that God made breathes," she had said thoughtfully on a rainy day in 1975. "You know, he must have been a tremendous somebody to think all these things out. Then comes man . . . how could anyone improve on God? They are letting the factories come down here, and most of them are tremendous polluters, making chemicals that are bad for people and destroying our nursery grounds. Everybody wants a shortcut, you know. They don't have enough faith to plant a seed in the garden and let nature take its course with the help of a little elbow grease. No, they want a miracle seed. Most of the seeds you buy now are coated with something so the bugs won't eat them. They sprout and grow faster. Then you spray chemicals on the ground to kill the crawling bugs. The birds eat the bugs and the birds die or lay eggs that don't hatch. You're breaking into the circle of life. That will eventually destroy us. Man is messing with God's plan. Sometimes I wonder why God even bothers. He sure don't have to."

The Warrens' tranquillity ended abruptly. "The refinery had a horrible smell all the time," Nora says. "We fought it in the courts from the beginning, but we only won a few small battles. One of the big oil trucks from the refinery hit a bunch of our chickens and did them all in. Then there was the flood . . . I was talking on the phone when I saw water shimmering all around the house. Our yard had been flooded with foul water. Who knows what chemicals were in it? The company drained it and flushed out the yard. They paid us eighteen hundred dollars in damages, but life was never the same after that. We always had big gardens. When we had the soil tested, we were told not to grow anything there for seven years and not to eat anything grown on the property.

"Our water well was tested unfit for household use, but no one would put the blame on one source. Eventually we got city water out there, but before that Margarette got very sick. She has a neurological problem. She went to work one day, had some kind of seizure, and passed out. She was unconscious for an hour. It happened many times after that with no advance warning. The doctors down here couldn't tell us what was wrong. The ony thing they said was that she had very heavy metals in her body. We figured it had a lot to do with the refinery, but no one would admit it. I was worried sick that she'd have a seizure one day that we couldn't bring her back from. I took her to a specialist in San Antonio and slept on the chair next to her hospital bed there for almost a month. They never told us exactly what was wrong with her, but they finally found some medicine that helps her a lot. The doctors told us Margarette couldn't stay near the refinery; it was making her more sick all the time. The refinery drove us all away. We moved into town (Ingleside) at the end of August, 1984. Bud and I found a man who would move the house Bud built for us that replaced our old trailer. We helped Margarette and her husband Mike to build themselves a nice new home right next to ours."

Unfortunately, that wasn't the end of family illnesses. "My mama got real sick, too. We had to put her in the hospital. When we went to bring her home, the doctors told us she had Alzheimer's disease. They told me I wasn't in good enough shape to manage her at home, and that I'd have to put her in a nursing home. It just killed me to do that. Mama is only in her early seventies."

Nora was mentally and physically exhausted when she returned from the nursing home. "I knew something was very wrong with her because her face was so flushed," Bud says. "Her blood pressure shot up with all the stress she was under. I told her to sit down and relax, but she couldn't." That night in November, 1984, the same day she put her mother in the nursing home, Nora had a massive stroke. She had just turned fifty-seven. "When they checked her blood pressure it was 240," Bud recalls. "She was paralyzed on her left side, couldn't talk, and could barely move. I started massaging all those muscles on her left side from that moment on. When you love somebody, you don't let them go. You take care of them."

Nora spent nearly a year in three different hospitals. To be with her, Bud retired from shrimping, accepting the penalties of getting his Social Security early. Their marine insurance had been axed in federal government cutbacks, so most of Nora's bills came straight out of their savings, their future. "Our whole world kind of fell apart when I had my stroke," Nora says at age fifty-eight. "It wiped out everything we had in thirty years of working."

Nora spent nine months at a rehabilitation hospital that specialized in stroke therapy. In her view, she was making very little progress. She was, however, one of the lucky ones. The stroke had left her with no brain damage other than some lapses of memory. She was speaking well, but one of the doc-

Nora and Bud have a special secluded beach where they sometimes go to enjoy some quiet time when they are not working.

tors told her she'd never walk again. She looked the doctor straight in the eye and said, "Don't count on it, old boy." From that moment on, Nora had a goal. She was determined to walk out of that place. She became an impatient, difficult patient, a stroke victim who once kicked a doctor across the room with her good foot.

"I was determined to dance with Bud on our forty-third anniversary in October, 1985," Nora says. "'I'll be damned if someone else is going to dance with Bud on our anniversary,' I told the doctors. 'I am.' They thought I was crazy. They insisted I couldn't walk and couldn't go home until I could. I told them to bring me a crutch. The doctor got me one of those crutches with five feet on the bottom. Out of sheer bullheadedness, I picked it up and shuffled off a few steps. They got so excited, they called Bud and Margarette to come get me. I could go home! I think I ran out of that place. And I danced with Bud on our anniversary at home, not too gracefully, but I danced."

The last hospital bill quickly zoomed up to seventeen thousand dollars. "We ended up trading our four lots by the refinery to the hospital for my care to pay that one. Bud said he didn't care about losing our place as long as he had me. I told him he'd just have to take me the way I am. I'm not all right, but's that's the way I am. There were several other ladies in this area that had strokes about the same time I did. They all died. So I guess I'm doing real good."

When Nora came home in the fall of 1985, she could barely walk. John's wife, Eileen, took out every book in the library

on stroke therapy and studied them. James rented videotapes. Bud and Eileen worked all of Nora's muscles every day so she wouldn't get stiff. They taught her to walk. Bud massaged her left side and facial muscles until his hands hurt. He stayed up nights to turn her three or four times in bed so she never got a bedsore or even a red mark. "Bud and Eileen did more for me than the therapists at the hospital," Nora says. "They never gave up. My left foot was so paralyzed and crooked it was practically turned around. They got it straightened up."

Today Nora walks well for short distances with a crutch or four-legged cane. Her conversations are punctuated by stretches and steps. On longer expeditions, like shopping trips, Bud puts her in a wheelchair. He takes Nora out every day to keep her spirits up. He has devoted his life to her care, and she gets a little stronger every day. The children and grandchildren don't come around as much now that the critical care period is over. Bud and Nora are together constantly, and they are not a depressing sight. They are a story of what love can do. They laugh a lot, uproarious laughter, much louder than they laughed ten years ago. And they hope. Bud still has the *St. Jo* tied up at the dock, looking forlorn from disuse. "I don't want to sell her quite yet," he says. "When Nora gets better, I hope . . . I think this is going to be a good shrimping season."

Bud has taken over all the cooking. "He had never cooked in his life, but he's become an excellent cook," Nora boasts. "He makes better piecrusts than I ever could." That's only an occasional splurge, however. Nora has learned to take care of herself and stay on a diabetic's diet. She's a slim 151 pounds, about half the size she was at her heaviest. They qualify for some fine state programs that ease Bud's labor. A lady comes to the house to clean for several hours a day, five days a week. She also helps Nora with personal grooming and often fixes dinner. A home nurse visits at regular intervals, and Nora attends therapy sessions for an hour twice a week, moving every muscle.

Nora's left arm and hand are still completely paralyzed and in a sling, but she's convinced they'll come back like her legs have. "I'm fighting and clawing every day to get back," she says. "The only way I'm going to get a nice fresh trout to eat again is to get well enough to get out in the boat and catch it myself. Don't be surprised if I do that someday. I'm bullheaded. I think I'm going to recover completely."

Nora
Dott
Warren

Mahala Combs

"Mahala Combs? She's a real good woman, but she's turned funny." That's a typical description of fifty-eight-year-old Mahala heard on Lotts Creek. To translate the old eastern Kentucky expression, it means she hears a different drummer. That just might be Mahala's salvation.

Deep in the Kentucky coalfields about fifteen winding miles from the nearest town of Hazard, Kelly Fork of Lotts Creek slices between mountain ridges. Mahala was born down the long, narrow hollow, and she will die there. Most of the families wedged into this densely populated strip of land have known more hard times than happiness. Poor roads have always isolated Kelly Fork from the mainstream, breeding chronic unemployment and poverty. In the 1960s and 1970s, once beautiful mountains were raped by coal-hungry strip miners. Traditionally this was an area of poor, but proud, subsistence farmers, but most of them have given up farming, defeated by landslides that bury their crops and threaten their homes. The atmosphere of failure hangs over much of the hollow like a thick, wet fog. It is obvious in the blank eyes of jobless men tinkering with their old cars and their nervous, overworked wives who try to keep the family alive. It is a place where men and women grow old quickly as the hope drains out of them. They pass their dreams to their children and grandchildren and pray that future generations will have a better, easier life.

Strikingly beautiful children are everywhere on Kelly Fork, transfusing it with life, laughter, and hope. Kids from Kelly Fork have achieved success, but they've had to leave to do it. That's the hard part. Close, loving families protect them from the knocks of the outside world, but staying on Kelly Fork is almost a death sentence for a young adult. Only the strongest survive. Most of the people left on Kelly Fork are old, jobless, or children. There are exceptions, people who refuse to give up. Mahala is one of them.

The dust of Kelly Fork's potholed main road coats houses and cars with a tan film. Breaking through the stifling cover of dust is the rhythmic banging of a single hammer rising from a bowl of land whose sides are the mountains. Building is an uncommon sign of hope in a hollow that has known much more destruction than construction. Mahala Combs, a row of nails protruding from her mouth, squats on the roof of her unpainted shack, pounding down tar paper. At 4'10" and ninety pounds, she is a wisp of a woman who seems unsuited for hard, physical labor. As she rises to stretch, hands massaging her aching back, a mountain breeze blows her thin, shoulder-length white hair, exposing a craggy face with sunken, tired eyes. But those eyes flicker with determination. She grabs her can of Prince Albert and the cigarette papers she has tied around her, and rolls a lumpy cigarette with tar-stained hands as she surveys her domain. There are two ragged acres littered with abandoned cars. A rusty creek polluted with mine acid flows through discarded bedsprings, stoves, and garbage, but Mahala sees beyond all that.

Hang Kelly Fork. Hang poverty. Mahala has a dream. She's determined to transform her three-room hovel, which leans and sags like the haunted houses in children's imaginations, into a comfortable six-room house that five generations of her family will be proud to visit. It's more than a dream. Adversity fuels her energy. The more impossible the situation looks, the harder

Kentucky mountaineer Mahala Combs, fifty-eight, refuses to let poverty defeat her spirit.

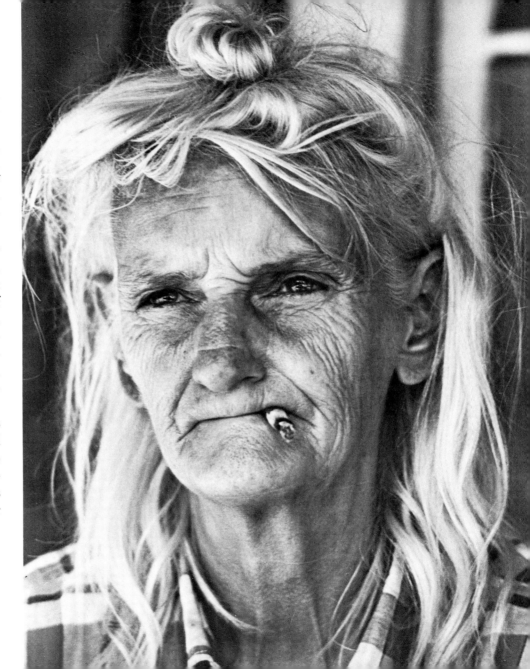

Perched on top of the new roof she is building over the bedrooms, Mahala lines up an ancient board to help support the roof. When she ran out of long boards, she used tree trunks to support the new roof.

she fights. She builds all day, every day, and usually all alone. For fifty dollars she bought all the lumber from an old house someone had torn down. That heap of scrap lumber is her building material. She has only three tools: a hammer, a bow saw, and an ax.

"I grew up in this house," Mahala says. "My daddy built it long about fifty year ago, I guess, but no one has lived here for a long time until we moved in last February. I wanted a home of my own on my own land, land my mommie deeded me before she died. No more old rental houses. This place was a mess when we got here, and it's even more torn up with all my building. This old house was flooded out by the creek and full of rats and mice before my cats ate 'em. It leaked a lot and was awful cold with rain and wind a-blowin' through all the holes in the walls and ceilings. I'm pluggin' those up. It's an old house that don't look too good, but it's gonna be right smart when I get through with it."

Poverty has been a way of life for Mahala since childhood, but her spirit isn't impoverished. "I don't know about them people that sit around," she says. "I don't know what their problem is. If I had to lay around, well, I just don't think I could live. I'm getting old and I don't feel too well anymore, but I'm used to work. My mommie raised me to work. From the time I was six and could climb up on a lard can and reach the stove and sink, I had to cook and wash the dishes. I can't remember playing much when I was a kid. I was too busy playing with them dirty dishes.

"I had to quit school in the third grade to stay home and help Mommie. She was sick most of the time and got so bad she couldn't fix anything to eat. She took spells falling and had to run to bed. I think she had high blood. She was a decent woman, decent about everything. My mommie never said a bad word in her life. She may have been sick a lot, but she

Mahala stands on the front porch of her home. She built the addition on the right, which is not yet finished.

raised us young'uns not to talk bad and not to take nothin' off nobody. She wasn't able to do much, so I did everything I could for her and Dad. Daddy worked in the coal mines shoveling coal. When he came home from work, he kept this little farm nice. He built fences all around it. I was the only girl in the family. I had five brothers. I don't know why the boys never did anything. We weren't what you'd call a very close family, all working together. I kept a home for my mommie as long as I could, almost until she died."

Mahala has been taking care of people ever since. Three of her six children are teenagers who still live at home. In addition, nine grandchildren and three great-grandchildren often stay with her; she has practically raised some of them. Her sixty-three-year-old husband Cullen depends on her, too. For twenty years he's been too ill to hold a job. As the head of the family, Mahala manages a meager household income of $216 a month. "We get Social Security and a little dab [$72] of welfare. I just hold on to the money as long as I can and buy only what we really have to have."

Just after dawn on the first day of every month, Mahala gets a ride to the county seat of Hindman and stands in a long line waiting for her food stamps. It often takes more than one day. "We pay $68 for $138 worth of food stamps every month. I go right out and buy all the flour, cornmeal, lard, dried beans, taters, and stuff I need for the whole month. Meat and stuff's so high I can hardly buy it, but we do buy a little bacon or

Cullen Combs, sixty-three, waits for the trickle of water from his hand-dug well.

hog meat. On the first days of the month, I buy a little hamburger and hot dogs to fix the kids a treat. We don't eat much meat, but I guess they get two or three good messes of meat a month. Soup beans, corn bread, and milk are our usual dinners. In the morning we make biscuits and gravy and sometimes an egg or two. When the garden is good, we get to have some fresh vegetables. I've got the sorriest garden I've ever had because of the flood this spring. I planted beans, taters, corn, peppers, cabbage, and tomatoes, but I ain't lookin' to get much from the garden this year. What the creek didn't drown, the locusts ate up awful bad. It'll feed the family, I guess, but it won't give us nothin' extra.

"I'm poor. I'd like to help other people if I had anything to help with. I ain't got no way to live myself, but if anyone comes in here hungry and wants something to eat, they're welcome to eat and share anything I've got. That ain't much, but maybe it's just as important to be nice to people as it is to help them out with money."

Mahala and Cullen have been married for twenty-six years, the second marriage for each. Affectionately, she calls her tan, whiskered husband "Old Man." "We have a good marriage because we like each other and always get along," Mahala says. "Bein' sorry for one is important. Cullen never had no one to take care of him. He was sickly and put out when he was a kid. He never went to school or learned to read and write. I think about those things a lot. I want to be good to him and do everything I possibly can for him, but a body can go just as far as they can, and that's as far as they can go. I hardly think there would be anybody else I'd ever want because

I don't think about nobody else. Sorry for anyone is more than love. It makes you think how to be good to them."

Mahala's first marriage, when she was only sixteen, ended abruptly a week after Ruby, their first child, was born. The proud father ran off with another woman. "I met Cullen before me and my first husband married, when I was about fourteen. He kept comin' round and comin' round but he ran off and married somebody else, so I went out with the Ritchie boy about three weekends and married him. He took out other women in front of me. I didn't figure that was right, so I told him if he wanted other women he should go get them and let me go. He did. Maybe that was the best thing for both of us, though it was hard on me raisin' that young'un alone until she was eleven years old. I used to wash for a lot of people on the creek, cleaned their houses and scrubbed their floors for $2.50 a week while Mommie and Poppy took care of Ruby. I packed coal right up to my stomach and piled it on the porches of the women I worked for. I remember workin' for Rose Whitacker, three mile up the creek. Dark was gettin' on, but she wanted me to finish up. I had to walk home in the dark. I couldn't see my hand before me that night. It was wintertime and the ice froze on me.

"All those years Cullen and his first wife had a good time, I reckon. I mean, they was happy, I reckon, as far as I know. Glad they was! But his wife, she went to the store one day and got killed on the railroad track. She left three little kids. Their baby was only three weeks old. Old Man's got three cute kids somewhere, but there are people who never wanted him to have those kids, so he could never get up with them. His oldest girl never did forget him, though. She's in Cincinnati, Ohio. Cullen came up and told me about his wife being killed. I felt so sorry for him. After that we got married."

Reflecting on their marriage, Mahala says, "I guess Cullen and I fell in love, something like that. Me and Cullen don't believe in lovin' on each other like some people does. We really think there's something more important when you start raisin' a family. Work and try to raise the kids, that's what we always thought about life. Some people can't forget the honeymoon. I never did believe in no foolishness. I always believed in something solid. When you get on the solid place, stay right there."

For the first six years of their marriage, Cullen loaded coal in the deep mines for twelve dollars a shift. Plagued by "blackout spells," which became more and more frequent, he would fall unconscious to the mine floor. The company forced him to quit. A twenty-year stint in the mines left Cullen with little more than a hacking, choking cough and lungs laden with coal dust—black lung, the insidious coal miners' disease much like emphysema. He has never received compensation for his injuries. Only recently, he hired a lawyer to plead his case.

"Back then when all the kids were small, we barely had enough money to live," Mahala remembers. "Old Man never made much money in the mines, then when he had to quit it put us in real hard trouble. I couldn't get a job and still raise the kids, but I got in good with Miss Slone and Bertha Whitacker at the school [Lotts Creek Community School, where all Mahala's children have gone, which has always helped the community through education, scholarships, food, and clothing]. They had some very nice clothes to give away. My neighbors, they like to wear pretty clothes, so I'd fix 'em up real nice and sell 'em to 'em very cheap. I kept my kids in food and school supplies for years just sellin' those clothes. That's about the only way we had to live until we got a little bit of welfare. Back then, things didn't cost too much. If it had been like now, we'd have starved.

"Cullen was an awful good father to the kids. He used to run around and play with them all the time when he was younger. Cullen still acts a lot like a kid. I really do feel sorry for him because of the way he does and the way he is. He coughs all the time and smothers with that rock dust on his lungs. When he goes to sleep, he rattles. He tries to work with me. Seems like he can't do much. He really don't know how to do anything like it's supposed to be done, but he tries everything. But really, he's just like a kid. Cullen don't have no worries. He seems very happy all the time. Just like a kid, you know."

When Cullen was younger, he missed the camaraderie in the coal mines, but age has slowed him down and changed his satisfactions. "I'd rather be stayin' here on the place, just takin' care of my animals," he says. At least three times a day he leads his large, raw-boned cow around their two acres, searching in vain for a clump of green grass "so she can pick." The sad-eyed cow is Cullen's prize possession. "I gave over two hundred dollars for her, but she's worth more than that to me," he says. Although he milks her twice a day, she provides less than a gallon of milk, barely enough for the family. A tiny yellow kitten claws up Cullen's pants and shirt and rides on his shoulder much of the day. She swats at his cigarettes as he rolls and licks them. At times she bites his ear, then licks it, winding her tail affectionately around his neck. Cullen grins widely. He proudly shows off two ponies, which he boasts can plow his mountain acreage better than any motorized plow or anything else on the hoof. Sadly, with the spring flood of acid water over the land, there was little use in plowing.

Getting to Mahala's home is a feat. It is accessible only by vehicles, bravely driven, which can manipulate snaky, single-lane dirt roads cut into the sides of mountains. Cars must creep slowly down the steep road for a quarter mile, bottoming out all the way and scraping rocks, then pass Mahala's impossible right-hand turn to turn around in a distant neighbor's driveway. Only then can a car head down Mahala's long, deeply rutted driveway. Few people beyond family make the trip.

The first impression of Mahala's environment is a shock to the senses. The smell of raw sewage permeates the air. Its source is likely a rusted corrugated tin outhouse with a striped sheet as a door backing into the creek. Unfortunately, it also backs up into the grandchildren's swimming hole. It is hard to imagine anyone swimming in the bright orange creek so obviously polluted by mine acid. "This creek used to be clear and have fish in it," Mahala says. "I don't imagine anything can live in thar now, not even a worm. I never seen nothin' anyway. It kills everything." The creek ripples over rocks, making placid country sounds, but soon it rushes over discarded stoves, abandoned swing sets, tires of every description, scores of Pepsi and motor oil cans, rusted car fenders, torn clothes stained with rust, eggshells, flour sacks, watermelon rinds, and twenty-five-pound lard cans. The creek may as well be the county dump. Each family's floatable garbage flows gently downstream to the

Cullen with his ever-present pet kitten.

next house and the next and the next.

The Combses have initiated their own system of flood control, lining the banks of the creek with abandoned cars. "This bottom gets flooded so much, the house would wash plumb away if we didn't put them old wrecked cars along the creek," Mahala explains. Additional abandoned cars surround the house like an army of aged men felled in combat and left to rot. There are twelve cars, each with a family history Mahala chronicles. "That's the '65 Ford Allen wrecked last month. Guy plowed right into him—smashed the radiator, busted the gas tank, broke the power steering, and smashed the fender

The grandchildren and great-grandchildren's swimming hole is directly behind the corrugated tin outhouse. Young mothers take their babies out to wade behind the outhouse in the orange creek, which is polluted with mine acid and garbage.

and side. Glad Allen got out okay. That one over there was a good car before we took the motor out. . . ." Mahala's two sons, Allen, nineteen, and Emory, eighteen, spend a good deal of their time coaxing the old cars to run, usually in vain. Only one, a beat-up, rusted '63 Chevy Impala, can climb up the hill and out of the hollow.

The Combses make use of the dozen abandoned cars.

Mahala stores clothes in many of them. Dogs sleep under others. Allen and Emory often sit alone in the cars dreaming private dreams. Occasionally, the cars are used as conference rooms since the old house has no privacy. Mahala dries the three-generation family's tennis shoes on one hood after she has washed them all in her wringer washing machine. The smashed car directly in front of the house is Mahala's roost. After building all day in the heat, she slumps there, cross-legged, trying to catch her breath.

Mahala's dream is believable when one watches the intensity of her work. She moves quickly, tossing her unruly white hair out of her eyes as she yanks a needed two-by-four out of the bottom of a pile of scrap lumber, pulls out the rusty nails, and pounds them straight for reuse. Soon she is climbing her homemade ladder of tree trunks with scrap lumber steps, hoisting a poplar trunk to the roof. Long boards are hard to come by, so she uses tree trunks to brace the new roof. She has a squint-eyed, lock-jawed determination that makes the dreary environment recede in importance. Mahala has a way of seeing the apple trees around the house and blotting out the junk cars that surround them. "I never get discouraged." she says. "I can't let myself look back on all the work I have to do on this house. I just do one thing at a time and get it done.

"I taught myself how to build houses by studying on it," Mahala said proudly one day. "I practice with a hammer. I just study what I have to do—don't go too fast on it. I learned to drive the nails good. I don't have no ruler or nothin', so I measure with a plank. Nobody told me what material to use. I just figgered it all out. Except for some roofing paper and drywall,

I can get by with this scrap lumber I bought. I just have to piece a lot."

Already Mahala has built on a new bedroom and raised the ceiling in the front bedroom from 5'5" to 8 feet. "I don't know why my daddy built ceilings so low," she complains. "He did that on all of his houses." Short on money to buy drywall, Mahala has covered the gaping holes in the walls temporarily with Colonial Iodized Salt boxes and a Do It Yourself TV Antenna box. The bedroom has two double beds, one for Mahala and Cullen and the other for Louise, their fourteen-year-old daughter. Mahala reroofed the room with tar paper though she still hasn't plugged up all the holes in the walls. "The roof doesn't leak now and storms don't usually blow that way," she explains. There are three windows, each with a different kind of curtain or sheet covering it. The windows provide the only source of light for that room. One naked bulb on the kitchen ceiling uses the only electrical outlet in the house. It has five extension cords plugged into it and taped in various directions across the ceiling. The bulb has a short life span because tall, handsome son Emory, who is preoccupied with thoughts of girls, constantly crashes into it with his head. Cullen would prefer having no electricity. He complains about the twenty-seven-dollar-a-month "juice bill" for the stove, refrigerator, two bare bulbs, and a TV and threatens to convert to coal oil.

The inside of the house is a disaster. Floors sag. There are holes in most walls and ceilings. Most rooms have three layers of wallpaper in various stages of peeling. Mahala is slowly remodeling the existing rooms as time permits, tearing up three dirty, splitting layers of linoleum, and laying wood strips, which

After a long day, Mahala rests on the hood of the old Ford that Allen wrecked. Mahala gives herself the dregs of food and clothes after everyone else is taken care of.

she planes with her long-handled ax. Cullen helps her saw the wood strips on the fifty-pound lard can in the kitchen. He tries to work outside, but he has little strength. When Mahala was building the bedroom roof, Cullen stood on the ground handing up her long, pieced boards. He hugged the lumber in his arms like a new father gingerly holding his first baby. He gasped and choked as he lifted it over his head. To Cullen, in his condition, they must have seemed like three-hundred-pound barbells.

Mahala Combs
111

Three able-bodied teenagers rarely help. Occasionally Allen or grandson Carlos Ray lends a hand on the roof. When Mahala is asked about her teenagers' inactivity, she jumps to their defense. "All my kids think about is school. They can't do these things. All I think about is work. They study school. I study work. I just want them to get their lessons in school. School's hard for my kids. Sometimes they have to stay up until one in the morning to get their lessons, but I've never had a young'un that didn't like to go to school. I want my kids to get theirs with a pencil, finish school, and get an education, then get a good, light job. I don't want them to have to leave Kentucky to work in some factory in Ohio or Indiana and I sure don't want my sons in no coal mine. Clifford Ray, he's my second cousin, he got mashed up in the mines and he's in the hospital now. The mines are dangerous. Look what happened to Old Man. I like to see my kids study hard, then take a good, long vacation in the summer. They need some rest and pleasure.

"I've worked all my life, and it never did hurt me. If it did, I couldn't tell it. But now I'm not as stout as I used to be. I can't put up as much work as I used to. I get tired, but I go on anyway. If you quit for tired, you'll never work much. If you quit for feelin' bad, you'll never work none either. I just go on and work like I done almost since I came into the world. That's all I know how to do. I can't see no other way but to just work until you die."

As if Mahala didn't have enough problems building a

Mahala builds an addition onto the old house her father built fifty years before.

house alone with no money, no tools, and no help, the strip miners started dynamiting the mountain behind her a few months ago. Although armed mountain men in some hollows successfully stopped the strip miners from beheading their mountains for coal, Kelly Fork has been devastated. Decades before, when the mountain people were isolated and few could read or write, many signed their mineral rights away with an X for a pittance. "I was on top of the house a-workin' when I heared them comin'," Mahala remembers. "They shot. Something blowed up. It made such a noise, I dodged down. I found out later that one of their motors blowed up and a pedal flew off a machine they was workin' on. Whatever it was flew by me pretty close and gave me a little shock. It didn't hit me, but when I dodged down, I hurt my leg and arm. If that thing woulda hit me, it woulda killed me.

"I never fought the strippers. I've never been one to argue with nobody, but they wanted me to sign a right of way through my place so they could get the coal out. I wouldn't sign it because I never sign nothin' for nobody. It's not legal, but they did it anyway. They destroyed the water and tore my land up there. If the strippers destroyed my house, I'm sorry to tell you what I'd have to do. A feller has to protect what little he's got. I'd shoot 'em. We haven't got any law in this part of the country. I hope the mountain doesn't scoot down on us after all they done up there."

These days, since Mahala works full-time on the house, Cullen has taken over the cooking. "Old Man, he helps a lot that way. Yeah, Buddy, he's a good cook. He can make pies, bread, and everything. He does right smart. If it wasn't for him,

it would be too hard on me. I do all the work out yonder because he can hardly see. He's goin' blind, you know. When he lifts and tries to do hard work, he smothers. We help each other."

The door to the kitchen is always wide open to grandchildren, dogs, cats, and flies. Mahala's first child, Ruby, now thirty-eight, lives directly behind them with her husband and children. The only water supply for some fifteen people in the two homes comes from a fifteen-foot-deep well Cullen dug on the mountain about fifteen years ago. A narrow black line of hose leads from the well to a washtub in front of the Combs house. Water flow is stopped by shoving a whittled broomstick into the hose. It took Cullen a month to dig the well with his hands, a mallet, and a shovel. Somehow, with careful conservation, the water usually suffices. On wash days, however, when Mahala seems to do load after load of clothes outside in her wringer washing machine for her family and grandchildren, the flow usually stops. Their backup water source is a mountain spring across the creek. Buckets in hand, patient Cullen wades back and forth to the spring bringing Mahala all the water she needs.

◄

Mahala, oversleeping, in the bedroom she shares with Cullen and fourteen-year-old daughter Louise. In this room Mahala has raised the ceiling and tried to patch most of the holes with boxes.

Inside the house Mahala attempts to lay a hardwood floor over three layers of dirty linoleum. She had patched the holes in the walls with G.E. appliance boxes. The hole in the sagging ceiling is covered by a Jeno's pizza box. ►

When Cullen makes his morning biscuits, there's usually a granddaughter beside him trying to help. In the kitchen there's a good electric range and an old, but working, refrigerator. A yellow table with chrome legs and no chairs serves as a counter because meals are informal. Cullen bakes his first round of biscuits about 10 A.M. He leaves the biscuits in an iron skillet on the stove for people to eat whenever they want them. "We use five or six twenty-five-pound pokes of flour and three or four twenty-five-pound pokes of cornmeal a month, plus twenty-five to fifty pounds of lard," Cullen estimates. "We have right smart company when all the family comes." Most of the family eats standing up, wandering around or sitting on Mahala's bed, but there's a big gray easy chair and a fifty-pound lard can in the middle of the kitchen floor if anybody wants to sit down. The cat leaves Cullen's shoulder to munch on any leftovers people throw into an old refrigerator produce drawer that serves as a garbage can.

During the building and remodeling, things are out of place much more than they would normally be because five people and their possessions are crammed into three rooms. On a kitchen cabinet, there's a bust of Lincoln and a row of college textbooks, heavy on sociology. They look incongruous in a kitchen with no running water, with ceilings that sag to five feet. The books belong to Allen, the first Combs child ever to attend college. He is a painfully shy nineteen-year-old who says he'd like to be a writer. Allen is an avid reader and con-

Cullen tries to handle a long board Mahala has pieced, though he has little strength and doesn't know how to grip a board.

sidered bright. Although he has only completed one semester in a community college in nearby Hazard, he talks about going on to study journalism at the University of Kentucky with scholarship help. In the same breath he says he should stay home to help his mother. His insecurities about emerging from Kelly Fork into a better-educated world are obvious, but Allen has come a long way, considering his father can only sign his name with a shaky X. Mahala will not admit to having a favorite among her six children, but she adores Allen. Of her family he has the best chance of breaking the cycle of poverty. She doesn't say that, just, "Allen is good at everything. He can do anything he wants."

Although most of the Combs children are grown now, the laughter and tears of small children still fill the house. Grandchildren and great-grandchildren love to visit Mahala. Appalachia is a land of extended families with strong family ties. Mahala's children have stayed close. The most distant one, a daughter, lives only an hour's drive away. "All my kids like their daddy and mommie," Mahala says. "They just don't want to leave us." Every weekend there's a large, spontaneous family reunion at Mahala's house.

"Raisin' a family is one of the most important things in my life," Mahala says. "I never did think too much about the number of children I had. I just took 'em as I got 'em. I always loved kids. I guess I spoiled 'em, too, 'cause I always pampered them a lot. Some people just lay their babies down and let them go. I never did my kids that way. I always had them in a tub or pan of water when they was little, cleaned 'em up and all that. They grow a lot faster when you bath[e] them a lot.

Mahala is worn out after a long day of building.

"All my young'uns get along good with us and with each other. I'm proud of my kids. They all turned out good. They all want to help somebody. I don't mind sayin' that's the way I raised 'em. We've always helped each other out all we could, all of us. Back when I was raising my other kids and my oldest girl, Ruby, was married, she helped me out a lot. When Old Man couldn't get no work to do, we stayed with them in their house. I've always loved all my kids, and they've always loved

Cullen "packs" water from a mountain spring through the polluted orange creek to Mahala for her washing.

'em up right, they'll straighten up. They won't depart from the right way. I think the Bible says that. I can't read the Bible, but the Lord, he gives it to me. I always had my kids in church. When they in church, they sure ain't in no bad place. God got us through the hard times. When he fur you, there's nobody that can be against you.

"Really, the most important thing in life is God. Lovin' is next and then a-eatin', but no drinkin' no whiskey, no beer, and no wine. Drinkin', killin', stealin', card playin', marijuana, it's all wrong. If it's not right with God, then it ain't right with me.

"I don't go to church much anymore because I can't afford to. I ain't got no money to give, but you don't have to go to church to be saved. I'm an Old Regular Baptist, have been for about fifteen years. Before that, I felt I was lost. My soul was a-goin' to hell. I believe the Bible says hell is many times hotter than a stove. We can't stand that kind of fire. I had a problem with drinkin' when I was sixteen or seventeen. All that had to be took away, and there was no one to take it away but God. I got down on my knees and prayed, and he saved me. It only takes God a crank of the finger to save you if you are earnest of heart. I felt so happy when he came into my soul. Then Brother Elzie Kaiser and Brother Andy Bates baptized me in Camp Branch. I know I'm saved. I never drank a drop after that. I don't know about Old Man. He's a backslider.

"After you get saved, it's wrong to cut your hair. Once I cropped a little bit, right by my face. When I cut that little tip end off, God showed me it was wrong. You know, disfigurin' up yourself awful by makin' up too much. Little ol' bath pow-

me. All my children and grandchildren always knowed if I had something, they had it, too.

"I never believed in being mean to kids. You have to just talk to kids a lot and tell them what's right and wrong. I told my kids they could never cuss, play cards, or drink, and I never had any of those things around them. Raisin' kids up right is very important. They get a little off sometimes, but if you raise ders, I don't believe that's wrong. Clean and nice is different. You need soap and water to wash up, bath powders, and clean clothes. The Lord wants you to be a nice person. He's nice hisself, and he wants you to be nice and clean. And clean your soul. You pray to the Lord to forgive you for what you've done, and don't never do it no more. He'll come right into your soul. Then you'll be able to shout and tell all the good things the Lord done for you.

"You are really livin' when you live for God. Be good to everybody. And don't ever look for it back from other people. If you give anybody anything, it's wrong to take it back. That's the reason I never did have very much. I never took nothin' off nobody, unless I gave 'em somethin' for it. My young'uns are like that. They won't ask for help. They try to live on their own, get by by themselves, so they won't owe anybody. That's what it is. None of my young'uns wants to owe anybody."

Eldest daughter Ruby lives in a simple home about thirty feet behind her mother and has to cope with even more problems than Mahala. For twenty years of her twenty-three-year marriage to a coal miner, she was happy, enjoying her seven children and three grandchildren. Then three years ago she says her husband got on drugs and nerve pills, lost interest in her and the kids, and started chasing other women. Ruby, who has a heart condition, sits back stoically, hoping her marriage will improve, but her pain often shows. She's a motherly woman who watches over Mahala as well as her own children and grandchildren.

Anna Lee, twenty-three, Mahala and Cullen's first child together, has a happier life with her truck-driver husband,

Granddaughter Rosa Jean, nine, and Mahala play with Elroy, Mahala's great-grandson. Rosa is Elroy's aunt.

though she quit school in eighth grade to marry. Their sons, Bartley and Boyd, are among Mahala's favorite grandchildren.

Rosalena, twenty-two, quit school six months before her high-school graduation to marry a handsome coal miner, Estill Noble. Estill worked hard and is now a coal mine boss. Like her sisters, Rosalena has never worked outside the home. Her strongest desire is to have children, something she has not yet been able to do.

The three children at home—Allen, nineteen, Emory, eighteen, and Louise, fourteen—are more studious and considered

Mahala does load after load of wash for her family in her old Maytag wringer washer almost every day.

smart in school. Allen is the only one who is interested in college. Pressed for money to pay his tuition after one semester, he dropped out of school, hoping to return soon. Although he was offered a loan from Lotts Creek Community School, which arranges for deserving mountain children to go to college, he turned it down out of pride. "Allen don't want to suppose up [impose] on anybody," Mahala explains. "He wants to get by by hisself, but he's stuck with no money to go to school

on." Allen wants to get back in college so badly, he'll likely accept the loan for the coming semester.

Both Allen and Louise are too timid even to eat with the rest of the family. They are loners who rarely say a word. Emory is just the opposite. The tall, sandy-haired boy is boisterous and flighty. He is about to finish high school and is considering going to vocational school to be a mechanic, but his main joy in life is chasing girls.

"Back when we was raisin' these kids we had our ups and downs," Mahala admits. "Life was hard when Old Man had to quit workin'—real hard, but we pulled through. All of my kids have had a hard time with no way to live. No checks much, you know. I couldn't buy for them like I ought to because I never had much money to buy with. They had love, though. All my young'uns and family are important to me. Really, there's nothin' else. I'll have to say this, though, I wouldn't want to raise any more kids. If I found one that didn't have a mother, I'd take it, if it needed takin' care of. I wouldn't want it cheated or treated dirty or nothin' like that. I think one of the most important things in this part of the country is to take better care of kids —tell 'em things, talk to 'em, try to get 'em straightened up. There's too many nervous kids in the world, and they make the other kids bad and cause all the problems.

"The most important thing to me is livin' a good life . . . workin' hard, tryin' to get along with everybody, and tryin' to be good to everybody. This is a hard life to take, no matter how you take it. I don't know how I got by sometimes in my life. I guess I always studied how to get by, how to make it. I always studied how to live."

JULY 1986

As hard as she has worked, it is remarkable how little Mahala has aged in the dozen years since she was pounding away on her ancient house, trying to make it livable. She's nearly seventy now. "I thought I was seventy-eight, because I feel like it sometimes, but the records say I was born January 19, 1917," she says. Mahala has probably dropped another ten pounds. "I'm healthy, just old and worked out," she says, but she still moves in double time, that straight white hair blowing in the wind. "About the only thing wrong with me is that the doctor says my lungs ain't too good. He made me quit smoking." She has replaced the lumpy, hand-rolled cigarette dangling out of her mouth with chaws of Red Man chewing tobacco.

Mahala still lives on the same two acres on Kelly Fork, beside the same orange creek that was choked with garbage and lined with old cars for "flood control." But the air no longer smells like sewage and the dozen wrecked cars that once surrounded her are now gone. Mahala's life-style has improved considerably since Cullen's black lung was finally officially diagnosed by a doctor. One day, some years ago, compensation arrived in a lump sum of twelve thousand dollars. To Mahala, it was a fortune. She had never held so much money in her hands at one time. Fortunately, a lifetime of hard times had taught Mahala how to spend their windfall wisely, wasting little.

"The first thing I did was go out and buy us a used three-

Mahala embraces Cullen's pet kitten, the one who rides on his shoulder all day.

bedroom trailer, so we could have more space, a roof over our heads that didn't leak, heat, and a real bathroom. It don't look like too much since the creek flooded us, but I paid six thousand dollars for it. Then I had a good deep well drilled so we'd never run out of water again. I bought a new refrigerator, a deep freeze, and a washer and dryer. I can get anything I want in town, even credit, because I pay my bills. We bought a big color TV for Old Man and the kids and got on the cable. I'm too busy workin' to watch TV much, but Old Man sure likes it. He's seventy-five and don't do nothin' now but watch television. He can't go out anywhere by hisself. If he got to a road where cars go by he couldn't see them or hear them fast enough to get out of the way. There ain't much for him to do since his animals got killed. His cat got in the car engine and died and someone shot his cow one night. He misses them awful bad." Cullen looks healthier than he did twelve years ago and coughs less now that he no longer helps Mahala with her work. He looks bored, glued in front of his big TV with its flawless reception, like a man who has ceased to have a function.

Mahala and Cullen's monthly income has jumped from $216 a month to $715. "It's all black-lung payments and Social Security," Mahala says. "We make too much money to get welfare and food stamps." Mahala is proud of their new-found self-sufficiency and the things they've accomplished, but she admits, "Life is just as hard as it always was, maybe harder. I go to the store and pick a little here, pick a little there, tryin' to get everything as cheap as I can. You can't find nothin' hardly cheap no how. I feed a lot of people. They all come to eat with me. I never turn anybody down. There's a lot of grandchildren

runnin' around here. They young, and it's harder. I wouldn't have to raise them, too, but they stay around me and I don't run no kids off. I wouldn't take nothin' for 'em."

In this part of eastern Kentucky, where families are close and steep mountains make building lots scarce, it is typical for some sons and daughters to return to the home farm and build their homes on a portion of it. No one is crowded on fifty or a hundred acres, but on about a half-acre semicircle, all the flat bottomland Mahala owns, the population density is more urban than rural. There are thirty-four people living in two trailers and seven houses, four generations of family. Four of Mahala's six children surround her, and three of Ruby's children have built around her. Small children run everywhere with their assorted dogs, cats, puppies, and kittens. No child will ever have to worry about having no one to play with, nor will any adult experience loneliness, but privacy is a commodity that's hard to come by. Mahala has twenty-one grandchildren and seventeen great-grandchildren now. Sometimes it sounds as if all of them are playing in front of their old red-and-white trailer. Their tiny pants and shirts are pinned on her curtains to dry. If family were not enough, Mahala has taken in a pale teenager with a listless baby and built her a tiny house. "I took her in because she had no place to go," Mahala says. The girl and her baby seem completely accepted by the family. Mahala loves the small baby as one of her own grandchildren.

Mahala's long building project may have been more of a learning experience to her children and grandchildren than she once thought, because they have built their own homes. They are spartan houses in matching black tar paper, but they appear to be competently built.

"I like havin' all the children, grandchildren, and great-grandchildren around me," Mahala says. "I like that very much. It seems like they all had a hard time livin' and they don't understand a lot of things. I've been livin' long enough to tell 'em what to do. I try to teach 'em how to stretch their money and how to keep their kids goin' with something to eat. I don't think that any kind of life anybody lives in the country, back in the hills, would be easy. It's hard, hard livin', when you have so little to live on."

None of Mahala's children holds a steady job at the moment, and it's unlikely any of them will as long as they stay on Kelly Fork. Unemployment in the area stands at 22 percent. Emory, thirty, who lives next door to Mahala and hauls old cars and scrap metal to a junkyard for cash, comes the closest to being employed. "Emory's not on welfare," Mahala says proudly. "He works for his kids. Sometimes he goes to Lexington to work when he can't make it here. I keep Emory's three little boys. He wants them to stay next door with him, but they won't do it. I don't think they like it there because their mother drinks beer. I guess I'll continue to have them on me for the rest of my life."

Even Allen, a thirty-one-year-old bachelor who fulfilled his dream of attending the University of Kentucky, but did not graduate, has no job. Still a loner, he goes into a back room of Mahala's trailer when strangers come, never emerging. "Allen is very shy; he don't like to talk," says his mother protectively. "He needs a few more credits to finish college. I'm sure he will go back to get his degrees when I'm dead. Right now he doesn't want to leave me. He helps me a lot. He can fix the electric stove, his car, anything he wants to. He helps these little kids with their schoolwork. I don't know what his major in college was. I never asked. I do know he wanted to be a writer and he's writin' every day on word puzzles and contests he gets in the mail. He won five hundred dollars once. He winned a ring the other day. Don't know how much it's valued. His dream is to win a brand-new car."

Except for Rosalena, who is still married to the same man and has the baby she wanted, all of Mahala's daughters' marriages soured. In some cases, drugs, and violence, once unheard of on remote Kelly Fork, played a role in their demise. Louise, a husky, capable twenty-six-year-old with only a ninth-grade education, is saddled with four young children to raise. She lives in a trailer across from Mahala's. Ruby, even more motherly at fifty, lives in the same house with a new man, enjoying a fresh brood of pretty grandbabies around her. Her youngest daughter, eighteen, already has three children.

"I wish my daughter Anna Lee was still here," Mahala says wistfully. "I miss her so much. She's in Florida. When she was here, she worked as a night watchman. Her husband would get jealous and treat her horrible. He'd hit her, knock her down, and throw skillets at her. She got away. There was this old man, old enough to be her daddy, who took her out of it and went with her. He tries to do everything he can for her. They have one child.

"When Anna Lee came here, she had no place to put her trailer but where my old house was. I felt sad about losing the old house after I had worked so hard on it. I had finished everything pretty well, but I hadn't put the siding on. I couldn't stand to tear the house down myself, but I decided to let the others do it because Anna Lee had nowhere to live. After she put the trailer there, it got burnt down. Some of them got mad at her old man for being so mean and they probably set fire to it. It didn't hurt anybody. She was working at the time and I was keeping her kids.

"My children didn't come out as good on their marriages as I did with Cullen. Cullen couldn't work, but at least we stayed together and tried to help each other. There was none of the pot, meanness, or shooting that some of my girls had to put up with. It don't do 'em no good to get married if they just get divorced. Maybe it's all right that their husbands left. I'm sorry to say that some people in the family live together now and have children without bein' married. I think it's dishonest, especially if they do it for the welfare payments. I think some of my children are better off with me than they were married. I'd say back in the hills here is the best place to raise your children and not get them destroyed. It's better than out in the cities. I teached all my kids that I love them and didn't want them to get out and killed or get into no trouble. I wanted them to work and try to have something. That's all you can do."

Unfortunately, even with so many young, able-bodied family members around, Mahala still does most of the work. Every day she washes five or six loads of clothes. Mahala was the one who planted a beautiful vegetable garden on the hillside which she will harvest alone. She does the canning and freezing, though much of the family will share in the eating. It is blackberry season, a time when Mahala makes daily hikes into the woods to pick. No one accompanies her. "I wouldn't want the kids to get sticky," she says. Care of the sow and the boar and the chickens behind the trailer are Mahala's chores. After doing her string of chores and while most of the young women are watching soap operas, Mahala climbs the hill to Kelly Fork's main road searching for aluminum cans she can redeem.

"My kids never did . . . well, I figure they have their hands full takin' care of all them little kids," she says defensively. "I do a lot of that, too, but I figure they have their hands full feedin' 'em and washin'. I don't ask them for much help. Kids today want more than you can hardly give 'em. I just figure they got their hands full."

Now that Mahala's children are adults, she thinks in terms of their children. "I give my grandchildren and children all I can, and when I die, they'll have it all. Cullen and I, we done all right, as well as anybody could do that has a hard way of livin' and is tryin' to get by. I want them little kids to have an education. I try to teach 'em to go to church and live the right kind of life and not steal nothin' nobody's got. I try to teach 'em all those things, and I hope they will get by."

Teresa Camarillo

On a sultry Sunday afternoon three generations of the Camarillo family crowd the front porch of their modest frame home in Villa Coronado, Texas, thirteen miles south of San Antonio. Fifteen people jam together on lawn chairs, the car hood, and wrought-iron porch railings, all joking and laughing with one another. Teresa Camarillo, thirty-five, mother of all the eleven children gathered around her, squeezes the accordion to the delight of Adam, Jr., her first grandchild, who rolls over in his walker to bounce to the music. Four separate animated conversations go on at once, some in Spanish and some in English, punctuated by the crows of roosters in the backyard. Fourteen-year-old Oscar puts on his boxing gloves and challenges his mother to a fight. Fun-loving Teresa calls for a pair of gloves and punches lightly at her son's ribs until Oscar gets carried away and lands a left jab squarely on her jaw. The family rises in unison, like a church choir on Sunday morning, eager to help, but Teresa waves them off laughing, handing the gloves to Oscar's next victim. The horseplay goes on for hours.

The Camarillos have a good reason to be happy. Teresa and her husband Ramon, forty-seven, were lifelong migrant workers, as their parents were before them. Two years ago they broke out of the migrant stream and found full-time jobs in the San Antonio area. Life is always difficult for a family of thirteen, but they are still celebrating their successes. Their lives have stability now. They can plot their future with some certainty rather than by the whim of hailstorms, torrential rains, and early frosts, which can destroy the incomes of people who follow the crops.

"We were never treated mean as migrants," Teresa says. "We were lucky to work for farm families in Michigan who gave us nice houses to live in with heaters in every room, but

being a migrant is a lot of hard work. Your income depends on the weather. It might be very good. It can also be terrible. Sometimes storms ruin the crops and all you can do is move on or go home. Every day it rains, you miss a day of work. In the last few years new machines have been taking people's jobs away. They have huge machines that shake the cherries right off the trees. It takes only five people to run the machine; forty or fifty families used to pick the cherries off the trees. A lot of families drive all the way to Michigan or Wisconsin just to find they don't have a job anymore.

"I don't regret going to Michigan to pick the crops. I learned a lot of things I never knew before. My English wasn't very good until we got up there and I made friends with Anglo teenage girls from that area who were working in the fields with us to make extra money for college. We'd go bowling together. They helped me improve my English and I taught them to speak Spanish. We still write to each other. We had some good times up north, but it is much better for all of us to be in one place now."

The Camarillo home, painted vivid aqua blue, is as cheerful-looking as its owners. "I wanted a color to match the big, blue Texas sky I remember picking strawberries on a sunny day," Teresa explains. Surrounded by flowers, Teresa's home is one of the few bright spots in Villa Coronado. Villa Coronado isn't a town, it is a forgotten settlement on the fringes of a

The Camarillo family gathers on Teresa's front porch. All are home-bodies; even the married children return every weekend and most evenings.

Oscar, fourteen, challenges his mother to a boxing match. Somehow he forgets he's fighting his mother and lands a left on her jaw. Another son rises to help, but Teresa laughs and waves him off.

beautiful city. Rows of shoebox homes on dusty streets pack in some two thousand Mexican-Americans. No one knows exactly how many people live there because most people board up their tiny houses and follow the crops half the year. Many houses are gray and shabby, but others, like the Camarillo home, are well tended and landscaped with two-pound Folger's coffee

cans full of marigolds and mums. Most homes are guarded by chain-link fences that have spikes on the top and are locked with padlocks on heavy chains. Hand-painted signs on the fences warn BEWARE — BAD DOG, whether or not a dog exists. There is little protection in a place where crime and vandalism run rampant and grinding poverty is the norm.

The streets in Villa Coronado have melodic names like Estancia, San Acacia, and Socorro, but they are little more than dirt alleys riddled with potholes. When it rains, they flood. Children wallow ankle deep in mud to board the school bus, which recently became mired in front of the Camarillo home. "I just call our street the San Antonio River," Teresa says with irony. During the hot, dry summers dust coats the homes with a dingy layer of tan. When the sun sets, the streets can turn mean. "People used to call Villa Coronado 'Vietnam' before the police started patrolling it, there were so many shootings and stabbings," says Ramon. "I wouldn't go near those bars on the corner. It was well known that the sheriff's patrol would never answer a call very fast. They always waited until the victims were dead in a big pool of blood and the murderers had taken off. When the coast was clear, we'd see about six squad cars speeding in with their lights flashing and sirens going. I think the police do more pop drinking and sleeping in their cars than patrolling around here, but it's better than it used to be."

Unpaved Estancia Street in front of the Camarillo home floods every time it rains hard, and Teresa calls it the "San Antonio River." She and her neighbors are fighting to get the street paved.

Teresa and Ramon rise above their environment. Most of the time it is hard to distinguish Teresa from the teenagers she most enjoys being around. She does not look or act like a mother of eleven who picked carrots, cotton, squash, apples, cherries, and strawberries on farms from Texas to Michigan for nearly twenty-five years.

Ramon is a little bulldog of a man, dark, lean, and muscular from a lifetime of stooped labor. He is probably the epitome of a macho man to his sons, but he is also a gentle man who is happiest being home with his family. Teresa calls him "Camarillo the homebody," because unlike most men in Villa Coronado, he doesn't go to the bars to get drunk every Friday and Saturday night. The Lone Star beers he drinks on weekends are consumed in his own yard. "I just like being home with Teresa and the kids, with my family," he says, surrounded by the smoke from his front-yard barbecue, where he grills his special "chicken—Camarillo style." He motions son-in-law Adam over to share some of his culinary secrets. "This is the best part," he says, grinning as he drowns the bird in beer.

"I married Ramon over twenty years ago when I was only fifteen," Teresa says. "We met because we were all working on the carrot harvest on a big farm near San Antonio. Both my mother and father were born in Mexico, but they've been in Texas a long time. My dad came in 1901. My earliest childhood memory was being carried into the fields to play while my parents picked the crops. When I got a little older, I loved bouncing in the back of a pickup truck with my brothers and sisters. I don't remember a lot about my childhood, but I remember the ice on the beet fields in South Dakota and how cold it was.

I can still see the curved knives they used to cut the beets. I had seven brothers and sisters traveling with me. That was a small family compared to Ramon's. He had seventeen. After picking the last crops in the north, we'd come home to San Antonio for the winter. It was a hard life and we were poor, but we were happy most of the time until my mother died when I was ten. That was very sad. She was pregnant with twins and died in childbirth. They all died—my mother and both twins. We went to stay with an uncle for a while. We were glad that Dad got married again soon so we could come home. I wish I could remember more about my mother. I was so young when she died. We loved our stepmother, though. She took good care of Dad and us. They live in San Antonio. When they stopped migrating, Dad became a house painter. He's seventy-four now.

"I started working in the fields when I was about ten or so, picking cotton in Eddy, Lubbock, and Taylor, Texas. I was always fat. My father complained because he had to pull me around on the cotton sack when he picked. How I loved to ride the cotton! I wasn't lazy, though. I turned out to be the best cotton picker in the family, stuffing the cotton down to the bottom of the sack with my feet so it would hold more. By the time I was twelve or thirteen, I could pack 115 pounds of cotton in the bag and carry it. Ramon never believed that. He thought it was just a big flood of talk, so the August after we got married we went up there to try it. Ramon couldn't take the hot weather. He got sunstroke the very first day and vomited all over the fields while I proved to him that I could still stuff all that cotton in a bag and lift it.

"When I first met Ramon he worked in the warehouse

Ramon and Teresa relax on their front porch. Their relationship is a very fun-loving, close one.

me a lot and I liked him, but he didn't last too long. He got leukemia and died at fifteen. There was nothing we could do.

"I'm glad I married an older, experienced man. If we had both been as young as I was, the marriage wouldn't have lasted. Ramon is a special kind of man. I'm lucky to have a husband who trusts me and lets me go out and do things on my own, even get a job. There aren't many men around here who'd do that. So many men are jealous and want their wives home all the time. The women never have a chance to do anything.

"I don't have any secret for twenty years of happy marriage. I just love Ramon. We've always trusted each other. I think that's what makes it good between a man and a woman. If you really love your husband, follow him and enjoy him. Be together and work together as much as possible. I guess that's my motto. I try to give Ramon what he needs and help him. We've always helped one another in whatever we wanted to do."

It is interesting to watch the dynamics of Teresa and Ramon's relationship on a daily basis. Teresa is a natural leader whom children and adults turn to for help. She's completely capable of running the family, but she usually talks all family matters over with Ramon and defers to him for a final decision. As the boss, Ramon's manhood, his machismo, is never threatened. "I don't let him feel bad," Teresa explains. "If he asks, 'Who's the boss in this family?' I say, 'You are—sometimes.' The truth is that sometimes I'm the boss and sometimes he is."

Teresa is very proud of Ramon and the accomplishments he's made with only a third-grade education. "Ramon has always had poor jobs because we were migrating at least half of the year. Until the last two years he never made more than

of Van der Walle farms near San Antonio building wooden boxes and icing down the carrots to go on the trains. When the owner saw how hard my family worked, he put us inside with Ramon. I put the carrots in plastic bags and packed them in his boxes. Ramon was twelve years older than me, but I didn't care if he was old. We waited only a month to get married. My father and stepmother didn't object. They liked Ramon and knew he'd take good care of me. He had been married before, but his wife died three days after their first child was born, when she was only sixteen. I helped Ramon raise his boy. He liked

$40 to $50 a week in his whole life. We'd leave for Michigan at Easter time and not get back until sometime in October. Every year he had a terrible time coming home and having to look for a job all over again to support me and the kids. We are far better off staying here in one place all year long. Ramon started out two years ago as a street sweeper for the city of Windcrest [an affluent suburb of San Antonio twenty-two miles from the Camarillo home]. He worked very hard. They really like him. Now he's street supervisor of all of Windcrest, making $3.25 an hour. He's the boss, with six men working under him!

"I didn't mind the migrating because I love working outside on farms where the air is fresh. I'm fast, so I did well in the fields, but migrating was very hard on Ramon and the kids. My older kids had to finish school every year in Michigan. The English they speak around here is kids' talk, not very good. In Michigan the children are smarter and the grading is harder, so my kids didn't pass. Every year we went, they missed another year of school. They were so big for their grade, they were ashamed to go to school and dropped out. I couldn't seem to stop them."

The Camarillo children are: Peter, nineteen; Lydia, seventeen; Isabel, sixteen; Carmen, fifteen; Oscar, fourteen; Estella, thirteen; Raul, twelve; Henry, nine; Ramon, eight; Rueben, six; and Albert, five. When Albert, the "baby," entered kindergarten, Teresa found a full-time job at a small chemical company. "It is the first job I've had in my life outside of working in the fields. I enjoy getting out of the house. I feel good about making two dollars an hour, but my seventh-grade education won't get me a very interesting job. It's an easy job and boring compared to working in the fields. In the fields, I rose from picker to foreman. At the chemical company no one advances. We make liquid and powdered fertilizer. All I do all day is fill the bottles with liquid and pour powder into plastic bags and seal them. Most of the time we work outside in the hot sun. When it rains, we go inside a shed where the roof leaks on us. It's a poor place to work. The fumes of the chemicals burn my nose. I know the dust is dangerous for my health. There are always accidents. Yesterday two people out of ten of us had to be taken to the hospital. I've been there only five months. It's a temporary job. I'll be laid off when there's less demand for fertilizer. I don't like the job, but I like the extra money, so I just keep working there.

"Ramon says he'd rather have me stay home. He's sure we can make it on his salary. I don't know. With this extra money I can buy almost everything I need for the kids. I used to go to the second-hand store for all their clothes, even shoes. Now I can buy them new. I'm taking advantage of that. Sometimes I see kids that come from small families. I wish I could have mine dressed that well. With things so expensive, it's hard for a big family to manage these days. The light bill gets higher. So does the water and telephone. When you have eight kids going to school at the same time and you buy one pair of shoes, you have to buy them all a pair. I just can't do it. You have to learn to manage on what you have.

"Sometimes I think it was better when we were poor because the more money you have, the more money you spend. We learned to manage on the money we made in the fields, and we did just fine. Now we have fun with the extra money—

give it to the kids to buy new clothes, go get hamburgers for everybody, buy fried chicken. The money goes real fast. We get our checks cashed and, just like that, the money is gone. We don't save any."

When the younger children were still at home, Teresa volunteered most of her free time working at a community clinic where she could take her children with her. "I really enjoyed that. I was never paid, but I couldn't wait to get over there every morning to help people. Time passed so fast. I was constantly running, talking to people, asking them about their children, giving them what they needed. At the chemical company, time passes slow. In the mornings now I wake up feeling lazy, almost too sleepy to go to work, but I go. I'm proud to have a job, even if it isn't a very good one."

At the clinic, Teresa met Josepha Aroila, a sixty-five-year-old diabetic with high blood pressure and a heart condition. She lived alone in a small house down the street, so the Camarillos adopted her as one of their family. Teresa helped her fill out the lengthy medical forms that she couldn't understand and took her to the doctor every Saturday morning. Oscar cut her lawn. Lydia made her laugh again.

"I like to help people because it sets an example for my kids," Teresa says. "We should all learn to help neighbors and make the communities we live in better places. It isn't important that you get paid. You'll be paid back somehow. Maybe when you get old, their kids or grandchildren will help you out."

Teresa takes Josepha Aroila to the doctor every Saturday.

Word spread quickly that Teresa was a natural community leader. She was elected to the boards of the Villa Coronado Community Center and the Southwest Migrant Association. Then a group of twenty-five concerned citizens in Villa Coronado asked her to lead the fight for the area's annexation into San Antonio. "There are some real active neighbors around here who really care for this community. I fought hard with them. We'd go speak to San Antonio's city council and mayor when they had a meeting. We'd tell them about our community, and they listened to us. They were real nice. I'm not shy or scared to speak out. You have to talk for your community and use your rights to get some of the things you need. We needed police and fire protection, paved streets, sewers, garbage pickup, and bus service out here, but we always seemed to be passed over because we were poor. The air in Villa Coronado smells like a sewer because the city sewage treatment plant is draining in here, making people sick. What benefit is it to us? Only a few families have a flush toilet."

Discussion about annexation went on for months, but Teresa and her neighbors won their battle. Living conditions are slowly improving. A city bus runs through Villa Coronado now. Some streets are being paved. Police patrol the neighborhood. "If we all work together, I think we can get more things now that we are in the city," Teresa says. "Everybody is paying taxes. You might as well get involved to get a decent, clean community out of that money."

Teresa's optimistic attitude boosted the family through all the years of migration. "We followed the crops for the money, not for the love of it. There were so many things we neeed that

we couldn't afford on Ramon's salary of forty to fifty dollars a week. We needed another car. We had to build on to our house. For a time we had thirteen people sleeping in two rooms! So each spring we left. We nailed all the doors and windows shut from the inside. Then we climbed out a back window and boarded it from the outside. No one ever bothered our house while we were gone.

"We picked strawberries, cherries, and apples up in Michigan. I liked being out in the fresh air meeting new people. We started at 4 A.M., when it was so cold you had to wear a sweater. The leaves on the strawberries were still wet with dew. There were seven of us in the family working in the fields. We could make five hundred dollars on a good week, but our average was three hundred.

"We were lucky to find a real nice farmer in Bear Lake, Michigan, who wanted us back every year the last few years we migrated. He gave us everything we needed and helped us in every way. We had a nice three-room house on the farm at first, but when he saw how big our family was, he bought the materials for us to build on two more rooms. He furnished and heated every room for us. It was a nice warm house. No matter how much money we made, he brought us extra food and helped us get food stamps.

"The farmer didn't boss us around. He would say, 'Ramon, I don't have to come to the fields to tell you what to do. You are hard-working guys. Just take care of my fields like you were the owner.' He made Ramon and me foremen over five families, including our own kids, about thirty field-workers. We made $1.90 an hour working from 4 A.M. to 7 P.M. I had to weigh in all the strawberries people picked and punch the cards. It was hard for me at first because I didn't know how to add and subtract. My kids taught me how to count fast. A few weeks ago the farmer wrote us a letter saying how much he needed us and wanted us to come back. I feel real bad about not going because he is so kind. I'm glad I didn't have to see his face or talk to him on the phone because I know I'd start crying.

"A lot of good things happened to me in Michigan. That's where I finally got the birth control pill. After eleven kids I started on the pill! I would have had five more kids by now if I hadn't. Every time a child was five months old, I got pregnant again. I have one for every month except April. Most of them are just a little over a year apart.

"I only wanted four kids. After that I asked the doctors to fix me so I couldn't have any more children. They told me they couldn't do anything about it because I was too young, I wasn't sick, and I had no problems having the children; they all came natural. I told them that my husband had a poor job and we had a very small house, but it did no good. The doctors just told me to talk to my Catholic priest, so that's what I did. I said, 'What am I going to do? I don't want to keep having kids.' The priest didn't understand. All he said was, 'Teresa, I can't do anything about it. All you have to do is watch the calendar.' Of course, that doesn't work. I was sick and tired of having babies every year. The pill saved us. I know there is a God up there somewhere and I think I'm religious, but I don't go to church every Sunday anymore. I go when I feel I need it, when I feel guilty. Then I go to confession.

"When Planned Parenthood came to Villa Coronado, they took a picture of me with eleven kids. They wrote a caption under it that after eleven kids I started on the pill. I was kind of embarrassed about the picture, but I did it because I thought it would give the young mothers-to-be around here an idea to have small families they can support easily. That's what I tell my own children.

"I'm proud of all my eleven children. They are the most important thing in my life. I care a great deal about every one of them, but it's hard to support 'em, hard to feed 'em, and hard to dress 'em. I manage because I'm used to being poor. I was always poor. You can't just give up because you have a big family. Sometimes I wish for so many things for my children. . . . Some things I can have, others I just can't have. You've got to keep trying. Some day you'll get there. You'll make it."

The Camarillos depend heavily on food stamps. They pay $43.50 for $141 worth of food. Married daughter Lydia and her husband Pete help the others by combining their food stamps with Teresa's, shopping together, and eating all their meals together. "We eat a lot of beans, ground beef, and macaroni," Teresa says. "When you mix them all up together, it stretches pretty far. It's only in the summer that my food bill becomes a problem. The kids are all home and hungry every hour." Teresa avoids the high-priced grocery stores and goes straight to the truckers' market to buy all their fruit and vegetables by the crate at wholesale prices. What they don't use, they sell.

In their migration days, Teresa would wisely buy most of the kids' school clothes in Michigan at rummage sales because the money they made had to stretch over much of a year's bills.

"I could get clothes for 5 cents to 10 cents up there at the yard sales. Here you pay $1 to $1.50 for used things."

The crops were especially good in Michigan in 1970, so Ramon had enough money to turn builder that fall, increasing their two-room home into seven small rooms and a carport. With the help of his brother, Ramon added a dining room, a living-room extension, and boys' and girls' bedrooms inside. "Before that we had kids all over the floor, on beds, on couches," Teresa says. "We were packed in like sardines." Fortunately, Ramon can build or fix almost anything. But he can only do what they can afford. After he built the addition and paneled, carpeted and tiled the rooms, just a few planks marked the site of their future, and first, indoor bathroom. The only running water they have inside is the cold-water line to the kitchen sink. "My big ambition now is to give the kids the bathroom they need," Teresa says. "That's what I'm working for. It's so much cleaner than the outhouse in back. Right now we don't have an extra four hundred dollars. I hope we will soon."

Furniture in the home varies in age and attractiveness. Peeling iron beds, ancient wooden dressers bulging with clothes, and sagging wooden shelves contrast with a long, attractive Spanish-style stereo cabinet, a portable color TV, and a cheerful red sectional sofa. Knickknacks and vases of plastic flowers decorate every room. On the living room wall they've stretched a large, velvet Last Supper rug and just across from that a sizable velvet portrait of Martin Luther King. This is unheard of in

Teresa combs her hair in front of her bedroom mirror.

Isabel, Estella, and Raul Camarillo sit in the living room making paper flowers as decorations for a party Estella is having.

a Mexican-American home. "I put him there because he helped his people, the colored people," Teresa explains. "I'm for anyone who helps people." Another velvet wallhanging pictures John and Bobby Kennedy. "The Kennedys are here because I read they grew up in a big family like ours," Teresa says. "Maybe they were once poor like us. Anyway, I think they really wanted to help poor people. They were not like Nixon, just out for

themselves.

"Everything in my house except my stove and refrigerator has been given to me—my furniture, my dishes, my clothing," Teresa says. "I use everything people give me, and I know how to take care of things to make them last. I never say, 'I don't want that,' and avoid something used. I grew up knowing nothing else."

Above each window and door in the house, Teresa has tacked a tiny palm cross. "It's the holy palm you get in church on Palm Sunday," Teresa explains. "It gives us good luck and protection. That's a tradition that goes way back in my family." A wealth of religious statues and pictures—Virgins, saints, crucifixes, and portraits of Jesus, including a three-dimensional one with blinking eyes—adorns the walls and tables, particularly in the children's rooms. Teresa may be opposed to the Catholic church's position on birth control and may not attend mass regularly, but she is more religious than anyone in the family when it comes to the superstitions, originating in Mexico, that were passed down from generation to generation in her family.

"They say when you build a new house, you bring the father over to baptize it," Teresa says. "I do it myself once a year. I get holy water from the church and sprinkle some in every corner, praying each time. It's good luck. Incense runs the bad spirits out of the house. I burn it at least once a year, especially if someone is trying to do us bad. As I burn it, I pray that my children will not get sick and I ask God to help us pay our bills.

"When all of our babies were small, I opened a scissors like the sign of the cross and put it under their pillows. It is important to do this before the baby is baptized so he will not get scared and start crying in the night. After they are baptized, I put a glass of holy water under their beds so they will have a peaceful sleep. We used to have bats outside that would hit the windows and wake up the children and scare them. They look just like flying rats. And they whistle. They go 'wh-s-s-s-t,' then swoop down. My father told me I'd get rid of them with the scissors and holy water. He was right. We never had the bats again."

When a severe thunderstorm warning is announced on TV or radio, Teresa assembles the whole family on the front porch. "I look out into the storm and pray a Hail Mary," she says. "Then I throw a handful of salt on the yard to cut the water while we pray. With a knife, I make the sign of the cross in the air. I won't say that it works for everyone, but a bad thunderstorm has never hurt us." Ramon and the children are skeptical about Teresa's actions, but they go along with the rituals to please her.

Behind the Camarillos' home there's a large backyard with a wooden outhouse, Ramon's toolshed, and a Maytag wringer washer that's always humming. The family built a backyard shower, a wooden cubicle with a garden hose spraying from above. Animals are everywhere. No Camarillo child can pass up a stray dog or cat. The yard bulges with thirteen dogs, three kittens, twelve ducks, three fighting roosters, three geese, three hens, fifteen baby chicks, and thirteen pigeons. The popula-

Thirteen-year-old Estella plays with a mallard, one of the many pets in the Camarillo backyard.

tion fluctuates constantly as dogs run off and new chickens hatch. The life expectancy of kittens around thirteen dogs is only three weeks, but all the animals get ample love and attention during their stays. Even the ducks get hugs and kisses. With all the human and animal traffic out back, the grass disappeared long ago. When it rains, the backyard turns into a muddy pond that the children can barely slog through in boots. In the summer the flies are so thick and sluggish that the boys' cupped hands capture them like lightning bugs.

The children care for the house and yard with the discipline of a crack battalion, never complaining. Each child must do chores every day, including sweeping, dusting, washing, ironing, lawn mowing, washing dishes, taking out the garbage, and cooking. The crowded little house with thirteen people may be worn in places, but it is always neat and clean. It's a responsibility everyone accepts. The girls fix dinner for the whole family almost every night now that Teresa's working. All the boys can cook, too, even tiny five-year-old Albert.

"A family as big as this one doesn't run without everyone pitching in," Teresa says. "I taught all my kids to work, and they work hard. They are considerate of me, saying, 'Mother, you sit down and take it easy. Let me help you.' I really have good kids. I think the work will benefit them. They'll be married someday. They'll be glad their mother taught them to do all these things."

The Camarillo children move in triple time on Saturday

Raul cooks breakfast for his brothers on a Saturday morning when Teresa and Ramon have gone to the truckers' market.

mornings, like Keystone cops in a 1920s movie, racing through their chores so they can play. Slim, barefoot Raul, twelve, sweats over the stove fixing his own concoction of scrambled eggs and hot dogs for his little brothers, a furry black-and-white kitten at his feet. Thirteen-year-old Estella, a beautiful, outgoing girl, is covered in bubbles washing nine loads of clothes in the backyard. Rueben and Ramon are there to catch the clothes as she squeezes them through the wringer. They hang them on the line in seconds. Oscar and Albert feed all the animals while Henry sweeps the bedroom floors. Isabel mops the front porch. The children do these chores on their own because Teresa, Ramon, and Lydia pull out of the driveway in the pickup at 6 A.M. to catch the truckers bringing semi-loads of fruit and vegetables into San Antonio's terminal market. Teresa bargains for the best prices on crates, bushels, and gunnysacks of fresh produce, a cheap and healthful family staple.

As if they hadn't done enough work for a Saturday morning, Raul and his four younger brothers anxiously await the return of the pickup truck. On their own, they devised a Saturday morning produce route to earn extra spending money. When Teresa decides what amount of fruit and vegetables the family can consume in a week, the boys carefully arrange the extra produce, putting it in plastic bags and pricing it considerably higher than the truckers' market but lower than grocery stores. They sell it door-to-door throughout Villa Coronado. When Teresa saw that they were serious about running the

At dawn on a Saturday morning Teresa is at the San Antonio truckers' market bargaining for bushel baskets full of produce.

A neighbor girl sits on Teresa's lap and pulls her nose. Teresa talks seriously with all the kids, helps them with their problems, and plays with them.

route every Saturday, she obtained a peddler's license for them, making them legal salesmen. In two hours, the boys come home five to ten dollars richer.

They take their work seriously. Raul keeps a copious notebook log of all his customers and what they buy each week so that he will have everyone's favorite fruits and vegetables ready to sell. They sell soft drinks in the same manner, bringing home a pickup-load of cases, undercutting the expensive neighborhood groceries and still making a dollar profit per case. He notes which families aren't interested so that he won't bother them again. On one page of the book he keeps a list of the meanest untied dogs and carefully avoids those homes.

Since no other kids in the neighborhood have the driving ambition of the Camarillos, they are always called on to do odd jobs. The older boys regularly cut lawns, spread dirt, and clean yards for neighbors. Whatever money the children earn on these projects is theirs to spend. "My children get all excited when they make a quarter," Teresa says. "They think that's big money. They really love to work."

Teresa is a magnet for children, her own and all the neighbors'. Wherever she goes, they follow her. "Kids trust me. I like being with them. A lot of parents don't care. They talk to their kids real loud in a heavy voice all the time, like they are always mad, running the kids out of the house. I don't get angry very easily, but my kids know they have to pay attention to me. Ramon doesn't know how to handle kids. He's either yelling at them or playing games with them. When the kids are growing up, you have to sit down and talk to them seriously to teach them. You have to watch your temper. Everybody makes mistakes. I think you have to be an example to your children to show them what's right. They'll learn.

"Here's another thing I think about raising children," she adds. "Care about them and love them, but don't be overprotective of them. Let 'em have fresh air. Let 'em grow. Let 'em live a normal life. The more you baby a child and keep him inside, the sicker he gets. Your sons will be mama's boys. The more you give them a chance to be themselves, the stronger they get.' This psychology must work. Teresa's children are independent, but never defiant. Like their father, they are homebodies. The young children rarely leave the yard, and the three married children, even Peter, who is in the army in Austin, return like homing pigeons every weekend.

Unlike most mothers in the area, Teresa doesn't gravitate toward babies. She prefers teenagers. Neighborhood teens come to her with their problems. No matter what she's doing, she always makes time to go off in a corner with them and listen. "I guess I'm like a mother hen," she confesses. "If anyone needs something, they come to me. I like to help people. Ramon and I just started three baseball teams to get the kids off the streets and give them something to do. On the street, all they do is fight. Baseball is more than a game, it teaches them sportsmanship, how to play and work together, how to help one another. I hope it carries over to their personal lives. No one has tried to organize the kids in Villa Coronado. We want them to learn something. I hope it helps."

Teresa managed to recruit even the toughest-looking young men in the neighborhood. Bandannas tie back their long, stringy hair. They may look frightening on the street, but they seem to mellow on the baseball field with Teresa as she jokes with them. In the beginning, they called her "747" after the big airplane because she was so fat. They were amused at

Teresa and daughter Lydia grill chicken in the front yard.

Ramon plays with Adam, Jr., their first grandchild.

Teresa hasn't been completely successful with her own teenagers. Although none of them has been in any trouble, their futures don't look bright. The oldest children, Peter, Lydia, Isabel, and Carmen, are the educational casualties of a lifetime of migration. None of them has made it past ninth grade before dropping out.

When they quit school, they immediately got married. Because Teresa and Ramon were violently opposed to the teenage marriages, three of the children eloped. Peter married a thirteen-year-old and had a daughter, but because he's in the army his future isn't too bleak. Lydia, seventeen, is happily married, but less happy being pregnant, wishing she had waited. Carmen, now fifteen, mother of Adam, Jr., was the heartbreaker, running off to marry at fourteen with only a sixth-grade education. Teresa changes the subject whenever the grandchild is mentioned. The hurt is still too deep. Ramon bounces little Adam on his lap constantly, but Teresa is more aloof. "Carmen says Ramon has a good heart and I have a cold one because I don't love her son the way he does. It's a problem. I love all my grandchildren. I'll soon have three. I tell my kids I'm tired because I have eleven of my own and I have no love for another one. That isn't true, but it's the only way I can stop my kids from fighting and getting jealous of one another as the grandchildren come. I don't care what anybody says, mothers and grandmothers have favorites. I just say they are all beautiful and try to avoid hugging one more than another, like I did my kids. Otherwise, I'll just get myself into trouble. It's hard when you have such a big family.

"I was both mad and hurt when my kids ran off and got

the sight of this 236-pound mother of eleven running barefoot around the bases with them, bulging out of her shorts. After five months of baseball, walks, and bike trips with the kids, she had lost 52 pounds and earned their respect. Teresa shouts louder than anyone when her teams win. Teenage vandalism and theft run rampant in Villa Coronado, but no one has ever touched the Camarillo house or yard.

married. They're so young, I think they'll be very sorry they started having kids early like I did. They'll be tied down and grow old quickly. If that's what they want, I guess it's up to them. I didn't run them out of the house. I'm lucky because I have a husband who trusts me and lets me do things, but not too many men do that. I would have liked my children to stay children longer and have more fun, but I can't complain too much about them. They are all such good kids. They treat us so well . . ." There's a sad, wistful tone in Teresa's voice as she chops off the sentence.

Teresa has given up opposing the marriages. Estella, thirteen, her fifth grader, will be the next to go. Like a high-school freshman invited to the senior prom, she's bubbly about her wedding. All the Camarillos like Larry, her nineteen-year-old boyfriend, a maintenance man with the park system. They call him "Chocolate" because he's several shades darker than they are. Teresa has reservations about the marriage. "I'm happy and I'm not happy," she confesses. "It's obvious to me that they are really in love, but Estella is just a girl, much too young for marriage. The first thing I'm going to do is take her to Planned Parenthood."

From experience, Teresa knows she can't stop the marriages, so she intercedes as the family birth control counselor. The pill is a frequent topic of conversation on the front porch. "I tell my daughters, take care of yourselves. Right now you have

Teresa combs a junkyard full of burned car parts to find lengths of copper wire, which she sells back to the owner for sixty-five cents a pound.

a good husband, but you can't tell what's going to happen later on. If you really want a little baby, have one. That's a good family. Wait at least three or four more years before having another one until you are sure you can support it. At least you'll probably have a house to put him in." The message seems to be sinking in. Carmen realizes that caring for Adam, Jr. is not as exciting as it once seemed. Lydia, who is about to deliver her first baby, feels "terrible." She adds, "I'll never get myself in this fix again. This is my first and last." Estella claims she loves other people's children, but wants none of her own. So far the teenagers have mustered the maturity to stay married, even as children raising children, but the years will tell if that love is strong enough to endure hard times, as Teresa and Ramon's has.

Now that she and Ramon have jobs and the stability of living in one place year round, Teresa is beginning to dream. She dreams that her remaining six sons will finish high school, though only six-year-old Rueben and five-year-old Albert are in their proper grade. They were still preschoolers when the family stopped migrating. "I tell all my children never to follow the crops up north, but in a way it was good for them. They all learned to work instead of loafing around home all summer like most kids. I tell my boys to stay in school, then look for a job and stay with it. Never quit to become a migrant."

Predictably, Teresa and her daughter Isabel, sixteen, who

Teresa and daughter Estella pick squash early one morning near Atascosa after Teresa was laid off from her job at a chemical company.

works with her at the chemical company, were laid off for two weeks in midsummer. For Teresa, it was almost a relief. She could be her own boss again. She borrowed Ramon's pickup, loaded up the kids, and headed for the junkyard to go "copper picking," a disagreeable but consistently lucrative money-making project. The huge junkyard resembles the face of the moon with hills of gray ashes, the charred remains of unsalvageable parts from demolished cars burned to make room for more. The air reeks of smoldering rubber tires as the Camarillos sink into ashes to dig for tiny lengths of copper wire. They sell it back to the junkyard owner for sixty-five cents a pound. Five Camarillos waded through the ashes for four hours for twenty-five dollars. "This is really livin'," Isabel said, expressing the viewpoint of all the kids. Teresa grinned every time she found a wire, like a prospector uncovering gold nuggets in a pan. Their profit was nine dollars more than she could make for eight hours of hot assembly-line work at the chemical company.

A few days later Teresa heard that a farmer in Atascosa, Texas, needed extra hands to pick his squash crop. At dawn she shook Oscar, Estella, Isabel, and Raul awake. They stumbled into the truck grudgingly. Bumping through acres of fresh, green fields brought back memories to Teresa, not all of them bad. "I still like the fields much better than the chemical company," she admitted. "Maybe I'm just used to it. It's great to be out here! The smell of the country is so much fresher than the smell of Villa Coronado." Teresa picked like a machine, tossing squash into a bushel basket she carried down the rows. She still outpicks the children two-to-one. "Come on you guys!" she yells, prodding them on. Oscar and Estella are barely awake. Their

hair stands straight up because they came directly from their beds to the fields. Raul, in his Lone Star beer rain hat and red cowboy shirt, balances squash on his shoulders instead of putting them in the basket. Estella scowls, then yawns. It is obvious the children never expected to be in another field picking squash, or anything else. That was a part of their lives they hoped was over. Forty-two bushels later, the Camarillos had picked the field bare. They were more than twenty-five dollars richer, each bushel netting them sixty cents.

Driving home slowly, inhaling big gulps of country air, Teresa turned philosophical. "I guess I think different than a lot of people. Some get defeated so fast. They keep sinking down and down. I keep trying. I can't say I'm doing bad. I'm just an average American. We're doing fine. At least the bills are all paid."

NOVEMBER, 1986

In the years since they stopped migrating, Teresa and Ramon have worked hard and prospered. In 1986, neither Teresa nor her children talk about being poor. The word seems to have disappeared from their vocabulary. Teresa, Ramon, and their eleven grown children, ages eighteen to thirty-one, struggled their way into America's middle class, and they intend to stay

Teresa, doing a little local "freelance" farm work in a South Texas field, laughs happily because she's finally made it out of the migrant stream.

there. Everyone works. No one is on welfare. Most of the children have forgotten their migration years, and San Antonio is home to all of them now. Ten of Teresa's eleven children are married, and each owns a home of his or her own.

Ramon's first full-time job with the city of Windcrest will be his last. Now fifty-nine, he intends to work there until he's sixty-five, then retire. "Ramon really enjoys working at Windcrest, and they like the way he runs things over there," Teresa says proudly. She is forty-eight now, much slimmer, and as lively as ever. "He's always answering some kind of call beyond street repair. When there's a fire, he volunteers to fight it. In the winter when the streets get icy, he stays there all night putting sand on them. He's even the dogcatcher. He catches 'possums and raccoons for people. He likes the people and they like him. On Christmas Day they give us turkeys and hams. The clothes they've given us over the years helped all my children until they grew up.

"I work at Windcrest, too. After I was laid off at the chemical company, I ended up having to have a nose operation. After that I decided to run my own business. It started by accident when a lady from Windcrest was going out of town and needed someone to take care of her plants, yard, and house. Ramon volunteered me. When she came back, she told me she had never seen her plants look as beautiful. 'What did you do to them?' she asked me. I told her I talk to them just like I do my grandchildren. I ask them how they are doing and what's wrong with them. Then I sing to them. After that woman started telling her friends about me, I've never had to advertise. Carmen, Lydia, and I have worked together keeping yards and houses in Windcrest for eight years now. We're fast. My daughters cut the yards while I do the trimming. We have done as many as ten yards in one day! When the three of us work together on a big house, we can clean it spotless in two to four hours. People look at us, like the way we do our job, and pass it around. With all our husbands working good jobs, we only have to work two or three days a week. We still find time to have fun together as a family.

"We are homebodies just like we were before, but worse than ever. All my kids are the same way. We don't go out drinking on the weekends. We all get together to party in Lydia's backyard most of the time. They've poured a cement patio where we can have music and dance. We bought a trailer and take it down to Corpus Christi to go fishing and camp. If we go, everybody goes. It's like a convoy. We go to Laredo shopping together, the kids and I. We all pitch in on expenses and go. We do almost everything together.

"Carmen is especially close to me. She's here every day. I remember how hurt I was when she ran off to marry at fourteen and had a child right away. She has two handsome boys now. It won't be long before she'll go through the same thing I did when her sons get married and bring their wives home. My girls have stayed close and are so helpful to me. They all have homes in Villa Coronado. Oscar and his family live right next door. Lydia and Pete are almost finished building their pretty new home next to Oscar's. It's all paid for, too."

Carmen and Lydia are good examples of a phenomenon that has spread through Teresa's family, enhancing their chances for success—a commitment to having small families. Each daughter has only two children and a firm opinion about having no more. And they are immensely proud of their children. Pictures of them emerge immediately. They tell of their successes in school, of how they can speak English fluently and write both English and Spanish, and how much fun they are to be around.

"Above all, I wanted to get the message through to my kids not to have more than two children. It's hard to raise four or five kids these days when everything is so expensive. You can't give them what they need. With seven or eight kids, it's impossible. If you want your kids to grow up to be somebody, you've got to give them a lot of attention."

With ten children marrying in their teens, Teresa could have scores of grandchildren by now. She has only eighteen. That small number does not reflect divorce. Every one of her children, even those who married at thirteen or fourteen, have stayed married to the same person, defying all the statistics on teenage marriage. "I don't believe in divorce," says Teresa. "Ramon and I have been married thirty-two years. Our marriage isn't perfect. We've had our ups and downs, arguments, and hard times. I tell my kids it will be that way for them, too, but if there's a lot of love, that's all that's needed. If you talk things out, you can work everything out.

"I tried my best to raise my kids well. I gave them what I had. I taught them the right things. My kids always worked hard. Three of my boys made it through high school. My kids won't be future presidents of the United States, but I think they'll all be somebody. They'll work hard to earn what they want."

All Teresa's sons have good jobs at plants, factories, and businesses around San Antonio. It is not white-collar work, but it is far from menial labor. "I'm proud that all of my married children have homes of their own," Teresa says. "I never wanted them to have to live with us or their in-laws. They do a lot better when they are married if they live by themselves. I helped them when I could. I bought the house next door, then sold it to Oscar. He pays me every month and it will eventually be his free and clear. That's the way they learn. I did the same thing for Albert. They work hard, pay me every month and take good care of the property. It's for their future."

With the help of both Lydia's husband Pete and Oscar, Teresa and Ramon's home has been completely remodeled. It is all stone on the outside now with a pretty stone goldfish pond in front. Visitors enter through an arbor. The plants and flowers Teresa grows so well are everywhere. Inside they've reduced the home to two bedrooms, greatly expanding the living room. Oscar and Pete made cathedral ceilings and installed ceiling fans. Their bathroom was built in the mid-1970s. The kitchen has new appliances and handmade oak cabinets. Four generations of family gather under Teresa's Last Supper rug to eat Thanksgiving and Christmas dinners, five turkeys' worth. Teresa still has her eighty-six-year-old father and stepmother, who join them for the feasts.

Villa Coronado is a better community to live in now, though it is far from perfect. It is no longer a migrant community. Mechanization on farms has forced most of its residents to find other work. In a more stable community, the neighbors have worked together to get most of the streets, including Teresa's, paved and to have a park built. "We still need more police protection, more streetlights, and a cleaner place to live,' Teresa says. "I guess every community has its problems. Crime is still very bad here. People get into houses and take anything they can get their hands on, and there are still murders. It turns mean around here at night. Last Father's Day, on Albert's eighteenth birthday, we had a big party for him in Lydia's backyard. He left early to get his child a special kind of soda water at the Texaco station's store on the highway a few blocks from here. As he drove up, a man he had never seen before threw the finger at him. When Albert walked out to his truck with the soda water, the man was waiting for him. He stabbed him with a knife or screwdriver for no reason. They hadn't even talked.

"It was terrible. We almost lost Albert. He was stabbed right next to his heart. The doctors told us he might not live until morning, but they had gotten him to a hospital with all the right equipment immediately. He survived without surgery and was home within a week. He's just fine now and back at work. It's a miracle. Albert got the license number, but the police never found the man. The car was stolen. It makes you realize just how precious your children are to you.

"I have no particular dreams or goals for myself now that my children are grown. I just wanted to see them happily married with good jobs and homes of their own. I say thanks to God—my dreams for my children have come true. They are all supporting themselves and doing just fine. Now any time God wants to take me, I'm ready to go."

Teresa
Camarillo
149

Gladys Milton

It was barely dawn on a chilly winter morning in December, 1975, when Gladys Milton's green Buick station wagon raced down Highway 331 between Paxton and De Funiak Springs in the gentle, rolling pine country of the western Florida panhandle. "I try not to go over seventy, but maybe I'll take it seventy-five on the straightaways," says the fifty-one-year-old midwife. "I don't worry about the road patrol. They give me a police escort when I need it." Gladys is a formidable woman with a fullback's shoulders. She stands 5′11″ without her size 12 B shoes and weighs more than two hundred pounds. As Gladys sped along the highway, she turned the volume up high on the radio so the 1 to 5 A.M. hymns on the Nashville station sounded as if you were in the front row of Ebenezer Baptist Church. "Spiritual music helps me dedicate myself on the way to each birth and ask God's blessings to give us a healthy child and mother." She poked her head into the bracing morning air, which woke her up like a cold rain.

It had only been five hours since she'd driven twenty-five miles home to Flowersview, Florida, from her nursing job on the 3 to 11 P.M. shift on the O.B. (obstetrics) floor at Mizell Memorial Hospital in Opp, Alabama. When she entered her long, attractive brick home, it was quiet and dark. As usual, husband Huey, a school-bus driver, had been asleep for hours. Gladys picked up her sewing basket and crocheted a few squares of the bedspread she was making for her daughter, "unwinding" in front of the midnight movie. She had managed only four hours' sleep when the phone rang and a jittery seventeen-year-old father-to-be rattled rapid directions to his parents' farmhouse deep in the pine woods many miles away. "Babies always like to be born in the middle of the night, but I don't mind," Gladys says. "After all the babies I've delivered, I still get excited. Every birth is miraculous. It's a gratifying experience, something only God could do. In the middle of his directions, that boy told me his wife's water broke. That means step on the gas!" Although Gladys didn't know it at the time, she was rushing to the most difficult delivery of her fourteen-year career as a midwife.

Gladys is always in demand. Covering six rural counties in her native Florida and nearby Alabama, she's one of the few licensed midwives left and the only one who's also a nurse. Over the years, she's delivered some seven hundred babies, about half of them white and half of them black, never losing a mother or baby. She's well respected in the little southern towns around her. As she shops, mothers with babies on up to teenagers often come up to hug her and show off their growing children. "That's one of mine," Gladys proudly proclaims to anybody within listening range. "I delivered him. I feel all the babies I deliver are my children, too. They belong to their mamas and me."

For generations, rural southern communities relied on granny midwives to deliver babies at home. By the mid-1970s, however, those old women were fast disappearing, and younger women were not entering the "old-fashioned" practice. Gladys works with the county health departments, which screen mothers carefully through prenatal examination. A woman with high risk factors or a history of trouble giving birth is required to have a hospital delivery. More than the poor come to Gladys. She's enjoying the growing trend toward natural childbirth where the father is present at the delivery. Hospitals in the area sedate mothers and ban fathers from delivery rooms.

"When a woman engages me, I tell her not to think she is taking second best because she can't afford first best. I like

Gladys Milton on duty as a nurse on the O.B. floor of Mizell Memorial Hospital in Opp, Alabama.

to work with women who have made up their minds not to go to a hospital, women who trust me enough to believe they'll have a safe delivery. I have the wisdom and foresight to spot any abnormality and get them to a doctor or a hospital if they need it. You can't sedate a mother without having everything

Gladys
Milton
151

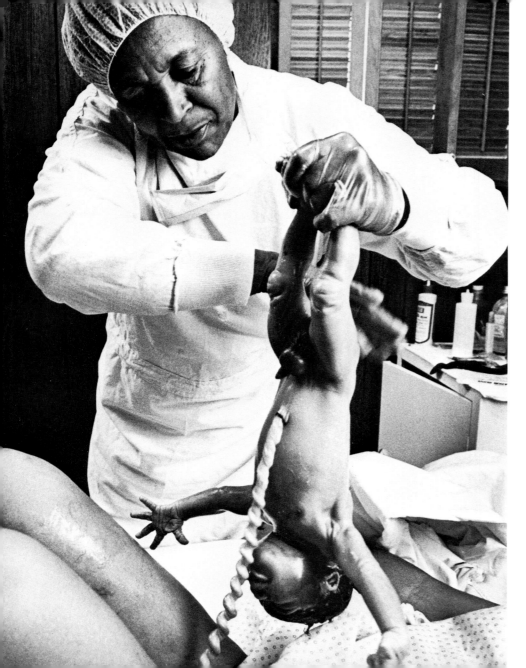

she gets going straight across the placenta. A sedated baby is slower to cry, slower to adjust. Becoming a mother is too wonderful to be doped up and not know about it. One look at your baby repays you for all the pain."

When Gladys arrived at that delivery in December, Joyce, the young, blond expectant mother, lay quietly in her mother-in-law's bed in a neat room warmed by a gas heater. "These were excellent, clean conditions for home delivery," Gladys says. "One time about ten years ago, the sheriff's department came to get me in a squad car at 2 A.M. A lady was having a baby in a bar. She was one of the acts in a carnival that was pulling out of De Funiak Springs. By the time we arrived, someone had moved her to an unhooked carnival trailer with no electricity or ventilation. Two policemen shined their great, huge flashlights on her for me. She had already given birth to the baby on a bed with filthy sheets. As I cleaned up the mother and baby, I almost threw up from the stench and the heat. Someone brought me a chair to sit on. It had a big pile of feces on it! Supposin' I hadn't looked . . .

"Joyce was as calm as she could be. We waited and waited. The first child is often slow so I didn't worry until I examined her closely to see what was going on inside. I found myself faced with my first double footling. The baby was in a position where the feet are down, not head-first like it's supposed to be. I was scared stiff, but I didn't show it. You must never upset your mother. I wanted to move her to a hospital, but it was too late. There were no hospitals or doctors nearby and I thought about

Gladys has delivered hundreds of babies, black and white.

the rescue squad bumping a fully dilated mother over miles of sand roads. The birth would be difficult and painful enough without taking place in the back of a truck. Way down deep I wanted to panic, but I called a doctor and got some further instructions. I knew what I had to do.

"Joyce was patient. It was slow and painful. At the hospital we give the mother gas, but I didn't have anything like that. It's natural childbirth all the way with me. I assured her everything was going to be all right as I kept praying constantly to myself. You can't have a frightened mother on your hands. She wanted that baby so much, she'd endure any pain for it.

"Finally I got a-hold of both feet. It was a big baby—eight pounds and four ounces. I told Joyce to press down, but she was so exhausted by then that she wanted to give up. The head got held up. I rotated it to the left and to the right and no way could I get it. If the head wasn't born immediately, the baby would die. Joyce said she couldn't push anymore, but when I told her her baby's life depended on it, brother, she got with it like a soldier. We got him born, but he was the most lifeless, chalky-looking baby I'd ever seen. He was so limp that he lay motionless on the bed. I was afraid I had broken his neck trying to get the head born. The two grandmothers who had been in the room with me the whole time began praying loudly, 'Lord help us. Please! Please!'

"I knew exactly what I had to do. You don't worry about

Every baby Gladys delivers is special to her. "They belong to their mamas and me," says this midwife. She is loved and respected equally by blacks and whites in her community in the Florida panhandle.

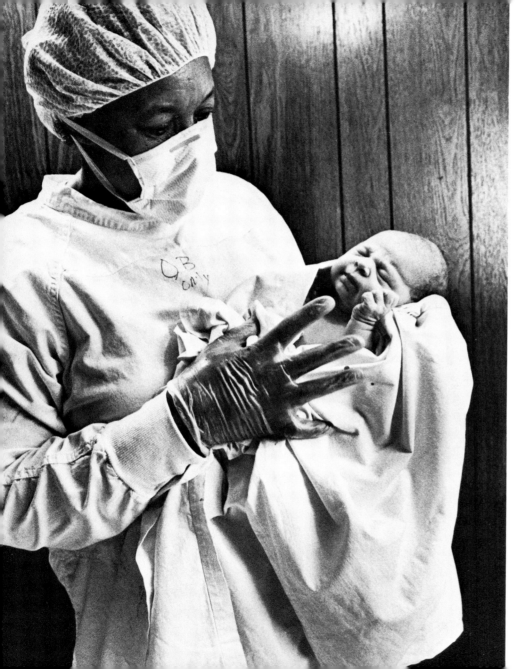

sterile techniques at a time like this; you can take care of the germs later. I got on him immediately with my big, black mouth and did mouth-to-mouth resuscitation to get him breathing. He breathed so slow, I had to blow extra oxygen into his face. Finally he started pinking up. He got so pink and pretty that all the grandmothers and I could do was lock necks and cry tears of gratitude. What a joyous time in that house! When we got one little peep out of the baby, I almost beat him to death. He had a red tail, I'm telling you."

Gladys entered midwifery through the back door. She had been a housewife, a cleaning lady, an insurance writer, and a substitute teacher. "When my twins were little girls, we had a schoolhouse up on the corner. They ran home one evening to tell me that all the mothers had to come up there to a meeting. When I got there, sat down, and looked around me, I realized I was in a room full of expectant mothers. I said, 'Wait, this is the wrong place for me. I'm not expecting and I don't want to be expecting no more.' The nurse from the health department told me to stay anyway. She looked right at me and asked if there would be anybody in the room interested in training to be a midwife. Nobody said a word. She never took her eyes off of me. Finally I said, 'Wouldn't that be kinda like going into the kerosene lamp business?' That was before midwifery had its revival. I found out how serious she was when she told everyone how much the area needed a midwife. Even if everyone could pay to go to a hospital, there weren't enough doctors in the area to deliver all the babies. When I had my first

Gladys holds a baby she has just delivered.

two children by midwife, none of the doctors would deliver black babies, to lay it on the line. I told her I'd think about it. When I got home, I discussed it with my oldest son Henry, who dreamed of being a doctor. All he could say was, 'Mother, what could be more important than that?' That comment stuck with me. I went down to the health department and agreed to go into training."

Gladys was the only woman accepted for midwife training by two white doctors, Clifford N. Matthews and J. Paul O'Neal, at their clinic in Florala, Alabama, very close to her home in Florida. Through the course of her training, she observed twenty doctor-delivered births. When she was ready to tackle deliveries on her own, the doctors supervised her every move until she became adept at it. "When I finished training, the doctors asked me to stay on with them. I worked for them for five years, sometimes sixty hours a week, in addition to doing my home deliveries. I'll never forget how much those doctors helped me in an era when midwifery was scorned by most of the medical profession. Dr. Matthews is gone now, but I still carry the bandage scissors he gave me for sentimental value, though it's old and dull. When the doctors built a new hospital in Florala, they took me with them to help in the delivery room. After the training they gave me, I passed the state boards by waiver and became a licensed practical nurse in 1968.

'Midwifery is my calling, just the work I want to do. I believe divine providence worked toward me becoming a midwife. I think it's what God wants me to do with my life. When you deliver as many babies into the world as I have, you develop a high respect for life. I believe in birth control, but not

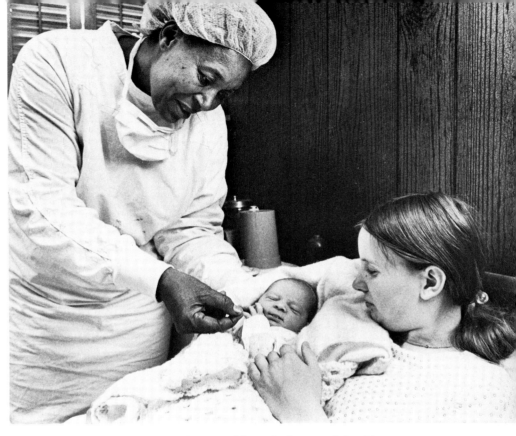

Gladys admires the baby girl she has just delivered, the second for this young mother. More white couples than black now come to Gladys looking for the warmth of a midwife delivery where the husband is present.

abortion. I think life begins at conception. One thing about poor people around here, they always keep their babies."

Gladys would love to be a full-time midwife, but she's prac-

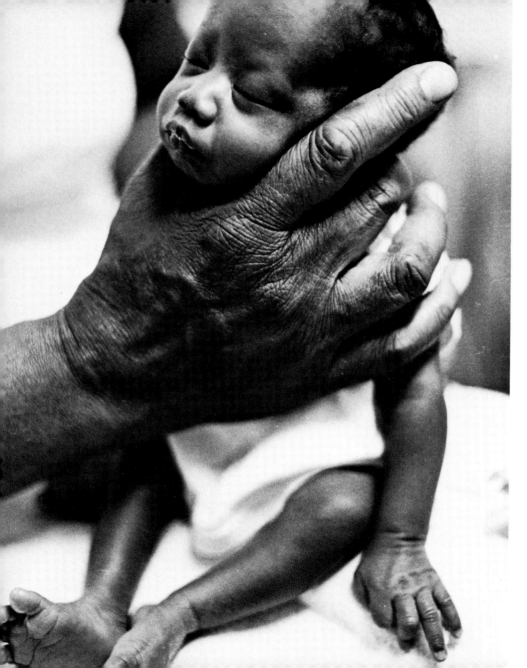

tical enough to know she could not afford to lose her hospital nursing salary and benefits. She only charges one hundred dollars per midwife delivery, keeping the fee within the reach of poor families. Besides, the hospital offers her other kinds of nursing roles she thoroughly enjoys—an opportunity to work with a broader spectrum of patients, assist doctors in the delivery room, and monitor the development of premature babies in the nursery. The hospital staff has always been remarkably supportive of her dual careers, knowing how important midwifery is to her and the community. Nurses are usually willing to switch days off with her on short notice when one of Gladys's mothers suddenly goes into labor. It's a juggling act, but somehow she balances both occupations with few conflicts.

The only serious drawback to hospital work is the fifty-mile round-trip drive she makes five days a week, piling up a few speeding tickets. Gladys lives life on a conveyer belt, rarely stopping. Often her mornings are filled making lovely ceramic pieces at a nearby shop, one of the few relaxations she indulges in when there are no babies to deliver. "I can come home and change clothes and be down the road to Opp in exactly seven minutes," she says laughing. "Sometimes I'll pamper myself and allow a whole fifteen minutes if I really want to get all gussied up and put on my warpaint." Usually she's braiding her hair and buttoning her white uniform on the way to the car, gulping a glass of Coke for lunch. Her days off are often jammed with volunteer work, taking blood pressures or visiting shut-

Gladys's enormous hand cradles a premature infant that she has just fed in the hospital nursery.

ins. "I like to do things for people. It's my friends who make me tick, always have. I love people and I care what they think of me. I'd feel awful if someone didn't like me."

While Gladys is gone, husband Huey, fifty-eight, paces around the house in his green work clothes and the matching green visor cap he wears constantly to cover his shiny bald head. He only removes it at church, where he's a deacon, at Sunday dinner, and at bedtime. Huey watches Gladys with an expression somewhere between awe and amusement, never saying much. Although they've been happily married for twenty-seven years, Huey and Gladys are direct opposites in personality. Gladys is always animated, laughing and talking constantly. Huey is silent, except around his close friends and the band of adoring ten- to twelve-year-old boys on his school bus route who call him "Uncle Huey" and visit him after school. Gladys's activities keep her on the road constantly. Except for necessary school bus runs, Huey stays home by choice, puttering around the house. "Huey's a pacer—pace, pace, pace," says Gladys. "He circles around the house a few times, then he hits the yard. That's the Milton trademark. All of them strut like peacocks, their arms bowed out, bumping against you. It's really amusing, but sometimes it drives me nuts. There are few people kinder than Huey or more honest. He's a deep thinker, very reserved. He doesn't communicate too well, but he enjoys people. He's a listener, not a talker. When he doesn't want to talk, I get my crochet and go off to myself. We respect each other's

Gladys is glazing a ceramic manger scene. Ceramics is her favorite hobby and one she is very good at.

Huey Milton, fifty-eight, watches as a boy who lives on his school bus route helps out.

individuality. Sometimes we just let each other alone—he go his way, I go mine." Gladys bids Huey good-bye at 1 P.M. and heads for the hospital, leaving him a big pot of stew or chicken she's cooked for him early that morning. She doesn't see him until the next morning when she awakens to his spoon rattling in his coffee cup and a sink full of dirty dishes.

The 102-bed Mizell Memorial Hospital is modern and well equipped, yet small enough to be friendly and homey. Gladys knows all the doctors and nurses and at least half the patients at any given time. One doctor labeled her the "Goodwill Ambassador" because of the rapport she establishes with her patients. The floor seems to come to life when Gladys is on duty. Laughter returns. Her nonstop patter of conversation relaxes even the most worried mothers-to-be.

"I know I talk too much, but a lot of people need talking to," she says. "I've been accused of spoiling my patients. So what? I pamper them. I like to share with them in their dull moments."

Many rural Floridians, including Gladys, are convinced that more babies are born when the moon is full. This full moon the hospital nursery is literally wall-to-wall babies, all howling at once, and Gladys is the only one free on the floor to feed them. Nursery temperature is a constant 84 degrees, ideal for babies who just left their mothers' wombs, but stifling to the overweight Gladys, who must don a sterile gown, cap, and surgical mask. Gladys feeds the normal-weight babies in bassinets on demand when they start crying, but the confusion is multiplied by three "preemies," each no bigger than one of Gladys's enormous hands. Every two hours she pokes her arms through the holes in their isolettes, gives them each a bottle, burps them, and diapers them. It's quite a feat. "What a poor specimen of woman you are," Gladys says to the wrinkled creature in her hand, conversing through the plastic wall of the isolette. "Believe me, you are really going to grow up someday and get out of here to go home with your parents." The monologue continues until she is summoned by the blood-curdling scream of another hungry baby. "Babies need a lot of stimulation," Gladys explains, tickling one of the infants to induce a smile.

Gladys is the only black nurse on O.B., a fact no one finds unusual. She's just one of the gang of nurses who work together, laugh together, and go to dinner together. Here in the Deep South, where integration was bitterly fought a decade before, there appears to be racial harmony. It is impossible to know if people in the area are unusually enlightened in racial matters or if Gladys's warmth and friendliness make people color-blind. "Any time I go downtown to the bank, store, or walk down the streets, white people come up to me. We always stop to discuss things. My best friends come from both races. I wish they'd drop the words 'black' and 'white' from the English language. We have good relationships. Nothing happens here because of race that I know about, and I've been around here a pretty good while. I've never seen any one of our staff of nurses treat black and white patients differently. Nobody cares. People are people." While Gladys's large number of white friends may appear unusual in some parts of the country, she has a simple explanation for it, "I have more white friends than black because there are more white people around here. We're small-town people. In times of trouble, you find all your friends will help you, black and white. We cry with each other, laugh with each other and hug each other's necks. That's the way it should be.

Gladys tenderly cares for a premature baby in an isolette at the hospital.

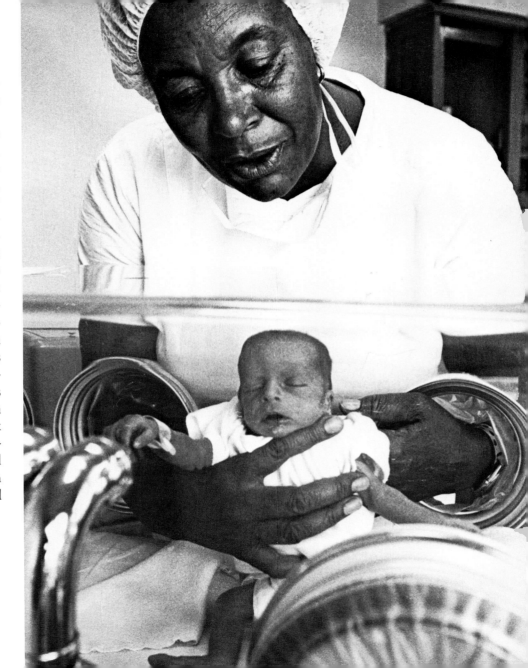

Gladys eats dinner with other nurses during a break on her shift at Mizell Memorial Hospital.

"A black can succeed here as easily as any white. There is nobody to stand in his way but himself. I've been accused of thinking too big. I do. I don't think I deserve anything but the best, and I've instilled that into my children. I have no patience with people who don't try. I'd beat my head up against the wall before I'd give up on anything. The oldest of my seven children, Henry, talked about being a doctor since he was little, but I thought it would pass. He used to bind up his grandma's chickens' wings. I suspect he broke a few to have something to doctor on. Mama used to tear him up with a switch when he messed with her chickens, but they were always very close. When Mama died of inoperable cancer, Henry came back from college and told me he had to be a doctor. We went for it. Together we came up with a mutual philosophy of life: 'The difficult things you do right away. The impossible takes a little longer.'

"Oh, I had a time getting up his tuition money every quarter. I'm no wonder woman, no brain. I'm just the dog who barks and keeps things going. This family has always worked well together as a team. I'd clean houses in the daytime and work at the clinic delivering babies at night. Some days I didn't sleep at all. In those days you could only make five or six dollars cleaning a house. I cleaned for the Holzhauers, an elderly couple in Niceville. They were so good to me. They'd advance me a month's salary when I was in a tight for tuition money. They also gave Henry four hundred dollars when it looked like he'd have to drop out of pre-med. It was the Holzhauers who bought Henry his first leather bag, a beautiful pair of pajamas, and a robe, those extras I simply couldn't afford. I have so much respect for those people. That's why I still go clean their house on my day off every other week, though I don't need the money. I always will. They helped me out when I needed them. Emil Holzhauer is a well-known painter, but he's eighty-nine now and going blind. I can't give him money because I don't have it and he doesn't need it, but he can't see to cut his toenails any longer. I'm honored to have his foot in my lap. Those feet

Gladys gives a talk to the attentive Laurel Hill, Florida, Girl Scouts about her career as a midwife.

Huey laughs as he outwits Gladys in a family domino game. It is unusual for quiet, reserved Huey to show this much emotion; he is more likely to be working independently on something around the house than joining in group activity.

have walked a million steps for me."

After Gladys got Henry through pre-med, she began to relax. Henry had proved himself. "Dr. Joseph Wilson and Dr. Henry White, two prominent white doctors from Fort Walton Beach, gave Henry his first five hundred dollars to go to medical school, no strings attached. They didn't even know Henry,

but on another doctor's recommendation they started helping him because he was smart and deserved a chance to go on. Henry was in tears. He went into a closet and prayed and thanked the Lord for that. He went to Meharry in Nashville, which was one of the top two black medical schools in the country. He interned in Nashville, then had a residency in St. Louis followed by two years at the National Institutes of Health in Maryland. Now he's both a pathologist and a specialist in internal medicine. I'm so proud of him."

Henry isn't Gladys's only successful child. "If I did anything, I presented society with some pretty nice children," Gladys says. "They are everything I wanted to be, and more. I never had to push my children, just keep them encouraged. Bein' a mama, I could tell when one would start getting discouraged. I always nipped it in the bud. We gave them all a happy home life. I think that's the basis for their success. I didn't choose a field for any of them. They went their own ways. All I wanted was for each of them to be something special and be good and honest at it. I think you kind of pass along to your children the same values that were instilled in you. I taught them the importance of doing things well and getting a good education.

"We didn't have enough money to send my second child, Mabelois, to college either. My Aunt Mag saved us by giving her free board and room in her home in Jacksonville so she could walk to college. Her field is English. She ended up with a master's in it from Peabody. Without Mabelois, our younger children wouldn't have college degrees. As soon as she got a teaching job, she sent us two hundred dollars every month out of her paycheck to give them a college education. Even after she married, she sent the children money directly to keep them in school."

Twenty-four-year-old Elinor, one of Gladys and Huey's twins, has a degree in speech therapy from Florida A&M. She has three children and teaches both elementary and high-school special education classes at De Funiak Springs. One year son Tyler Kent, the twins Elinor and Eleanor, and Debbie all attended Florida A&M.

"Kent was 6'3" and a basketball whiz. He could pick up a basketball in one hand and throw it like most people do a baseball. Of course he wanted to be a coach. Eleanor's major was special education and Debbie's accounting and finance. On the evening of February 4, 1973, they all hopped in Kent's Volkswagen and headed home to Paxton High's big homecoming. That's our newly integrated high school, where Kent had been a basketball star and Debbie a cheerleader. As they drove near De Funiak Springs, a sixty-five-year-old drunk woman pulled out of a beer joint in her big 1959 Cadillac and drove the wrong direction on the divided highway with her bright lights on. Kent was so blinded by her lights, he just stopped. She plowed right into them and bent their car like an accordion. Kent died instantly and Eleanor the next day. Debbie was in the backseat sitting sideways. Her pelvis was broken on both sides, but she survived. Kent was a junior and Eleanor had just enrolled in graduate school. Their deaths were so senseless. They had so much promise and so much ahead of them . .

"I almost didn't make it through that tragedy. I was numb for weeks. The first week after the accident I got only twelve hours of sleep. I refused to take the tranquilizers and liquor people offered me. I just prayed through it all. The church was packed with all their friends—black, white, green, brown, and red. They came from everywhere. My friends, black and white, saved me. They cried with me and hugged my neck. I would never have survived without them. Everyone was so kind and thoughtful bringing food and comforting us. Hundreds of people came. I will never accept my children's deaths or understand them, but death doesn't end fellowship. I have a beautiful fellowship with Kent and Eleanor. That's what keeps me going."

Debbie recovered and returned to Florida A&M, where she made the highest grades in accounting and finance in the history of the business department there. Scouts from major corporations wooed her. "She knew she was really up in the world when she flew to her first interview with the Chase Manhattan Bank in New York," Gladys remembers proudly. "Then she went to Westinghouse, Shell Oil, Caterpillar, Pittsburgh Glass, and more than I can remember. I told Debbie she was riding her southern hips off. I was worried one of those big jets would fall down with her on one of her rides to see the world. I was relieved when she finally settled on B.F. Goodrich in Akron because they gave her the best offer."

There is still one more Milton. Youngest daughter Maria, a dignified, intelligent girl, is a freshman in pre-med and destined to follow in Henry's footsteps. He's already given her his first black bag.

When the children's careers were launched, Gladys finally considered her own dreams. "My ambition was to become an

RN-midwife. I commuted to Pensacola for two years to work on my degree at a college there. I planned to intern in a special midwifery program in Arizona delivering Indian babies. It would have given me in-depth training and more experience. My dream was to come home after that and get a job as a public health field-worker and midwife so I could do home visitations and encourage black women to seek proper medical care at their health departments—regular Pap smears, prenatal care. I'd do family planning, too. There's a great need for a black field-worker who can really communicate with her people. A lot of black families close their doors to white RNs. I got so near my dream, even without completing RN training. Such a job opened up in Alabama, covering three counties. I was asked to apply. Two weeks before that, Huey was burned terribly, third-degree burns. He was a human torch. I couldn't leave my job and the Blue Cross/Blue Shield when he was facing over a three-month hospital stay. All those bills . . . just when the job I had been waiting for all my life turned up. I could have helped so many people. I'd have driven all over those Alabama woods up there and been happy to do so. I almost cried, but my hands were tied. I later realized it wasn't meant to be. The funds were cut before the job even started. I would have been unemployed. My children were killed when I was in the middle of RN training. I never went back. I've got as much as this old soul can do before the Lord calls me without going back to college. Now my second big dream is becoming reality.

"I knew there had to be a better way to practice rural midwifery than driving all over two states and delivering babies in less than sterile conditions, sometimes without running water.

I came up with the idea of building a maternity clinic onto the back of our house which would provide the clean, controlled conditions of a hospital with the warmth of a home. It requires a delivery room, a two-bed recovery room big enough to hold familes, a big bathroom, and a cleanup room. People without insurance just can't afford a thousand-dollar hospital bill, but they deserve sterile conditions and a midwife who's also a nurse. The clinic is a more businesslike venture. I can take on more girls. Suppose I have to drive to De Funiak for a delivery when my girl in Laurel Hill goes into labor. I am only one person. If they come to me, I could watch them both at one time. They won't deliver at once."

It wasn't easy, but Gladys banked a slice of her paycheck for more than two years, saving for her dream. Then in the spring of 1976 she hired local contractor James Reeves and his men to build the clinic. In little more than two weeks of constant hammering and sawing, they built her four-room addition. The construction was completed on trust, without a contract. On the last day, Gladys surprised all the carpenters and bricklayers with a four-course banquet, then handed Mr. Reeves a check for thirty-seven hundred dollars, the full amount.

Although Donald Nelson, hospital administrator at Mizell Memorial, must have known that the success of Gladys's maternity clinic could lead to her working part-time or quitting altogether, he helped her equip it. The hospital was remodeling, and for $165 Gladys bought from him three of the old adjustable hospital beds in good condition, with three matching tables and chairs. He'll soon sell her an incubator he's replacing and a delivery table, professional equipment

Gladys never dreamed of having.

"I'm the one with the big dreams around here, but Huey always goes along with them. He supported me all the way on the clinic. The financial tights we get into are all my fault. Huey never believes in doing more than he can pay for. I jump up and overspend myself. Huey's a stronger person than I once gave him credit for. If I had listened to him, I would have made fewer mistakes. The older I get, the more I respect his way. I used to get mad when I suggested something he wouldn't do. I accused him of not wanting anything, not being ambitious enough. He's sensible, but if poor people do only what they can afford, I'd like to know what the heck they can do. I think I deserve a little more than I can afford. I believe in setting your stakes way out there, then scuffling as hard as you can to get there. When people see you're trying, they respect you. Ain't nobody gonna put you in jail if you get a second notice on a payment. Brother, I run to get the mail first that day because if I don't, I know I'm really going to get a lecture from Huey.

"We were poor in my childhood, but thrifty. We were never sorry. I was born in May, 1924, when my mama was only fifteen. My mama was fourteen and my dad was sixteen when they married. It didn't work. Dad deserted us in 1929. He just went off to find a job and never came back. I saw him only once after that. I was bitter toward him when I was a child, but I don't hold that against him now. He was backwards and couldn't make a way. He was too young to accept that much responsibility. Although mother remarried years later, she died of cancer in 1959, still loving him.

"Mama was still very immature after the separation and couldn't keep us well. My Aunt Mag came to visit us and found us all sick and undernourished. Can you imagine me undernourished? Mama was just a kid. Aunt Mag decided she really shouldn't have us children until she grew up, so she took me and my Uncle Simon took my brother. For seven years when I was five to twelve, Aunt Mag and Uncle Buddy raised me as an only child because they never had children of their own. Aunt Mag was such a gracious lady, my idol. I don't know if I could ever be the woman she was. She's where I got all my big ideas, my start. I can take a toothpick and make a lumberyard out of it. I don't want anything little. I have the biggest ideas in the world and nothing to back them up! It was in Aunt Mag's home, when I was eight or ten, that I first thought about being a midwife. She kept a book with pictures on how a baby was born hidden in an old trunk. My aunt had wanted to be a midwife, but she realized she didn't have the nerves for it. I kept sneaking back to read that book. It was a wonder to me how women had babies, something miraculous. All my life I kept coming back to that.

"We lived in the pine woods in rural Escambia County, Florida, on something like a plantation. Actually, it was a turpentine operation. Uncle Buddy worked the pine trees for turpentine, chipping them with a hack. It was work only blacks did at the time, for very low pay. When the sap flowed out of the pine trees, they collected it in pails, poured it into barrels, and took it to a turpentine still, where it was turned into resin, then spirits of turpentine. Uncle Buddy was one of their favorite workers because he was clean and honest. They paid him

$6.20 a week. Back in depression times, that was *money*. We lived in one of the best company houses.

"Aunt Mag and I washed for the wealthy family who lived in the big house, the main gator who ran the turpentine operation. We'd wash and iron for them for $2.50 a week. It took us two days to iron everything. I did the handkerchiefs and napkins and Aunt Mag did the rest, in addition to cooking and cleaning for the family. Aunt Mag taught me to do things right. She insisted on perfection. I had to fold those napkins so the corners didn't vary and the monogram was up in just the right place when she set the table. I appreciate those things.

"Aunt Mag had a way with people. Everyone loved her. The family gave her scads and scads of beautiful dresses, some hardly worn. When it came to sewing dresses for me, she'd buy the most expensive material and eyelet piqué for the collars. These were times some people didn't have anything to eat. She spoiled me, but I had to toe the mark. She instilled honesty in me, and the importance of a good education. I used to get the perfect attendance award every year because she made me go to school when I was actually sick. Aunt Mag spent a lot of time with me. I think she wanted to make sure I got started on the right train. I was so devilish that she had to keep an eye on me. I'd climb trees higher than all the boys. I'd climb so high I could look up and see all the neighboring towns.

"I was fair with flaming red hair until I was sixteen. That, and the way Aunt Mag pampered me, always made me a little different. We really wanted to be something. Though we were in a situation where we couldn't be anything, we never gave up trying. People respected us for that.

"I always wanted to get ahead. I'd come to church early so I could lead the lesson. We didn't have a church bell. It was a big circular-saw blade hanging up. When the preacher hit it with a big bolt, it would ring over the whole community. The preacher reminded me that when I turned twelve all my sins would be on me. Aunt Mag threw me a big twelfth birthday party with homemade ice cream and her perfect jelly that a knife would stand up in. I was sick through the whole party worrying about all those sins I'd be responsible for. I got saved the next month.

"That was the year my mother wanted me back. She had remarried and taken over my grandfather's farm in Flowersview. I wanted Aunt Mag to be my mother, but she was so unselfish she wouldn't let me think that way. She always said she wasn't my real mother and she wouldn't take me away from her. I hoped Aunt Mag would fight for me. She said she wished she could have adopted me, but she didn't have the legal papers, so she'd have to give me up. It was the right thing to do, but I wanted her to object. When Aunt Mag put me on the train, I cried all the way to my mother. I was bitter. It was such a drop in life-style. I thought Mother had sent for me and my brother just to have someone to help work on the farm, but that wasn't it. She had matured enough to want her children back. I came to love both her and my stepfather very much, though Aunt Mag had more impact on my life than anybody ever has or ever will. I'm afraid my mama didn't get too much work out of me. I hated picking cotton. I'd get out in the field and pick me enough cotton in the sack to sit on, then I'd plop there and tell jokes to the other pickers in the patch to distract them."

Gladys adjusted to Flowersview better when she started making close friends and her hair finally turned black. "Someone told me that if I rubbed my hair down good with castor oil before I washed it, it would turn black. I spent all my money on castor oil, but the more I rubbed on, the redder it turned. It was such a relief to be sixteen and have black hair. I've considered Flowersview home ever since. It was all hills and woods around our homes when I was a teenager. I was best friends with Bertha, my next-door neighbor. We'd whoop and roll down those hills together. There were two big stumps out in the woods between our houses where we had spoons stashed. I'd entertain Bertha's mother while she crept into the canning cabinet to steal some preserves. Now Bertha's mother would have given us her preserves, but they always tasted better when they were stolen. Bertha ran out to hide them in the bushes. When she came back singing, I knew the coast was clear. Then we'd run down to the stump and eat them all."

Flowersview, like most of the Florida panhandle, is gentle land. Wind-tossed fields of bright green wheat and rye warm under the March sun. Slash and longleaf pines are reflected in placid farm ponds. The first white blossoms of dogwood peek through dense pine forests just about the time the pink azalea bushes in everyone's yard begin to flower. Panhandle people, both black and white, seem as gentle as their land. Soft-spoken, with a hint of drawl, they extol their small-town lives. They are people who wave at you on the roads, whether they know you or not, are members of the Baptist church, good neighbors, folks who never fail to invite you into their kitchens for cake and coffee. "We all know each other's business, but we wouldn't have it any other way," said a middle-aged white friend of Gladys's over coffee. "We care about each other." Unfortunately, it wasn't always that way.

"Flowersview started sometime around the turn of the century as a turpentine community called Flowers Quarters," Gladys says. "When men tired of that sort of work, they turned to farming, buying land and clearing off the trees. They farmed for years until large companies wanted to plant groves of tung oil trees on the land starting in the late 1930s. Tung oil trees have poisonous nuts that when crushed have a very fine oil that was used in varnishes. The blacks were swindled out of their farmland by whites, one man in particular. As I understand it, most people trusted this man to drive to the county seat with their taxes every year. They gave the money to him because he had a car and all they had were mules and a wagon. He never paid their taxes. Huey's family had nearly sixty acres and were literally thrown out into the road. It was a real massacre. They tried to fight it in the courts, but black men had no power in the courts back then. The lawyer they hired had been bought off. My parents ended up with three acres; some got as much as five. Most blacks kept their houses, but lost their farms.

"That land deal was the worst thing that ever happened to people here. Outside of that, relations between blacks and whites have always been good. It was just the general trend then, the way things were. I will say it was a paradise around here with all the tung oil trees. People came from everywhere to see them. Blacks picked the nuts for seven to ten cents a bushel. I picked a few myself. Then everyone went off to World War

Gladys plays with grandchildren Felycia, Ahmal, and Ahmad at her Flowersview, Florida, home.

II. When the blacks returned, they had no interest in farming. They stayed in their homes in Flowersview and commuted to work in defense plants or Eglin Air Force Base. The tung oil trees eventually got sick and died and were uprooted.

"This is home. People think nothing of driving fifty miles a day to work like I do to live here. Part of the world's problems is that no one has a sense of belonging to a community anymore. Here everybody knows everybody, and they take an interest in you in an old-fashioned way."

Except for a few white families living on the edges, Flowersview is still a black community. Most homes are on two or three acres and range from simple frame houses to fancy brick colonials. It's a quiet, pleasant place to live now. "I guess the population of Flowersview might be 250 if you count all the men, women, children, dogs, and cats," Gladys says. "Everyone has a roof over his head, and although it's not always a good one, it belongs to him. No one's renting, and few, if any, are on welfare. You sure won't find any tenements here. People have nice things. They aren't tackily dressed country folks. They've been to town. I'd say they've all done pretty well for themselves."

Huey and Gladys "courted" briefly in Flowersview when they were young, but they both married other people. Neither first marriage worked out. Gladys was only sixteen when she married and had just finished the eleventh grade. Although the marriage produced both Henry and Mabelois, it's a period of her life she doesn't discuss. "I came back to Flowersview often with Henry and Mabelois to visit Mama on the farm. Huey still liked me and I knew I needed someone for the children. They all consider him their father. We married in 1949, the same year I received my high-school diploma.

"Huey may not be everything he ought to be, but I respect him more every year. I've always trusted Huey. Above all, he's a truthful man. I think he'd hurt himself before he'd ever lie. If you so much as insinuate that he's lying, I think he'd rather you called him a dog or a son of an anything. He has that much respect for the truth. A lot of people see me as the pusher, making all the major decisions. Like heck I do! If Huey says we aren't going to do something, brother, we don't do it.

I have a high respect for manhood. I think a woman is supposed to walk side-by-side with her husband and not particularly get ahead of him. I guess I belong to the old school. I'm satisfied with my role as a woman because I can be strong and do most anything I have time to do. Huey goes along with most of my big dreams. When he doesn't, sometimes I can puff and cry and make him change his mind."

The spartan six-room frame home Huey originally built slowly grew by necessity as he and Gladys had five children to add to her two. Even now that the children are grown, the house is often full on weekends and holidays. It's a close family with all three generations coming together often. Sometimes on a weekend, they'll spend hours huddled up by the piano in the den singing gospel songs. The Milton home is now one of the finest in Flowersview, an all-brick home with four bedrooms, three baths, kitchen, dining room, den, and maternity rooms. It's a warm, personal place, filled with family antiques, early American furniture, photographs of children and grandchildren, and many of the lovely ceramic bowls and figurines Gladys has made over the years. She has a knack for crafts. In the ten months since she's learned to crochet afghans, she's made eleven of them, three of which add color to her own home.

'I never cared if I had the finest things, but I appreciate having nice things," Gladys says. "All little girls have a storybook idea of marriage. You get your Prince Charming. When he comes home at night, you cook a lovely supper then watch TV or show home movies of the kids. I had it all pictured out, but sure as heck, the money ran out. I spend money like I got some. It's the only thing worse than my vicious appetite. Huey

Gladys loves to fish, and she laughs at herself when she pulls in a small one like this. "Fishing is my relaxation," she says. "Water is serene to me. I forget what's on my mind because I spend so much time watching for snakes. I never have time to worry when I'm concentrating on catching a fish. I call it giving my troubles to the waves, letting them carry them out to sea."

would buy only what we could afford, and that would be about half of what we've got. Some way or another, I work it out. As the children kept coming, I could just picture them needing food and clothes, but that never happened. We always managed to have enough, even in the hard times when we were poor, when I only worked one or two nights a week at the clinic. I cleaned houses, lots of houses, for extra money for twenty

Gladys Milton

169

years. That's part of what Aunt Mag instilled in me. It's not degrading or beneath me. We don't have that much now, but it tickles me to have three or four choices of clothes to wear every morning and several different kinds of meat in the freezer to choose for our dinner."

The Milton home is built on almost two acres of high land overlooking endless fields of soybeans. Although the soybeans belong to white farmers and they'll never recover their parents' farms, Gladys enjoys her environment without bitterness. "I don't think blacks in this area have wasted their resources. We haven't had much, but we've done a lot with what we had. I've got a country streak in me that I can't get satisfied anywhere else. I've just got to pull off my shoes and step on a few rocks and sandspurs to really know I'm here. I like big-city advantages—plays, operas, things like that—but if I lived in a city I'd spend most of my time outside of it at the fish ponds in the country. Mind you, I like to live as modern as I can up here in the country. I still want my air conditioning and color TV. I don't want no tar-paper shack. And I'm lazy. I don't want a big garden taking up all my time. I just want a patch big enough to grow me a few greens. As far as the rest of it goes, I'd rather wait until they have a thirty-seven-cent sale at the grocery store and stock up the freezer that way."

Gladys has always been deeply involved working for the betterment of her community and others around her. "I think

Gladys and Huey Milton are both deeply religious. Huey is a deacon at the Flowersview Baptist Church, where Gladys is giving this lesson. She is a very impressive, moving speaker.

you should live your religion. Go to church to worship, but when you go out that door, *serve*, in your home, in your work, and in your community." For thirty-two years, Gladys has been clerk of the Flowers Quarters precinct, one of two all-black voting precincts in Walton County. She's never missed an election. She's secretary to both the Walton County and Tri-County Community Action groups and a member of their executive and policy-making committees. They sponsor programs like Head Start, meals for the elderly, and other emergency food and medical programs. "We all come together to iron out our problems," Gladys says. "I feel I should give some time to civic duties, and I can't think of any better way to spend it than this." On many of her days off, Gladys volunteers to check the blood pressures of seventy or eighty senior citizens who come for free hot lunches. "Here's the way I look at volunteer work," says Gladys. "I occupy a lot of space around here, weighing two hundred plus. This is the way I pay my rent.

"We all leave footprints in the sands of time. I really want to leave impressionable ones." As she looked down at her size 12 B shoes, she burst out laughing. "I know I'm going to leave big footprints! I just hope they are good ones. I want to do things that will live in people's hearts long after I'm gone. I care what people think about me, and I want them to remember me. I think the highest tribute you can make about a person is to say that she was kind, loved people, and helped them out."

DECEMBER, 1986

Nothing keeps Gladys from helping people. After delivering

Gladys is active in two local community action groups and freely dedicates much of her spare time to volunteer work helping the area's less fortunate people.

her seventh baby in the new maternity clinic on the morning of August 12, 1976, and stabilizing the mother, she drove to a community action meeting in Chipley that night in a crashing thunderstorm. Driving home, she watched the storm intensify. "The lightning was so bright, the road was white. I couldn't tell if I had my headlights on. The hot pavement smoked all the way home as the rain hit it. It was raining so hard when I pulled into the driveway that I couldn't get out of the car. I just sat there, waiting for a break to run inside.

When it lightened up, I noticed the house was smoking just like the highway. Smoke was pouring out from under the eaves. I ran out of the car and flung open the door of the maternity room just as Elinor, her children, and the mother and baby fell out screaming. They weren't hurt, just terrified. It was awful. They ran to my station wagon as the fire got worse. Huey was trying to douse the flames with a garden hose while we waited for the fire department, but it was no use.

"Suddenly Huey asked me if they had gotten our grandson, Tyler, out. That's Debbie's son who was staying with us. I ran to the station wagon. He wasn't there! In all the confusion, they'd forgotten him. The roof started breaking in as I ran through the den door to his bedroom. I felt all over the middle of the bed and I couldn't find him. I panicked. I was afraid he had run through the smoky house and collapsed somewhere. Walls were falling in. I went into that house to get him and I wasn't planning to come out without him. I could never get over losing Tyler. Finally, I felt him rolled up on the side of the bed against the wall, still sound asleep. I wrapped him in my arms and ran. Somehow, we made it through the flames and smoke without getting burned. Ten minutes later the gas line in the kitchen exploded like a volcano. We had run right across there. Except for the grace of God, we'd have been killed. I had no idea all that can happen when lightning strikes a house.

"I was in a state of shock after the explosion. I just stood there with Tyler in my arms, thanking God for him. There wasn't a man in those two fire departments who wasn't my friend. I call them all my little white boys. I helped deliver most of them at the clinic. They are the same age as my children. They tried so hard to stop the fire, but it had gone too far. 'Don't kill yourselves,' I said. 'Don't you see that it is gone? Just try to keep it from catching one of the neighbors' houses on fire. Nothing in the world can be saved here.'

"I hated to see my house and clinic burn to the ground, but I had peace of mind. Dreams don't burn. Time will heal the loss of all the material things. I can do without everything, except life. I would never have gotten over picking up Tyler's burned body. Having him safe in my arms was all I needed. My friends all stood around me crying, wondering why I was so calm."

When they picked through the rubble after the fire, the only thing that was left was one set of dishes inside a chest that had somehow survived the heat. Gone were the priceless antiques, Gladys's Thomas organ, years of ceramics, all the pictures of her dead children, all the furniture and appliances she had scrimped so hard to buy when she really couldn't afford to. The estimated loss of the house and its contents was thirty-five thousand dollars. Huey only had twenty-five hundred dollars' insurance. He had never increased the coverage all the times they had added on and improved their home.

Friends in three states came to their rescue, contributing five thousand dollars. Others brought clothes and shoes. A close friend in Flowersview gave Gladys and Huey rent-free accommodations in an old house she owned for as long as they needed it. "It had no sink inside and the bathroom was on the back porch, but it started to look like a home when friends brought us furniture, a TV, an electric stove, sheets, blankets, bedspreads, pots, pans, and a crockpot. We were grateful to have a roof over our heads. Everyone we know was so good to us. It was the encouragement of friends, not just their contributions, that made all the difference."

With the twenty-five hundred dollars' insurance money and some of the contributions, Huey, a retired carpenter, and Gladys's brother started building the framework of a new house on the old foundation. Soon others joined them. It was like an Amish barn raising in the Florida panhandle. By late 1977, Gladys was back in business in a rebuilt clinic, deeply in debt, but happy.

"My main dream was to deliver babies full-time, nothing but that. Just before the fire, I was about to reach the point where I could afford to work part-time at the hospital, have someone manning the phone here, and really be open for business delivering babies for three county health departments." Gladys' dream would now take a little longer.

It was therapeutic for Gladys to spend many mornings in the ceramic shop, replacing some of her favorite pieces destroyed by the fire. When the police called her to come home on a morning in May, 1979, it didn't seem unusual. "I'm always called home to deliver babies. I was waiting for a girl to deliver her tenth, so I burned up some fifty-five and got on. When I turned up our road, I saw a crowd standing around our place. It scared the pants off of me. I was afraid the baby had been born in the police car and the mother or baby were dead. Then I saw the fire truck. Everybody hated to face me as I drove up. When I got there the house had just about quit smoking. It had burned to the ground again. The fire marshal thought it was an electrical short. No one was in the house at the time.

"I felt so bad, I didn't want to face people and show my inner self. When I'm depressed, I'd rather not see anyone. I asked, 'Why me?' I hated to question my Maker. All things happen for a purpose, but TWO fires? That's too much. When the second house burned, I went into a deep depression and meditation. I asked God to reveal to me if I was really doing his will or if I just thought that. I'd be willing to quietly drop the idea of a maternity clinic forever if it was wrong. I got a divine revelation that the clinic was his will for my life. I told God I didn't have the strength, the money, or the patience to rebuild this time, but if he would open up a way and give me the strength, I'd start again. He gave me enough miracles to last until 1990."

Mizell Memorial raised money for her, and as the word spread, three or four more hospitals donated equipment, some almost brand new, to make the third clinic a reality. White and black women's clubs in the area came together, throwing a big shower for Gladys in Florala. County commissioners sent their trucks to pick up donated furniture and hospital equipment for the Miltons. Insurance, boosted since the last fire, paid for the rest. Again, patient Huey started rebuilding. This time he could afford to hire subcontractors. Friends helped, too. They built the clinic first.

"When you have no problems, you're D-A-D-E!" Gladys laughed, maintaining a sense of humor through the tragedies. She is thinner in the 1980s by almost forty pounds. Her hair is white now, in a fluffy Afro. Her spirit never changes. "I'm one of those old-timey born-again Christians. It was my faith in God that sustained me through all the crises and gave me the strength to get up and try again. I'm an optimist. With all the federal programs being cut, I think more women will come to me to deliver their babies. As long as they believe in midwifery, have faith in God and in themselves, and trust me, I welcome them. I won't take anybody with a negative attitude. They might haul off and die, sure enough."

Like the others, Gladys's third midwifery clinic was named in honor of daughter Eleanor, the twin who was killed by a drunk driver. Eleanor loved midwifery as Gladys does and had accompanied her to many home births. The well-equipped clinic was dedicated at Gladys's new home on August 31, 1980. Bill Harker, one of the hospital administrators who helped Gladys tirelessly, encouraged her to hold a formal dedication, an occasion. "All my children came home for it and warned me to start crying a few days early so I wouldn't flood the place. I'm a May chick. I cry at everything, especially things like that. It was one of the most beautiful days in my life. Several hundred people came. Maria read my favorite poetry and Debbie sang. The newspapers sent photographers and writers. People in this area are so good to one another. When a need arises, they respond. My theme for the dedication was 'Great Is the Lord.' God has been good to me. More good happens to us than bad. Whether life polishes or grinds you depends on the material you're made of."

The clinic became a big success. Gladys left her job at the hospital in 1982 to deliver babies full-time. Although the laws and restrictions on lay midwives have become increasingly stringent, Gladys is always busy filling a great need. With malpractice insurance rates rising, fewer doctors are delivering babies in her area. More families want natural childbirth with the husband present in a less formal setting than a hospital operating room. "I'm pleased that couples come to me by choice, not because they have no other alternative," Gladys said in December, 1986, at age sixty-two and with seventeen hundred births behind her. "I'm waiting now for a mother who is due who has two kinds of insurance to pay hospital bills, who doesn't want to go to a hospital. I have a commercial pilot with insurance from his company whose wife is coming here by choice. It is just as I hoped it would be."

Actually, Gladys got more than she hoped for. Daughter Maria came home and started helping in the clinic. "All along I had hoped one of my children would say, 'Mother, I have so much respect for your profession, I want to be a midwife.' No one would say it. I believe in letting children follow their own path, so I had given up. Elinor is good at communicating with the mothers, but she has yet to see a baby born. She'll come back there with me, but when things get hot, she has to leave. One day Maria saw a miracle. A mother came in about 1 A.M. kicking and screaming. When I checked her out, I realized she was going to have a breech delivery. I'm not authorized to do breech deliveries, but it was too late to get her to a hospital. She scrambled over the bed trying to get away, but I got her calmed down and got the baby born. The baby was white and chalky, born dead. The mother was screaming. I said, 'Don't scream—pray! This is praying time.' I got on that baby and started doing mouth-to-mouth resuscitation on her. The Lord raised her up. In a second she was pink from head to toe. The daddy rushed in when he heard her cry and said to me, 'Doc, you got her to work.' I said, 'Not me. I didn't get nothing to work. The good Lord got your daughter breathing.'

"It had a great impact on Maria. She was silent about it for several days. Finally she said, 'Ma, I want to be a midwife.' I knew it. She entered midwifery school in Gainesville. It takes three years for most people, but since she had a degree in biology and lots of science, she finished in a year and a half. She'll take her state boards in April. She only has two more babies to deliver under Henry's supervision. Henry has come back home to Flowersview, too, in the last year because there's a great need for doctors here. He still goes back to the city to work in a clinic two days a week, but he has an office here and will be building a home. Maria, Henry, and I will all be working together.

"I've been discouraged, but I'll never give up. God wants me to alleviate the situation down here and deliver his babies as I was called to do. I intend to do his will as long as I'm able, until the good Lord says, 'That's enough!' I've got a lot more mileage in me."

Dorothy Smith

OCTOBER, 1976

"This isn't the real me!" forty-year-old Dorothy Smith shouted as she stretched a lump of gooey bread dough with the heel of her palm. Four other Zuni Indian women in her family laughed as they rhythmically punched and pulled dough with her around a long table. They were dressed for the job. Dorothy looked incongruous with a glob of dough in her hands, wearing a pretty pastel pantsuit. As usual, she was impeccably neat. After dismissing her kindergarten class, she had rushed over to her Aunt Flora Belle's home to prepare an old-fashioned Zuni dinner. She had grown up in this long, flat sandstone home in the heart of the Zuni reservation in west-central New Mexico watching her grandmother labor over the bread for two days, then bake it outside in beehive-shaped clay ovens.

"Grandma was a wonderful, witty woman in handmade dresses with long sleeves and rickrack borders," Dorothy remembers. "I never saw her without her apron. Zuni bread was one of her specialties. The sourdough starter goes on and on. Before she died in 1971, Grandma taught my sister Sadie all her secrets of bread making, so she's in charge now. About all I know about making Zuni bread is that you have to knead it for four hours. For me, that's entirely too long!"

Dorothy and the other women chattered constantly, slipping back and forth between Zuni and English. They ranged in age from twelve to sixty-one, but there appeared to be no generation gap, no awkward silences or sighs of boredom. The women didn't see each other as often as they'd like, so they enjoyed being together even if it meant kneading dough for hours. Dorothy's arms gave out first. "I'd much rather be doing the hokey-pokey with my kindergarteners," she snapped, belting the dough with a few hard punches.

"Is that how liberated women take out their aggressions?" a cousin teased Dorothy, the only college graduate in the family. Since Dorothy is probably the only Zuni woman who subscribes to *Ms.* magazine, they like to rib her about being a feminist. Dorothy has no plans to lead a women's liberation movement in the small, sandy village of Zuni. "I saw *Ms.* in Albuquerque, and thought it had some interesting articles, so I subscribed," she says. "I think the average Zuni woman is quite liberated without *Ms.* Their husbands don't hold them down. For years it has been the women who drove forty miles north to Gallup to work while their husbands stayed home making silver jewelry. Zuni men know how to feed and diaper babies."

Answering her cousin directly, Dorothy replied, "Come on, now, you know I think that much of the women's movement was created by ladies who had time on their hands and needed something to do. But really—is it necessary to knead bread for four hours and bake it outside when it will be eaten in thirty minutes? We could pop some loaves of brown-and-serve into the kitchen stove for ten minutes instead."

The banter continued for hours as Dorothy laughed, obviously enjoying the camaraderie with her family. Working full-time and having a husband and three children to care for doesn't leave as much time as she would like for special occasions like this, when the whole extended family, some twenty or so, sits down together to eat in the dining room of Dorothy's childhood home.

When Dorothy was small, she, her sister, and two brothers lived in the middle of the long sandstone house with their parents and grandparents on their mother's side. Aunt Flora Belle and her family lived on the right side of the house and an uncle and his family on the left. "We didn't see many outsiders

For Dorothy Smith, the only Zuni Indian teacher in Zuni, New Mexico, getting an education was an ordeal. She had to leave home at fifteen to go to a boarding high school run by the Bureau of Indian Affairs and then on alone to Oklahoma for her degree in elementary education.

back then because the roads to Zuni were unpaved," Dorothy says. "Traditions were stronger. Zuni family structure is based on matrilineal clans. When my father married my mother, he

Dorothy
Smith
177

was expected to move to his wife's home with her parents and family. We all shared the kitchen, which stretched along the back of the house. At mealtime, everyone in the family ate together—eight adults and nine children sitting around a big table."

Today Zuni families are much like those of other Americans. "Children now like to get married and move away from their parents into government housing or a mobile home," says Dorothy. "Maybe that's just as well. It was overcrowded here with our big family. We had no privacy. All the beds were in one room at first, though we built some partitions when we were teenagers. My grandmother told us the story of her honeymoon spent in the same room with her folks. Her husband was chosen for her by her parents. She had never dated him and hardly knew him. They had to sleep on a mattress stuffed with cornhusks right there next to everybody else. Grandpa was quite a character. Every time Grandma told that story, he'd pipe in and tell us that whenever he tried to do anything it would make such a racket that it wasn't much of a honeymoon."

No matter how modern or educated Dorothy may be, she says, "My Zuni extended family, my clan, and our traditions are all very important to me today though I've been to Oklahoma to college, married outside the tribe, and have a family

Dorothy Smith and her Zuni family stuff cornmeal paste and a chili mixture into cornshucks to make hot tamales, one of the traditional foods in their old-fashioned Zuni dinner. Left to right: *Aunt Flora Belle Enote; Annette Lorenzo, a cousin; Dorothy; Sadie Sanchez, a sister; and her daughter Karen Sanchez.*

of my own. It's nice to be part of a loving, close-knit family with cousins as close as brothers and sisters. If anything happens to one of us, everyone helps. There's no such thing as a lonely old age. The younger ones never fail to take care of the old folks."

Dorothy's husband Doug, an assistant principal in Zuni, is a handsome boy-next-door-type blond from Big Cabin, Oklahoma, who is accepted completely within Dorothy's big family. "My family is very open-minded about those things. One of the things I most admired about my grandparents is that they stuck to the old Zuni traditions but were good at conforming to the culture of the white man. When I first brought Doug home from college, my grandmother just said he was the best-looking boy I had ever dated. She liked him from the beginning. We're all mixed up. My family married into the Navajo, Laguna, Pima-Maricopa, and Cherokee tribes. Why not a white man? I went home with Doug a lot of weekends and stayed with his folks. We got along very well. They were used to Indians."

"Back in Oklahoma where I lived, everyone has some degree of Indian blood," Doug says. "My grandmother, who is eighty-seven now, has a Cherokee roll number. It doesn't matter to me. We don't even know how much Indian we are. There have never been any problems about our marriage within our families. I have to admit, I've even had a little fun with it at times. I had one Jewish friend in college who probably believes to this day that I had to give Dottie's father six horses before marrying her. Some Indian friends of mine and I told him that was the custom."

Dorothy helps fire up the beehive-shaped clay ovens in front of her childhood home in Zuni. After the fire roars for two hours, the hot coals are removed and the bread placed inside to bake for an hour.

While the men and children talked inside, the women continued preparing their old-fashioned dinner. Their mutton stew simmered on the stove while they formed an assembly line to make hot tamales, wrapping cornmeal paste and a chili mixture in cornshucks. They laughed at each other when a tamale bulged out of its cornshuck. They were all out of practice. It had been a year since the last old-fashioned family dinner. Even Dorothy was impressed by the sight of twenty-eight round loaves

of bread they had kneaded and shaped rising under white sheets. Getting into the spirit, she helped her sister fire up the old beehive oven, throwing juniper and cedar branches in until the fire roared. She promptly singed her hair and retreated to the modern kitchen. After the fire burned for two hours, Sadie performed the ancient tradition of sweeping the hot coals from the oven with a wet cedar branch tied to a stick. She tested the temperature by throwing in a handful of cornmeal to see if it would brown evenly or burn. When the oven was just right, she carefully loaded the bread in to bake for an hour. When the remaining red-earth ovens in Zuni disintegrate, most people think they'll be gone for good. The old women from Dorothy's grandmother's era who know how to build them are dying off fast. Younger women aren't interested in learning to build beehive ovens they'll never use in their fast-paced life-styles. The two-day ritual of making Zuni sourdough bread will soon be history in a Wonder Bread world.

Most Zuni women already wear the same pants and jeans the rest of America wears, watch the same popular TV programs, and consume hamburgers, french fries, and pizza more often than mutton stew. The 400,000-acre reservation with some six thousand Indians was once an isolated pueblo of two-story adobe buildings with no running water or electricity. Now, modern ranch-style homes are scattered over the rocky hills as more affluent Zunis search for panoramic views of the wildly beautiful sculptured pink-and-tan mountains that rise out of the arid plains around Zuni. Federal money and the national popularity of the distinctive Zuni inlaid stone and silver jewelry have transformed the reservation. Zuni may remain small, but when the forty-mile highway to Gallup was paved in the 1950s, its isolation ended forever.

Few outsiders would weep for the plight of the American Indian if they drove down Zuni's paved streets, admired its beautifully equipped schools or toured its new fifty-bed Public Health Service hospital. Some people like the Laselutes, Dorothy's family, have thrived in the last twenty years, rising from a simple life-style to become successful middle-class families. Dorothy is one of perhaps five Zuni teachers and one of a handful of Zunis who graduated from college. Her brother Edison, the oldest of the four, is the governor of the whole Zuni tribe. Another brother, Ervin, is an auto-body repairman in Window Rock, Arizona. Sister Sadie, the youngest, is a fine silversmith, following their father's tradition.

Zuni's problems aren't obvious from the new paved streets in the pueblo. "The pendulum just swung too fast for most Zunis," Dorothy explains. "The people were isolated farmers until the jewelry boom. A lot of poor families suddenly got rich and had no idea what to do with their money. If they had saved it instead of blowing it, they'd have something today. I know one family that paid a band three hundred dollars to play for a few hours at their child's birthday party. Roads, electricity, and television all came in at the height of the jewelry boom. These drastic changes in life-style were more than most people could handle. The family, which used to be Zuni's greatest strength, is breaking down. Tuberculosis used to be the number-one killer here. Now it's alcohol and suicide. So many people in their twenties are dying of cirrhosis of the liver. Alcoholism is such a problem here that some parents are abandoning their

Dorothy admires the paper halo one of her kindergarteners has just pasted and put on her head. The discouragement Dorothy feels about the educational futures of children in Zuni melts when she's teaching these happy, innocent kindergarteners.

kids. That was unheard of when I was growing up. There was no such thing as a foster home in Zuni. Children were always well taken care of by their parents. Losing that is very, very sad.

"I consider myself a modern woman. I say that it doesn't bother me to get away from the old traditions. That's not completely true. I can see some of the strengths and values I learned in my childhood that are missing in kids around here today. I wouldn't want to go back to living like we did in this house back then, not even for a day. The old times were not that great.

We didn't have running water, electricity, or TV. Our house was lighted by Coleman lanterns and warmed by a wood stove. In the wintertime I froze on my way to the outhouse. I like all the gadgets that make my life easier—my dishwasher, my washing machine, and my dryer. I don't want to go back to the time when I had to scrub my brother's Levi's on a washboard. Now is the best time for me, but I have some wonderful memories of my childhood, too.

"In the summers we all went to Ojo Caliente, a little farming village that gets its water from a natural spring. I'd fish in the lake and climb mountains around there. Grandpa farmed in the sandy soil and raised sheep. We butchered our own sheep for mutton stew and grew all our own corn, so everything for our special meals came off the farm. Both my grandma and my grandpa were very religious and belonged to medicine groups that heal the sick. They participated in many of the dances and ceremonies that were held in the pueblo. We went to see them all because all the adults went and they would never leave us home alone. At some of the night dances, I'd get so sleepy I'd nod and wish I was in bed. I could just picture my bed as I sat there trying to keep my eyes open. It was bad when I got too old to be held. They had a special dance called the Homecoming that was the beginning of the summer rain dances. Grandpa put a cover on our wagon at the sheep camp, loaded us all up, and drove us fifteen miles to Zuni over dirt roads. That was exciting. We almost felt like pioneers riding across the West in a covered wagon pulled by two horses.

"Our sandstone house in the middle of Zuni was a Shalako house built free of charge for my mother's family in the 1930s by the men who belonged to a certain dance group. They worked for a whole year on it. All the family had to do was provide food for them. All the women relatives came to help with the cooking. Shalako is one of the most dramatic Zuni ceremonies, which takes place in late November or early December and marks the end of the old year and the beginning of the new one with the blessing of the homes. Six men train for a year in religious rites for the honor of being the main dancers. Their colorful costumes make them ten feet high. These masked men portray ancestral spirits.

"It's so impressive when these giant figures rise over the hill. They have beaks that snap and horns. When it's dark, they start filtering into the homes. You are not allowed to follow them into the village. When I was a child, I always wondered how they got there. After a while they resorted to flashlights. Now the ceremony is a big tourist attraction, so they have police escorts. That really spoils it for me. Having a Shalako house is exciting, though. When I was a child, my aunt had one. The women in the family would cook solidly for two weeks before Shalako. They feed everyone who comes to the house, even the tourists, hundreds of people in each new home. The masked figures perform several ceremonies and dances in the homes from midnight or 1 A.M. until sunrise. Then we rush home and try to catch a few hours of sleep before the races start in the afternoon. Those ten-foot-high Shalako figures run back and forth across a dry riverbed. If one falls, it's a bad omen to their family and the whole community. Two of them ran into each other two years ago and fell. They were later whipped with yucca sticks. Anybody in the audience who sees the fall can be whipped, too, so you run right after it happens. I think they hit you to get the bad spirit out, but I've never stayed around long enough to find out."

Most of Dorothy's childhood memories center around her grandparents because her mother died when she was only seven. "Both my mother and my father were in a bad car wreck. Mom jumped out, hit her head on a rock, and died instantly. My father hurt his neck so badly he couldn't turn his head for a year. Dad worked most of his life as a silversmith and on and off he worked for the Forest Service scouting fires. He herded sheep on the side. I was crazy about my dad, a real daddy's girl. We used to fight over who would sit next to him at the table. He was so good to us. He never married again. I think my mother was the only one for him. I don't even know how old my mother was when she died. My grandparents grieved so long, I could never bring myself to ask questions about her. The memories were just too much for them. They even burned all her pictures. When she died, a part of their lives died, too. I remember them crying every morning for a long time. We cried, too, but eventually got over it. We were all so young.

"After my mother's death, my father went into mourning in the Zuni way and left our house for four days. Zunis believe that when somebody dies, their spirit goes to the Lake of the Dead some sixty miles away in Arizona on old Zuni hunting land. A relative, usually an aunt, takes the widower to his old boyhood home and watches him closely so the spirit of his wife doesn't return to get him. Something could happen that he would die, too. He practices a four-day series of religious rites. I really don't know the details of this, but I do know that in the Zuni way the husband usually moves out after his wife dies and goes back to his own family. My father got along so well with my grandparents that he stayed and took care of them when they grew old. He was good to them. They said he treated them better than their own kids did. He treated us all that way. Even if I didn't have a mother, my childhood was never lonely. Our father, grandparents, and aunts and uncles loved us so much, we didn't miss out on anything. We were always wanted, always a part of a big family. That's what makes the Zuni way so nice. You never miss out on love."

It is still very hard for Dorothy to talk about her father without crying. He died so recently, in 1974, that time has not yet softened the memory. In the 1970s, when Dorothy was in her thirties, she lost both grandparents and her father in four years.

"Religion for the Zunis isn't something we practice one day a week. It goes on all the time. Reverence for the dead is part of it. Even before you eat, you feed the dead. Almost everyone takes a little from his plate—beans, bread, meat—and throws it in a fire outside as an offering to the dead. I do it only at Shalako time when the spirits of the dead are supposed to come and watch the dances. I think our religion has been preserved through the generations because of our close family ties and our history of isolation. We've had a lot of people come in here to try to convert us—Catholics, Presbyterians, Baptists, and Mormons. A lot of Zunis go to those churches, but I think a Zuni is always a Zuni. There's something in our religion that we can't part with. I'm a long way from the traditions I grew up with, but I just can't throw them all away. I keep a few of them out of respect, if nothing else."

When Dorothy was ready for high school, she faced a dilemma. The Bureau of Indian Affairs school had closed its upper grades in Zuni, leaving her two alternatives: stay home and drop out of school or move away and go to boarding school. "I was fifteen when I went away to Albuquerque to the Albuquerque Indian School. My dad had to go to boarding school, too, but in his time they had regular military companies, uniforms, and drills. Fortunately, we didn't have to march or wear uniforms, but it was plenty strict. We were locked up in our dorms from 6 P.M. until breakfast. I was homesick for a few weeks but there were so many more things to do and see in Albuquerque than Zuni that I quickly got over it. It was a new world to me, the big city. I even stayed there in the summer working as a live-in housekeeper and babysitter to make money to buy school clothes. The school had Indians from all nineteen pueblos in New Mexico and some from Arizona. Our education wasn't the best because we were limited in subjects, but it was adequate.

"Only one teacher ever really talked to me about college. She was an Indian home economics teacher who went back to college in later years and had a rough time of it. She convinced me that if I worked hard enough and really studied, I could make it, too. I think that's when I began to realize the importance of an education. She had a profound effect on me."

Dorothy struggled with the decision between being a nurse or a teacher. She started out at the University of New Mexico taking general subjects plus a few nursing courses. "I got a job in a hospital in Albuquerque. One night I watched a patient die. It bothered me so much, I knew immediately that nursing wasn't the career for me."

Dorothy promptly changed her major to elementary education and looked for a smaller college. "My sister-in-law, a Cherokee, had grown up in Oklahoma and gone to Bacone Junior College in Muskogee, Oklahoma, a small Baptist school which was once an Indian university. She thought I'd like it. I really enjoyed it. I didn't know a soul when I arrived, but I made friends quickly. I worked my way through school in the library and by singing in the school choir, which paid ninety dollars a month. We toured the country and even appeared on TV. I shared a house with five girls. No one in my family had ever gone off to college, but I never thought of myself as a pioneer or a liberated Zuni woman. I never thought anything of it, really. I met a lot of people from other tribes who were doing the same thing I was. I had been away from home since I was fifteen, so I was used to being on my own, working, and living with strangers. I've always fit in easily wherever I went. All my roommates were white. None of us had any problem with that. I first met Doug at Bacone, but we never dated there. I had another boyfriend. We really got to know one another when we both went on to Northeastern State Teachers College in Tahlequah, Oklahoma. We dated for more than three years before we married.

"I knew I would never quit school until I finished college and had my degree. Perhaps the greatest educational influence I had was going home to visit and seeing my grade-school classmates in Zuni. They looked like old ladies. Those girls never went on to boarding school. They married at fourteen or fifteen, and now they're grandmothers five times over. I never wanted that to happen to me. I've always hated the idea of growing old. I want to have fun. Sitting around quilting and fanning the flies horrifies me. I hope I'm never like that. It's even hard to face the fact that I am starting to get tired now doing the bunny hop with my kindergarteners.

"When I came home with my degree my grandparents never said anything. I'm sure they were very proud. They told all their friends they had a granddaughter who was a teacher. They thought that was really something. Neither of them had ever gone to school. My dad got through tenth grade.

"I started teaching in a rural school in Thoreau, New Mexico, on the Navajo reservation about seventy miles from Zuni. I taught what they called 'pre-first,' the beginning. Things were primitive there in the early 1960s. The children didn't know what a bathroom was. I managed to teach the girls, but there was no way I could teach the boys. I'd point out the toilet and show them how it flushed, but I'd always find them in the bushes. Teaching there was a real challenge because the children spoke Navajo and very little English. I couldn't speak Navajo. I worked very hard with them on English as a second language materials—all oral—and had them speaking English pretty fluently by the end of the year.

"Doug and I were 'unofficially engaged' by then, but he couldn't afford a ring. He's three years younger than I am and still had another year of college to finish. After that he joined me teaching in Thoreau for a year, the first year of our marriage. Opportunities to teach in Zuni opened up after that, so we left the Navajos." The Smiths spent the next six years in Zuni, then returned to a modern school on the Navajo reservation in Crown Point, New Mexico, because Doug was offered a job as principal. During Doug's four years there, Dorothy taught. Taking some time off to have three children, she's in her twelfth year of teaching, and they're in their third year of a second stint in Zuni's schools. Doug is now the assistant principal of the high school in Zuni.

Doug is a gentle family man who often has all three of his children piled on top of him. He's soft-spoken, with the hint of an Oklahoma twang in his speech, but his softness shouldn't be mistaken for reticence. Zane Douglas Smith is a man of definite opinions. "Before we got married the preacher took me aside and put me through a sermon on the pros and cons of a mixed marriage," Doug recalls with obvious annoyance. "He asked me whether I was aware of the problems my kids would face because Dottie was a Zuni and garbage like that. To me it was irrelevant. If we hadn't loved each other and felt that it was right, I'm sure we wouldn't have gotten married. We've always been happy together, all of us."

"I can tell you what makes our marriage happy after thirteen years—a lot of love," Dorothy added. "We're just a very loving family, hugging and kissing each other all the time. It has always been that way. Doug and I never fight, and on those rare occasions when we have a disagreement, it's over right away. I'd have to describe my temperament as very mild. I can only remember chewing someone out once in my life. If I really get mad, I cry. When I was younger, I used to be very sensitive and easily hurt, but I'm not like that now. Our marriage works well because Doug and I like the same things and have similar goals.

We're both family-oriented stay-at-home types. Neither of us drink. We don't go out to party on the weekends. If we go somewhere, we usually take the kids."

The three Smith children are handsome. All are lanky, with dark eyes and their mother's shiny black hair. Terrence, nine, is a serious, intelligent boy who explains everything in great detail. Melissa, eight, loves everyone. "She has never known a stranger," Dorothy says. "The other day we were in the dimestore and she ran up to a gray-haired woman, threw her arms around her, and said, 'Hi, Grandma!' The woman was delighted, hugged her back, and introduced her to her thirty-year-old son. Another time we were in the grocery store when she yelled, 'Hi, Grandpa!' It was a colored man. I had a hard time holding her back and keeping her quiet. Everybody is grandma and grandpa if they are old and white-haired, regardless of skin color." Pretty six-year-old Franchon is the Smith's dramatic child in inflection and expressions. Doug swears she must have some Italian blood in her. Perhaps she's a budding actress.

"Melissa has the best personality because she's so loving," Dorothy says. "Educationally, I'm afraid she won't do as well as the others. She was slow to walk and talk. We took her to two neurologists, but all they could tell us is that she's slow. We already knew that. She has a short attention span and tires easily, but she has an exceptionally fine memory, especially for

The Smith children love to wrestle with their dad, Doug Smith, in their apartment in Zuni. Franchon is standing while her sister Melissa rides on Doug's shoulders. Terrence climbs on his hips.

people. When we go to the store, she'll recognize someone we've seen three weeks before and say, 'Hi, it's nice to see you again. Come see us again.' She has a lot going for her with that friendliness. She's in special education now, and I suppose she'll always be a little behind, but maybe she'll snap out of it. She's doing better. I think she'll get into a trade school, learn a skill, and have a happy, productive life. That's our hope for her.

"All the children have brought such joy into my life," Dorothy says. "They are so much fun to be with. I wouldn't trade them for anything or any other kind of life. I don't know what I'd do without kids."

"Our children are pretty good, even if they are ours," Doug boasts. "I like being with them. Children . . . well, they're your eternity."

"We love our kids a lot, but we believe in discipline, too," says Dorothy. "We don't let them go like Dr. Spock. One minute we'll be spanking them for something, and the next minute they'll be hugging us and giving us sugar. They forget. In raising our kids, we hope we're giving them a chance to have their own identity so they won't have to go off and 'find themselves' as so many kids seem to. I want them to know themselves, go to college, and get good jobs."

Home for the Smiths these days is the teacherage down the road from Dowa Yalanne School, where Dorothy teaches. It's an unpretentious-looking flat-roofed series of crumbling pink stucco apartments that look much like the urban renewal projects that sprang up in the cities during Lyndon Johnson's Great Society. Their apartment is small, but it has three bedrooms, new carpeting, and freshly painted white walls. Dorothy and

Dorothy is taken by surprise with a big kiss from six-year-old daughter Franchon.

Doug collect Indian art, which makes their simple apartment a fascinating place to be. Colorful *ojos* (eyes of God) in geometric patterns of bright-colored yarn hang in every room. Doug's collection of sand paintings and Dorothy's kachina dolls give the apartment warmth and personality. They are both knowledgeable in collecting the best Zuni and Navajo jewelry pieces, too, and have opened up a small shop on the main street in Zuni to sell it.

The Smiths are surrounded by interesting people because just about every teacher in Zuni finds an apartment at one of

Dorothy Smith
187

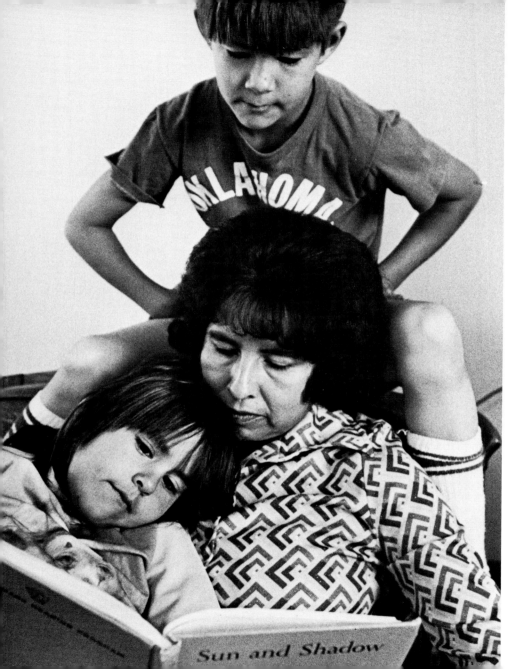

the teacherages. Hoping their work will be an adventure in another culture, young teachers arrive from all over the country. Dorothy can count up teachers from seventeen different states in her elementary school alone. Few of them, however, consider settling in Zuni and buying a house. They stay an average of two years, then go back home. The teacherage is convenient for these short-term residents and so inexpensive that they can pocket most of their salary. Dorothy and Doug pay only $127 a month for their apartment, all utilities paid. With Dorothy's salary of $11,900 and Doug's $17,000 salary, they have plenty of money left to invest in potentially valuable land in New Mexico and Oklahoma. "Most of our money is tied up in real estate," Dorothy says. "We have lots on Blue Water Lake in New Mexico, sixty acres in Oklahoma, and some land near Grand Lake in Oklahoma that we're trying to get commercially zoned for development. We think the most solid investment we can make for the future is in land rather than buying a house in Zuni. Zuni is home, but we don't intend to stay here forever. We need to be in a place where the children can have more opportunities as they grow up."

Rising up behind the teacherage are the jagged peaks of Dowa Yalanne, the Zunis' sacred mountain. It is a quiet, hauntingly beautiful place to climb over pink rock and look up at stone sculptures created by the erosion of time, wind, and weather. There's real grandeur and a peaceful quality on the mountain. Zuni legend says there was a great flood that forced

In their apartment in the teacherage in Zuni, Dorothy reads to Terrence and Franchon.

people to take refuge on the top of Dowa Yalanne. The water rose rapidly, nearly engulfing the terrified Zunis. To save themselves, the Zuni high priest sacrificed a virgin man and woman to the waters, his own son and daughter. As the legend goes, the water immediately receded and the Zunis were saved as the chosen people. Two spires are left standing on the mountain, images, the Zunis say, of the sacrificed man and woman who turned to stone. The Smiths often climb around the area. Dorothy points out the spire that looks like a woman wearing a shawl and the suggestion of water marks down the mountain where the floodwaters receded at various levels.

"I've climbed to the top of Dowa Yalanne about four times," Dorothy says. "A few years ago Doug and I went up. It's a strenuous climb that takes half the day. You have to scramble down before dark to avoid stepping into a rattlesnake den." Unfortunately, the trail up the mountain is littered with broken glass and beer cans, like many of the streets in Zuni.

Underneath the touching legends and colorful religious rites, there's an undercurrent of restlessness, boredom, and futility in Zuni, particularly in its teenagers. There's a pile of broken glass in the street in front of the Smiths' apartment. Dorothy claims she forgot to clean it up, but she may have left it there as a reminder of what's wrong in Zuni. "As assistant principal, Doug has to handle most of the disciplinary action at the high school," Dorothy says. "The kids get mad at him. The first time they came they smashed the taillights out of both of our cars. Another time they shattered the back window out of our Toyota. It made a terrible crash. We saw kids running off in the dark, but we couldn't recognize them.

Dorothy, Doug, and their girls play a game of keep-away in front of their apartment at the teacherage. The apartments are grim on the outside with crumbling pink stucco, but they are very nice on the inside.

What do you do? We replaced the window and about a month later the whole thing was shattered again. That time they sprayed the Toyota with white enamel paint and threw eggs at both cars. That's when I decided that Doug should get out of this kind of job. The future for our children is outside of Zuni."

Dorothy
Smith
189

"I'm very idealistic about education and moral right and wrong," Doug says. "I think vandalism is a direct result of having nothing to do, no parental guidance, no real values to live by. One of the most disappointing things is that the kids in Zuni and their parents really don't realize what's happening to them. You can trace most of the problems to alcoholism. Kids have walked into my office and told me that no one really cares about them or what they do and haven't for years. They turn to alcoholism and drugs for recreation at a very young age. If these kids ever reach high school, they'll probably drop out. We see it all the time."

"We're going to move away in two years when Terrence gets into seventh grade," Dorothy says. "Zuni is my home, but I can't change it. The kids at high school don't care about education the way we do. I don't want my children growing up in that environment. We'll adjust wherever we go. We always have. Life changed too fast here for most Zunis to cope with it. Zuni isn't alone. It's part of what's happening everywhere. Families break down when life-styles change so rapidly. I look at my little kindergarten kids and know half of them won't make it through high school if they stick around here. That's discouraging."

The discouragement melts when Dorothy enters the classroom. The way she smiles at those twenty-five round-faced kindergarteners and pats each one on the back when he or she does something well indicates that teaching is far more than

The Smiths climb rocks at the base of the Zunis' sacred mountain, Dowa Yalanne. It is a peaceful, haunting place that the Smiths love.

Dorothy acts out a song with her kindergarteners. Her school on the Zuni Indian reservation is extremely well equipped by the federal government with all the new teaching aids and educational toys.

a job for her. Something about those children tugs at Dorothy. It may be their wide accepting smiles, their innocence, or their spirit. Whatever it is, it keeps her energy flowing. One minute she's doing the hokey-pokey, the next she's reading a story, then she's elbow deep in paste and construction paper.

Dorothy runs to the record player to put on Zuni dance music, the real stuff recorded at ceremonies. Its rhythms are contagious. The children are up in an instant, hopping from one foot to the other while Dorothy beats on a handmade tom-

Dorothy Smith

191

The highlight of Dorothy's kindergarteners' day is when she plays a recording of ceremonial Zuni Indian music. Dorothy's helper beats the tom-tom with his fist and looks for approval. In Zuni the traditional dances have not died out. By junior high school many of the boys will have joined dance groups called "kivas."

tom with a stick. Her little helper uses his fists. Dorothy is surrounded by ear-to-ear grins. The Lasiloo, Kiyite, Siutza, Edaakie, and Cachini kids are a happy bunch at that age. They make everyone around them glow with their warmth.

When it comes to their lessons, Dorothy is strict. She wants her pupils' vision to extend beyond Zuni. Though only about half the class speaks English fluently, Dorothy rarely lapses

back to teaching in Zuni. "This is an English-speaking world," she says. "They can't get anywhere without a command of English. I only use Zuni as a last resort when they can't understand something. They get enough practice speaking Zuni at home."

The ten-year-old Dowa Yalanne Elementary is a modern, well-designed school with a congenial staff mostly of teachers from many states. At times Dorothy feels like a matriarch to them. She's the only Zuni teacher in Zuni, and she's taught there for many years. The federal government has lavishly endowed the school with every modern teaching tool, all the newest games and elaborate educational toys. They put a teacher's aide in every room and provide free lunches to all the kids, whether they are poor or not.

Apparently, that's not enough. One Saturday morning when Dorothy was packing a lunch for a family outing into the mountains, a teacher beat on the kitchen door. "Come quickly," she shouted. "Your room has been broken into. The police need you to assess the damage." School break-ins are common in Zuni, but most of them occur in the summer when the schools are empty. "One summer Zuni elementary had almost all its windows broken out," Dorothy says. "They came for those big magic markers. They sniff them and get high. They've never hit my room. Until now."

Dorothy winced at the devastation. It looked as if a tornado had touched down in the classroom. Fragments of broken

Dorothy strings beads with her adoring kindergarteners. She is constantly in motion in the classroom.

crayons and books were strewn all over the floor. Records had been pitched like Frisbees. Raggedy Ann was covered with green paint. Jars of paint were heaved against the walls, splattering all the children's favorite toys and their playhouse with globs of color. The white ceiling was full of purple spots. Broken glass lay everywhere, just as it does on the streets of Zuni. The new record player that provided music for the class to sing and dance to five or six times a day was smashed on the floor, its arm broken loose. The tape recorder had been stolen. Four filing cabinets were pushed on their sides. As Dorothy and the other teachers cleaned up the mess, they cried. "What will my kids do on Monday without music?" Dorothy asked. "How will they feel? There's too much damage here to hide."

The police attributed the vandalism to drunken teenagers bent on destruction. Nothing of value except the tape recorder was stolen. They were just getting their kicks. Something happens to the innocent, sweet-faced Lasiloos, Kiyites, Siutzas, Edaakies, and Cachinis by the time they enter junior high school, if they get that far. "The problem is their parents' drinking," Dorothy says. "They don't know what their kids are doing. If the parents are out drinking or home drunk, what's the kid going to do but start stealing drinks from his parents' supply? That's how it starts. I look at all the alcohol and drug problems we have in this small community and hope everything somehow changes back to the way it used to be. It's probably too late. I caught two fifth graders smoking pot during recess last year. It's frustrating. On the bad days I wonder if I can go on teaching forever, whether I really want to be in this profession. People around here just don't value education as we do.

With things like this, I don't think there's any alternative for us but to leave Zuni soon."

Dorothy and Doug seem to be running to something, rather than running away. Even before the vandalism started, Doug planned to teach twenty years, then go into real estate or insurance. Buying land for years was part of his well-thought-out master plan for the future. "I think it would be fun to have the opportunity to go show acreages and farm properties, to walk over the country with people in an atmosphere where they don't feel pressured. Sometimes I dream about the ideal place for me and my family. It will be west of the Mississippi River. I won't go east—unless somebody sends me there in a pine box. I'd like a pretty piece of land with trees where grass could grow without constant watering and where we could have a garden. I'd like a lot of room so the kids could have a dog, maybe even a horse. The best thing I can think of is some land with a creek running through it with a lot of privacy. If you wanted to take a dip in the creek, you could do it any time you want to. It's your creek and nobody's going to bother you."

Dorothy's dream revolves around a house, the house she's never had. "I want a big house, but a simple one with an upstairs and at least four bedrooms and a den. I worry about age because I'm getting older and so are my kids. Time is running out. I'd like to have my house now while the kids are young and all at home so we can enjoy it together. You don't need a house when you are old and the kids are married and gone.

"We'd like to give our kids more options socially and educationally, expose them to some culture. There's nothing here for kids to do but create their own recreation. That seems to

include alcohol and drugs. I'd like to see our children partici-
pate in sports, if they'd like to, go ice skating or swimming, take
in a museum. These are things most kids take for granted, but
ours rarely experience them except when we go on vacation.

"I'll miss Zuni because it's home. I know we'll come home
to visit my family often because we really care about each other.
I don't know where we'll move, but I'm not worried about it.
We'll be happy anywhere."

SEPTEMBER, 1986

The Smiths didn't leave their apartment in the teacherage in
Zuni until 1980. They didn't have to go far to find the happiness they were seeking. "We bought a three-bedroom, two-bath
home with a big backyard in a subdivision just east of Gallup,"
Dorothy says. "I really love it here. I guess you could say I have
the best of two worlds. I'm only a forty-five-minute drive from
my family in Zuni, so we've stayed very close. At the same time,
we are free of the problems we faced in Zuni. We moved so the
kids could have more opportunities as they grew up. There's
so much more to do here. I wanted the children to go to a high
school where they could be exposed to a wide variety of courses
and activities. Their subjects were so limited in Zuni. I think
they've really taken advantage of that. Franchon is taking drama
classes and loving them. Terrence wants to start his own business. Melissa will be going to trade school. Those things weren't
possible for them in Zuni when we were there.

"Doug is an assistant principal in the one high school in
Gallup. It's a good school. Kids here don't seem to be interested in breaking into schools. Doug has never been a target
for vandalism. They don't do that here. Getting away from that
changed our outlook. I realized that teaching was what I really
loved most. I teach first grade in Gallup in a well-equipped school
with a variety of kids, including Indians. I can even expose my
little first graders to computers, and I do, though I only know
the basics. This is my twenty-second year of teaching.

"New Mexico passed a new law that teachers can retire
after twenty-five years of teaching. That's exactly what I plan
to do. Our retirement isn't that great, but it's good enough to
make it worthwhile for me to retire at fifty-three while I'm young
enough to enjoy it. Even then, I don't plan to leave teaching.
I'll substitute, but I can be choosy about when I teach. I won't
have to go every day. I want to stay busy, but I don't want to
be tied down. I'd like to do more traveling, maybe some volunteer work, too.

"I think Doug will retire the same time I do, though I think
he likes education better than the other careers he's explored.
He's decided against going into real estate, in Oklahoma, anyway. Our kids still love Oklahoma and would probably move
there in a minute, but I don't want to live there. I could never
put up with those hot, humid summers. It's so cool here. Oklahoma is no place to sell real estate now after what's happened
to the oil industry there. Doug is more interested in insurance
and has been learning the business, but it would involve being
on the road a lot. I'm not sure he'd like that. We both love to
travel, but together as a family. Doug wants to do something
on the side, but I don't think he's found exactly the second

career he wants. We'll stay here. We're all happy in Gallup."

At fifty, Dorothy is an active, modern woman with a deep feeling for tradition. Two nights a week she sweats through aerobics classes. "I really get tired, but it's worth it. It makes me feel good. If you do aerobics two nights a week now, maybe you'll be able to jump rope at seventy-one. I have to keep limber to teach my first graders P.E. I'd love to do aerobics until I'm ninety. I don't worry about growing old now. If you stay active and have a lot of interests, age doesn't mean much anymore. There's even a fitness craze in Zuni now. So many ladies there were fat. Diabetes was widespread. One brave woman started an exercise class and it really caught on. Now there are all sorts of running clubs, fun runs, races, and walks. A lot of people have gone off insulin. It has been a positive change."

These days when Dorothy talks about Zuni, there's a different tone in her voice. The pride is back. "Zuni has changed," she says. "Things are better now. Oh, the drinking and suicides are still going on, but they've settled down since the jewelry boom. The most positive change I see is that people are more interested in education now because they understand what it will mean to them. A lot of kids are going to college now. One great thing is that there's now a Zuni branch of the University of New Mexico. I was once one of the only Zuni teachers. Now there are a bunch of them. There's a building boom in Zuni. Kids are staying and making something of themselves.

"The Zuni religion, dances, and medicine societies haven't died out. The younger people are interested and keep them going. Even the beehive ovens are popular again! They have a very active senior citizens group in Zuni that will send ladies out to build them. My sister Sadie just had four of them built at her new house. She's a wonderful cook who has taken over all the traditional meals in our family. She has a Shalako house this year, so I'm spending more time in Zuni than I usually do.

"My children never really became interested in the Zuni religion. Terrence didn't want to join a dance group. Our move was right for them. Terrence is nineteen now. He went to high school in Gallup, then on to New Mexico State in Las Cruces. He was coming home every weekend, so he transferred to the University of New Mexico in Albuquerque, which is much closer. He came home to marry his high-school girlfriend, a Navajo. We wanted them to wait, but they wouldn't listen to us. They're happy together and have a baby girl now. Terrence works at a truck stop filling up the big trucks and his wife works at a doughnut shop, but that's only temporary. He's going back to college next semester to study business.

"Our daughters are both juniors at the high school. Melissa is eighteen and in special education classes. She's about two years behind her age group, but she's doing well. She's happy and well adjusted. She'll learn a trade and get a job. Franchon wants to go to college, then become an actress. I'm trying to encourage her to go into something else, but she loves her drama classes.

"I think things have worked out well for all of us. I had two main dreams—giving the kids more opportunities and getting a house of my own. Both of those have been fulfilled. Now I think I'd like to travel more, see more of the country. Before Terrence graduated we took a vacation to the Smokies, up the Blue Ridge Parkway and to the Biltmore House in Asheville,

North Carolina. This summer we're off to California, Oregon, and Washington with the girls. It may be the last trip we'll have together before the girls graduate, Franchon goes to college, and the family breaks up. Our kids all seem to want to settle down in the Gallup area when they finish school. We'll be here. This is home now."

Dorothy
Smith
197

Nancy Smidle

Nancy Smidle doesn't fit the image most people have of a Wisconsin farm wife on a large dairy farm. She's terrified of cows. That doesn't imply that she retreats to the kitchen to knead bread dough and cut cookies every afternoon. She's in the kitchen, poised under the Old English–lettered Bless This Mess sign husband Dave gave her as a present, discussing farm legislation with a Michigan farm wife. She stretches the ten-foot-long telephone cord across the kitchen table, entangling son Dusty, eight, as she gripes about a Jack Anderson column she dislikes while her daughters cook dinner. She chain-smokes Benson & Hedges at the rate of four packs a day. Nancy hasn't planted a garden in years because she hates to pull weeds. Hay throws her into sneezing fits. And she'll be the first person to tell you that your "ordinary farm wife" is a figment of the urban imagination, a nostalgic stereotype of rural simplicity that doesn't exist on a large, complex family farm these days.

"Everybody thinks farming is such a bucolic existence," forty-year-old Nancy says. "Not long ago I was returning to my Washington hotel room after a day of lobbying for agriculture when the elevator operator stopped me. He had spotted my Wisconsin Women for Agriculture button and knew I was with a group of farm women. 'You don't look like a farm wife,' he told me. I guess he thought he was paying me a high compliment. Then he asked, 'Does your house have a bathroom?'"

The Smidles' large three-story farmhouse near Kewaunee, Wisconsin, has plenty of bathrooms. They also own about four hundred acres of some of Wisconsin's finest cropland near the shores of Lake Michigan, and they rent more. Their home is surrounded by modern fire-engine-red farm buildings, an eighty-stanchion barn that they designed, and 300 valuable registered Holsteins. Four silos loom high. Smidle Farms is impressive and prosperous-looking, the result of hard work, daily problem solving, and plenty of heartaches along with the satisfactions. The pretty picture on the outside doesn't expose the tedious three-hour-long milking sessions when Dave, his daughters, and one hired man pull six thousand pounds of milk out of 130 cows. Nor does it show the many 11:30 P.M. dinners Nancy rustles up after crisis nights in the barn. Nancy and Dave regularly play midwife to their cows in the middle of the night. Nobody sees the ten-thousand-dollar Holstein that gets mastitis and has to be sold to a mink ranch the next day for eight dollars.

"People are always amazed when I tell them what farming is really like," Nancy says. "It shocks them that we rarely make a profit over expenses. I know. I keep all the books. If we were paid the proper price for the products we produce, we'd be very, very wealthy. As it is now we have very little cash. We are always in debt. We've never been out of debt and never expect to be. Any agricultural economist will tell a farmer that whatever amount he's in debt today will be multiplied five times in ten years if he remains competitive, buying more land, new equipment, more cows. We're probably $200,000 in debt now. Everything we make is turned right around and put back into our investment. Last month I wrote $20,000 worth of checks and I couldn't pay all the bills. Take machinery, for instance. The average dairy farm in Wisconsin has to have seventy-five pieces of machinery. Some are big and expensive like tractors

Nancy Smidle frequently wears these I'm Proud to Be a Farm Wife sweatshirts. Modern farming has ceased to be a bucolic existence, and she finds herself having to be on the road telling consumers and politicians what farming is really like these days.

and combines. We have five tractors and a combine. Each has a function. We need them all. Some tractors cost as much as five family cars. We have a big disc in the barn that cost us nearly $8,000. It chops up the land and makes it easier to plow. We probably use it four hours a year, but it is absolutely essential.'

Nancy's husband Dave, forty-one, added, "My grain bill for one week is $1,100, just the grain, not figuring the cost of homegrown hay and feed. I feed a ton of grain a day. We might gross $150,000 a year, but we rarely show a profit. Last year, when we made $11,000, it was one of our better years. There isn't a gambler in Las Vegas who would play the odds we play farming."

Dave is a highly competitive man who runs his farm the way his idol, Vince Lombardi, ran the Green Bay Packers. "You have to be winning all the time if you are going to survive and stay in this business," he says. "There's no room for error." In the last fifteen years a third of the farms in the United States went out of business, and in Wisconsin, the number of dairy herds dropped from 132,000 to 53,000.

"About five years ago it was so wet that we couldn't get our crops out of the fields," Nancy remembers. "Tractors would just sink in. You couldn't even walk through a field without being knee-deep in water. Dave wouldn't give in. He devised an idea to put dual flotation tires on the combine. That was

Nancy picks up the mail on the highway in front of their attractive three-story farmhouse. The main barns are in the background.

unheard of. We drove all the way to St. Louis to pick up the special tires one morning and loaded them in our station wagon. There was so little room left that our little Dusty had to ride home in the hub of a tire. As soon as we got home, Dave put the tires on and combined into the night until he got it all. Dave has worked twenty-four hours a day without stopping when a crop has to come in."

At times Dave is on edge and exhausted. "I think I'm under more stress than the big city businessman," he admits. "At least he usually has a board of directors and some partners and somebody else's money to play with. We make all the decisions in this family and lose our own money."

Facing those odds on a daily basis, would Dave consider leaving the farm? "Let's say a guy comes to the farm and offers me a million dollars for it. [This is not an unreasonable thought. Good moisture-holding red clay farmland with drainage like the Smidles own is almost impossible to find in Kewaunee County. It sells for at least $1,000 an acre. Their cattle are worth another $250,000. One of their new silos cost $35,000. Add buildings, machinery, a home . . .]. What the hell would I do with a million dollars? Take it to the bank, sit there, and pick my nose? I like the challenge of being a farmer. I hate monotony. I like something with guts to it. Every day is different here. Sometimes when things go real well for about a week, I feel like I'm in a rut. I almost wish there was some trouble so I could cope with it."

"I have a college degree," says Nancy. "I could probably get a good job in a city, but I'd never go there. I'd feel too confined. My business is farming. I would miss it terribly if I

ever had to leave it. I grew up in Oshkosh, a town we consider a city, hating every second of it. When I graduated from junior high school, my dad asked me what I wanted for a graduation present. 'To get the hell out of Oshkosh,' I told him. We did. We moved to Kewaunee the next week. I had good friends in Oshkosh, but Kewaunee has only three thousand people. I can walk down the street and talk to everybody I see. I like that."

Kewaunee is a picturesque little town on the shores of Lake Michigan, as pretty as a New England village with casual midwestern friendliness. Fishermen flock there to catch coho salmon, trout, and perch, and hikers and campers gravitate toward the birch forests. The culture is rich with fun-loving Germans, Bohemians, Poles, and Belgians, all good beer drinkers. *Time* magazine once heralded Kewaunee as one of the great American capitals of beer consumption. One longtime resident remarked that there is a tavern and a Catholic church every square mile in Kewaunee County. She underestimated the taverns.

"Dave and I met when we were in eighth grade and went together all through high school," Nancy says. "Dad started out as an agriculture teacher and ended up as one, but between that he did some public relations work, was a county agent, and farmed. We owned farms in my childhood, but they were what you might call hobby farms, with a hired man helping

This is very typical of Dave Smidle, an intense, competitive man who takes every problem on the farm hard. He runs his farm like his idol, Vince Lombardi, ran the Green Bay Packers. "Vince Lombardi said winning isn't everything, it's the only thing," says Dave.

during the week and Dad farming on the weekends. When I was in high school, the word 'farmer' was a downgrade. It meant you were a hick. To marry a farmer was going downhill. When I was in college at the University of Wisconsin at Stevens Point, Dave was already a farmer. I knew I was going to marry him, and I was very proud of it. I married Dave on June 8, 1958, the same day I received my Bachelor of Science. I know a lot of my sorority sisters wondered what I was doing in college. Dave and I have something special here. We are both vitally interested in the farm and work together to keep it going. He has a lot of respect for what I say and do, and I think he's a fantastic farmer, one of the best in the business.

"Dave was a star athlete in high school. He wanted to be the first pro-football player from Kewaunee County, and I think he would have made it. He had two football scholarships to college. After that he wanted to become a vet. Dave's dad was a wonderful farmer, and his mother was a shrewd business-woman who helped manage the farm. Their farm had no debt on it. It was right down the highway from here. During Dave's senior year in high school, his father became critically ill and knew he would soon die. Dave is an only child. His dad gave him the choice of selling the farm and going to college and vet school as he had planned or running the farm with his mother. With some regrets, he decided to keep the 110-acre farm going. The house and barn burned to the ground before his father died. On top of that, his dad had no hospital or life insurance, and the hospital bill climbed to fifty thousand dollars. They were fortunate to have bought this house when it was a very good buy, so they had some place to move and begin again."

Predictably, as soon as Nancy gets close to one of their Holsteins, she gets bitten.

So Dave started farming at age sixteen with a debt that has increased every year.

"We started out farming with 110 acres," Nancy remembers. "For years we milked forty to fifty cows. I used to do everything on the farm but milk. Cows hate me. They know I'm scared stiff of them, so they kick me and knock me down every chance they get. I did all the feeding, bedding, and cleaned up the barn. I did tractor work in the fields. I never could bale hay because of my hay fever. Actually, I was kind of subdued back then. Up until I was thirty-four, I never drove a car. I never

Nancy Smidle

203

Nancy lobbies a state assemblyman, Lary Swoboda, at a meeting of farm wives.

thought I had to. I had everything I wanted right here on the farm. I enjoyed my four kids, being with Dave, and working on the farm. I went shopping when Dave needed to go downtown for something. Back then, I didn't belong to anything. I detested most women's organizations because all the women did at meetings was talk about their kids, exchange recipes, or discuss clothes. I don't give two hoots about any of that. The

only thing I was ever interested in outside of the home was something political."

The meat boycotts in 1969 shocked Nancy into activism. "Urban consumers decided that they didn't need farmers and could get along without meat. I found myself in an unbelievable situation during the boycott when I was asked to be on one of those small-town radio talk shows expressing the farmers' point of view. A lady called up and said, 'Look, Mrs. Smidle, we don't need you farmers. Everybody should go to Oscar Mayer like I do and buy their meat.' Before that my sister, who teaches kindergarten in Washington, D.C., told me she had a pupil who asked how farmers picked the cans of peas out of their fields. You expect that kind of mentality from a five-year-old, but not from an adult. It hit me like a bolt of lightning. Some people don't know where their food is coming from. They think it originates in supermarkets. I think that's when our movement really got started. We had always depended on our legislators to take care of us and on the consumer to appreciate farmers and want them around. Throughout history there was the 'Farm Bloc' when it came to voting in Congress. Most of our legislators came from farm communities. I think at last count there were only eleven senators who knew anything about agriculture. The dairy farmer better know what's going on in the migrant situation in California, and California growers better worry about imports of dried milk and cheese. We have no voice unless we work together. Politics, education, the whole ball of wax. We can't depend on anybody doing it for us anymore.

"We have to educate ourselves, our legislators, and the consumer. There are days when I wonder if I should stay home and clean the cupboards where I can see my accomplishment right away or stay on the road where legislation and changes grind away slowly. Domesticity is fine, if that's what you want to do. I'm a partner in a large, complex business. I'm going to do everything I can to save it. There are more important things to be done than housekeeping. If people come here to see if I have dust on the tables, cobwebs, and dirty floors, they don't have to come at all. If they come to see me or my family or the farm, that's fine. If they come to see a fantastic house, they've come to the wrong place. The cupboards can last another two years, but the things that are going on around us can't wait.

"Like every other farmer, Dave's so blasted busy that he doesn't have time to get out and fight. He concentrates on production. The average American farmer produces food for himself, his family, and fifty-seven other people. We're only 4½ percent of the population! A lot of meek and mild farm wives are getting off their duffs, branching out, and telling their story firsthand. I used to go to some farm meetings where the only thing the farm wife was good for was serving coffee and cake and possibly taking the minutes. That's not true anymore. Now if you want something done, you get a woman to do it. It is the farm wife who is going to take the time to fight. She's tired of being a second-class citizen."

Beyond the meat boycott, Nancy's transformation to activism was stimulated by a tragic event on the farm. "It was a terrible winter day—January 7, 1969—when the silo unloader froze up. Dave was the only one in the barn area at the time, so he turned off the switch and kicked it, hoping it would start when he turned it on the next time. The motor started on OFF,

which it never should have done. Dave's foot and leg were ground up by the sharp metal blades of the auger. None of us in the house could hear his cries hundreds of feet away through the howl of the blizzard. He managed to slide all the way back to the house in snow, leaving a path of blood behind him. We felt helpless watching Dave lying in pain on the dining room floor in a pool of blood. It took the ambulance an hour to get here. A snow plow had to blaze a trail in front of it.

"For ten days they debated on removing Dave's leg. It was just hanging there. The pain was excruciating. Dave couldn't even sit up for months. He was in the hospital on and off for two years, but a very capable doctor with front-line experience in the war saved the leg. Everybody advised me to sell the farm. They knew Dave might never be able to run it again and told me to face the fact that there was no way I could keep it going alone, a woman with four small children, including a baby. We were milking forty to fifty cows at the time. I decided there was no way I'd ever sell. Dave put his whole life into this farm and built it into a fantastic place. I wasn't about to let it die. I found myself a hired man who wanted to farm so badly that it worked out perfectly for both of us. We kept things going. Some neighboring farmers helped us in the fields as Dave had done for them when they had tragedies. People around here are friendly and helpful even if they are running their own big farms. Chuck, the hired man, and I milked fifty cows together. I'm not the greatest milker in the world, and he wasn't too keen on me, but you do what you have to do. When Dave improved, he helped run the farm by telephone from his hospital bed. We pulled through. I realized what a hell of a job Dave had been doing when I was forced to become both farmer and manager. 'By God,' I said, 'Someone's going to know about it!'"

From that point on, Nancy's toughness, drive, and aggressiveness blossomed. "I get very upset over injustice. Nothing makes me more angry than apathy, people who couldn't care less about what's going on in the world. That really gripes me. I get steamed. Stand up for what you believe in, whatever it is. Fight for your beliefs." Nancy was one of four founders of the three-hundred-member Wisconsin Women for Agriculture in 1973 and is in her second two-year term as president. She's assistant coordinator for American Agri-Women, a two-thousand-member national organization, and one of two planners of its first big convention in Kansas City.

Following her parents' example, Nancy naturally emerged as a leader and a spokeswoman for agriculture. "I had a great childhood and have always been close to my parents and my two younger sisters. Dad was a vigorous man who worked hard for agriculture day and night. He made a lot of speeches. I used to travel with him whenever I could and sit in the audience and listen. I know I picked up the bug from him. Mother was very outgoing and involved in things, too. She was a teacher all her life and very active in women's groups, the church, and the League of Women Voters. She still is. Some of that had to rub off on me."

In the last few years, Nancy has been a sought-after speaker on farm issues. People are impressed by her intelligence, her quick recall of facts, and her ability to communicate the complicated business of farming in terms laymen can understand. She is in her element lobbying on Capitol Hill, but she also talks to groups as diverse as the American Association of University Women, swine producers, the League of Women Voters, and grade-school children. "I'll talk to anybody who'll listen and let me get my story across," she often says.

It was only a few years ago that she made her first paid speech—to the National Organization of Farm Broadcasters in Kansas City. "It was the first time I had ever traveled out of state alone and my first flight. Flying still terrifies me. I never thought I'd find my way in the massive O'Hare Airport in Chicago, so I decided to fly out of Milwaukee. It was a big mistake. Connections to Kansas City were awful. I ended up on a bumpy, low-flying feeder plane. I could have picked the corncobs right out of the field, it was so low. I thought we were crop dusting. When we finally arrived at the Kansas City airport, I found I was still twenty-five miles away from my hotel. Since cabs are expensive, I waited for a bus. I hadn't heard of limousines then. No bus came. Finally a tiny black man in his seventies who had been watching me came up and asked me if I wanted a ride into the city. 'You bet!' I said. I was anxious to be permanently settled on solid ground. So we went off on the expressways in his '57 Ford with no fenders. He pointed out landmarks all the way, then dropped me off right in front of my hotel. All this for five dollars!"

Nancy's trips often turn into escapades. Recently, after a speech in Newton, Iowa, she tried to get to Des Moines. The only transportation available was a Greyhound freight bus crammed with packages from floor to ceiling except for two seats behind the driver. A personable nineteen-year-old youth occupied the seat beside Nancy. They immediately struck up a conversation. "I asked him if he'd like to get up and stretch and swap seats since there wasn't much room for comfort. He told me he would if he could. He was a prisoner handcuffed to the bus seat! When I told him it was my fortieth birthday, he kissed me. The bus driver caught a glimpse of us in the rearview mirror and swerved, almost hitting a tree. 'Everything is just fine back here,' I assured him. 'Just fine.' It was simply a friendly kiss from a worried teenager.

"Fortunately my husband and kids have gone along with all this travel. Not every family would. Working together and sharing mutual interests has made a big difference in the quality of our eighteen-year marriage. I can't think of anything worse than having a husband who walks into the house from his office and tells his wife that he doesn't want to talk about his business at all. It may be fine for him, but it leaves the woman out in left field. She doesn't have the slightest idea what he's doing. It amazes me that some women don't even know how much their husbands earn. If anything happens to the male end of the partnership, she'd be in tough shape. We've always worked as a team around here. When I'm gone, the girls take over the cooking in addition to working in the barn. They'll gripe like hell, but if you ask any one of the four if they'll give up farming or agriculture, they'll give you a resounding 'No!' without qualms. They take a fantastic pride in what they are doing, the way we live and what I'm trying to do, even if it means I'm not home all the time."

If Dave is upset about Nancy's travels, he doesn't admit it. "I think these women are doing a hell of a job," he says proudly. "Most men will not admit they have problems, and

Nancy rides eight-year-old son Dusty on her back.

they sure won't talk about them to a group. Women are more honest and they'll let their emotions show. They admit farming has its problems and we're losing money, then they'll go right out and attack the problem head-on. Nancy is great help to agriculture, but she's become a great liability to me. Her gas bills are staggering, and our long-distance phone bill looks like the national debt. It costs money to keep her out on the road, but I'm sure it's worth it. It's like everything else. Everybody wants to reap the harvest, but nobody wants to plant the seeds.

Nancy loves people. I think she's found her thing and she's doing her thing. It makes her happy."

Though Smidle Farms is a big, complex operation, it is also a family farm in the old-fashioned sense. "We have two hired hands to help with the milking and fieldwork, but if all our kids didn't pitch in to help us, I don't think we could make it," Nancy says. "Labor is too expensive for us and not worth it because the kids are so capable and take a lot of pride in what they do. There is no doubt in my mind that our daughters Bobbie, seventeen, and Tracy, sixteen, could run the whole farm. They are just excellent, much better at most things than I ever was. They can run all the machinery, milk cows, do tractor work, run the silo unloader, feed cows and calves, and give them pills and shots. They've assisted in the birth of calves. Even Becky, twelve, and Dusty, eight, are good workers and absolutely vital. Farm kids learn responsibility at an early age. We have a standing rule on this farm for the kids, Dave, and me. No matter what time you get home, check the cows. When a cow is about to freshen [give birth] we check her every hour, twenty-four hours a day. In this country, people don't realize the expertise of rural kids. They have such great potential. We need these kids sitting on boards of trade."

"I prefer girls working on the farm," Dave says. "They have much more concentration and do less clowning around than

Nancy and Dave walk around the farm discussing things that would make them more competitive and productive, though theirs is already one of the largest farms in the county. Nancy is involved in every decision and keeps all the records.

Tracy and Bobbie lift bales of hay to the mow.

boys. Today the girl is no longer weak. She can do anything that boys do. Girls will check and double check what they do while boys will make the damnedest mistakes you've ever seen."

At haying time Bobbie and Tracy recruit their high-school friends to help. In his usual spirit of competition, Dave got the kids fired up to see how much they could bale in one day recently. "We attacked 150 acres in one day," he says. "We had two balers, mine and the neighbor's. On the average a baler can put out about eight bales a minute. We were pushing it as high as twelve. This would turn out a load of hay—120 to 150 bales—hauled to the barn, unloaded, and mowed in seven to eight minutes. We started at 10 A.M. and quit about 8 P.M.,

Nancy gives daughter Becky, twelve, a final inspection before she mounts her horse and rides in the Kewaunee Trout Festival Parade.

but there was downtime for eating and heat exhaustion. Overall for the day we put in 4,761 bales! If they hadn't run out of dry, cut hay, they would have easily put in 5,000 bales."

"Our kids get $10 a week spending money apiece plus a salary of $2.50 an hour when they work making hay and things beyond their normal chores," Nancy says. "They could make more money working elsewhere, but we buy everything for their horses and all their clothes, the ones I don't make. Sewing is

my tranquilizer. When I'm really uptight I can go make something for myself and the kids and completely relax. The kids have always wanted horses. We started out with one Welsh mare, but when my dad died four years ago, we inherited all of his horses. The kids have thirteen horses now—Arabians, Appaloosas, and quarter horses and wall-to-wall ribbons and trophies in their rooms. Horses are their passion. We buy their $800 saddles and $1,000 riding outfits and decoration, but they feed, groom, and take care of their own horses. Dave and I don't touch them. Farm kids work full-time for the business, but there's no way we could pay them a salary commensurate with their worth. We'd go broke. So we compensate with something valuable to them. Beyond the horses, they all know their college is paid for. If they decide to stay home, they get a car. If they room here, they don't. During the last week of haying the kids each made $125. That's their money. If they want to blow all $125 on malted milks, that's their privilege.

"People tell me I'm much too permissive with the kids, but it doesn't bother me. I've never hit one of my children. They have a free hand. I think that kids are individuals who have to live their own lives. I don't want them to be just like me. They have to develop themselves. If they ask my opinion, I give it. If they don't, I don't. About the only thing I ever come down on them for is being late for chores.

"My children are on what I call 'independent study.' They've been on their own from the beginning. I never put them on a schedule. They ate when they were hungry. They potty-trained themselves. If they want to run around at sixteen and not be potty-trained, that's their problem. I stopped changing them when they were old enough to know what they were doing. They changed their own pants when they were wet or dirty. That fixed that in a hurry. We don't live on any routine. I fix a noon meal but if they aren't here to eat, they can fix their own. They have no hours. They can come and go as they want as long as they are home for chores and get their homework done on school nights. I think they react well to this. It has taught them responsibility. They've never failed me. Bobbie and Tracy are normal teenagers, though, who gripe like hell when they have to work in the barn until 10 P.M. on a Saturday night instead of going out on a date. You can't anticipate the problems you'll have on any given night on a dairy farm. They know that, and they bend. They love farming, and I think they'll always stay close to it. Because of their sex, the chances of Bobbie and Tracy going into farming is not great. Bobbie plans to study forestry and Tracy is determined to become a vet." Their youngest daughter, Becky, twelve, is interested in nursing. Dusty is just the fun-loving little boy everyone in the family adores. Tracy totes him under her arm and Dave spends hours wrestling with him on the couch. He's the child who makes everyone laugh, even in the tense times.

Although Nancy says she prefers to view animals from afar, she ends up right in the thick of things with the kids, feeding the calves, herding cows into the barn (prodding them at a distance with a cane), and cheering on her daughters at horse shows and parades. When one of the old mares she had as a child gave birth and died the next day, Nancy was determined to pull the colt through the critical period. "A colt is very touchy to raise because mare's milk is much different than

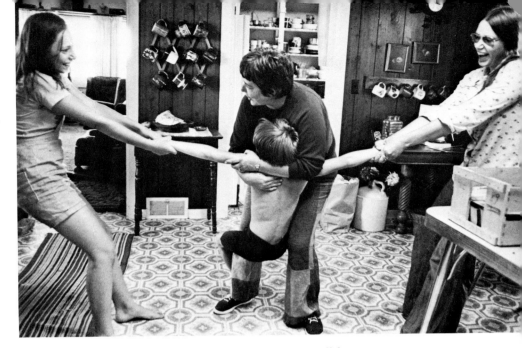

Nancy holds Dusty while Becky (left) *and Tracy* (right) *pull his arms. This kind of horseplay is typical with Dusty, who keeps the tension down in the family.*

cow's milk. The closest thing to it is goat's milk, so I went out and found a bunch of kids from the University of Green Bay who were trying to farm. I swapped them our cow's milk for their goat's milk. I fed that colt every hour on the hour, twenty-four hours a day for four weeks. I didn't get much sleep that month. My goal was to save the little guy. He was a beautiful colt, half Arabian and half Appaloosa. My dad had an old veterinarian book with a recipe for a formula to raise a colt.

Nancy
Smidle
211

Dave wrestles with son Dusty in the living room.

It called for lime water. I finally found some in a drugstore in Manitowoc. When the druggist brought out a small bottle, I asked him if that's all he had. I needed a gallon a week for four weeks. He turned white when he heard that.

"'Lady, do you know what this is used for?' he questioned nervously. 'It's a powerful old remedy for constipation!'

"I answered back, 'Well, it's a very large colt.'"

Nancy bottle-fed the colt from August until January, tapering off the feedings gradually until he was on his own. Dumas

thrived. In the 1976 Kewaunee Trout Festival Parade he won Best of Parade over all the other horses. Tracy has a whole wall of ribbons and trophies they've won together at horse shows.

A family working together on a large farm, as the Smidles do, has a lot of cohesion, but the headaches of modern farming create tension. Nancy is the easygoing one in the family who often serves as a moderating force for some of the others. "When I'm out on the road fighting for a cause, I'm aggressive and have ice water in my veins," she says. "But I have an even temperament. Things bother me, but I never argue with people in face-to-face combat. I think the number of fights Dave and I have had could be counted on one hand. Those have been battle royals, I admit, but they were over and done with fast." Stress shows more on Dave. He is both a simple man and an aggressive competitor, and sometimes those two sides of his personality are in conflict.

"I love nature," Dave says. "Many times I'd like to take a week off and go out in the woods alone and not be on call or responsible for anything." In the next breath he says, "I'm competitive, competitive all the way. From the time I was old enough to throw up a stone and hit it with a stick I've loved sports, competition, and winning. Vince Lombardi said winning isn't everything, it's the only thing. I believe that when it comes to football or farming. Everybody likes a winner, even if he's a son of a bitch. If you're not a winner, you don't stand a chance.

The Smidle girls ride in the Kewaunee Trout Festival Parade. Tracy, in the middle, rides Dumas. Becky rides on the left, and Bobbie is behind her on the right.

This newborn little calf is still wet, and her mama gets help licking her off.

"Our primary concern here is dairying because everything comes out of it—Nancy traveling around the country, the kids going to a horse show, my mother, Grandma, the hired men. There's a lot of people living off this farm, and it all has to come from the cow. All my interest is devoted to cattle—input, output—everything has to be go. We watch them twenty-four hours a day. We feed them twenty-four hours a day. This is where I concentrate my efforts. We do a good job of cropping in the fields, but it's a sideline, almost something you have to do in your spare time. Any time you start neglecting the cattle, you cut off your paycheck and that's tough."

The Smidles spend about $1,000 a year for a complicated-looking document called the Dairy Herd Improvement Association Report in which each of their cows is graded once a month on butterfat and milk production. That way Dave can tell which cows to keep to improve the herd and which ones to sell off for hamburger. Dave can no longer afford to get attached to a cow. They go by numbers, not names. A geneticist comes once a year, studies the report carefully, and decides which bull should be bred to each cow to produce the finest daughters. There's no romance involved, not even a nuzzle. Smidle Farms has no bulls. All breeding is done by cold, scientific artificial insemination. The inseminator comes every day with his shot of frozen bull semen from prize bulls throughout the country. The Smidles pay $6.50 to $50 for each insemination. If the semen doesn't take and the cow fails to become pregnant, the Smidles lose. They buy another shot of semen and hope for the best.

"Sometimes we get a real special calf," Nancy says. "One of our best cows was bred to a terrific bull. The bull wasn't producing a lot of daughters, so each one was very valuable. We had the most beautiful heifer you ever saw. The day the calf was born we had a man here offering us three hundred dollars for her before she was even dry. We refused. The calf grew up and we had her bred. She was due to freshen in less than a month when she hung herself in the middle of the night. She's the only cow we've ever had get her head stuck in one of the feed bunks. How she did it, we'll never know. We could have sold her for three thousand dollars like a shot or milked her for years and got a lot more daughters out of her, deriving a whole line of cattle from her. Then suddenly, she was dead. That's the way farming goes. . . ."

"I seriously thought about quitting farming when I was lying on my back in a hospital bed," Dave admitted. "I contemplated going to vet school again, but I decided I was too hooked on the challenges of farming. Many times I'm a vet to my own animals. You have to develop a certain amount of veterinary knowledge or you'll lose a lot of cattle. The vet can't come out in time for every crisis on every area dairy farm. I know a lot of farmers who can't stand to give one of their cows a shot. I can inject 15 cows with this three-dollar bottle of medicine. No vet will come out to give a shot for less than fifteen dollars. I save a lot of money in vet bills. The greatest cure is prevention. You've got to have a seventh sense to be able to tell what a cow is coming down with before she gets it. It's like a mother being able to hear a baby crying at night while her husband sleeps. You have to have that sense, especially with the calves. They are the most important part of the dairy operation and the hardest animals to work with. The old cow can take a lot of abuse and get pretty sick and you can still bring her out of the woods, but the little calf is about the touchiest thing there is. Feeding calves may look easy, but Nancy and the girls must carefully consider bottle height, complete cleanliness in bottles and nipples, the amount of liquid, and

Raising calves is one of the hardest jobs on a dairy farm because calves are prone to disease and everything must be kept sterile. Here Nancy watches the amount of milk the calves consume and bumps them on the head when they've had enough.

the amount of feed given to each calf. They watch each one carefully for any trace of disease. Last year out of 176 calves, I only lost three. That figures to a 1.2 percent loss. The average loss is 30 to 35 percent. Some farmers lose 50 percent of their calves."

Again the simple man is in conflict with the competitor in Dave as he says sadly, "We've put these cows under a hell

Nancy Smidle

215

of a lot of stress. Old mother nature designed a cow to have her calf and feed that calf, producing 10 to 12 pounds of milk a day. They've taken that same cow and refined her and bred her for everything we want that nature never intended her for. We've got her giving birth to a 110-pound calf when it used to be 40 pounds. She's producing 100 pounds of milk a day instead of 10. The poor animal is under stress from the time she's born until the time she dies and we ship her out. Maybe when you put an animal under stress just like a person, all kinds of illnesses set in. . . ."

As an active partner in the farm, Nancy feels Dave's pressures and celebrates his fragile successes. Her self-appointed mission is to stay on the road as long as she can to educate urban legislators and consumers to the realities of farming. "I know a lot of urban consumers don't care much about farmers," she says. "Some think we are far below them in any kind of class system. We know they can't do without us. They just don't realize it yet. Things have got to change so the American family farmer can survive."

NOVEMBER, 1986

Nancy traveled the country for eight more years, speaking out about the problems family farmers face until the situation on her own farm grew critical. "When the farm economy completely went to heck, I had to get off the road and come home to help Dave try to hang on to our farm. I was often on the road two or three days a week and paying my own travel expenses. We couldn't afford it anymore. It was really hard for me to leave the front lines after all those years of fighting, but I had to make that decision. The greatest challenge now is to stay home and try to help save our farm. It is the most important thing I've ever done.

"We're in an almost impossible situation here. Dave and I used to worry about making it on the farm from year to year. Now we worry about surviving from day to day. We may not be farming tomorrow. I can honestly say that I don't know what's going to happen to American agriculture and I don't know what's going to become of Dave and me.

"Our biggest problem has been that the people we put our faith in let us down. When I was crusading around the country, the Farm Credit System people were our financial advisers. We listened to them and took their advice. They told us our cash flow was fine and that we should expand. There would be no problem. Bobbie and Tracy both married in the 1970s and wanted to come in to work for us with their husbands, so we doubled everything. We're running a thousand acres now and six hundred head of cattle. I remember having meetings with 'experts' in the late 1970s. They told us how important it was for us to feed the Third World countries because they have so many people and so little know-how. 'It's up to you to help them,' they told us. Now those same guys come back to us and tell us that the Third World doesn't need us anymore. They add, 'You're in tough shape. I don't know what you are going to do.' They never offered us suggestions on getting out of 'tough shape.' Now it's too late."

If Smidle Farms looked prosperous in 1976, it now gleams with the patina of a huge, successful agribusiness operation. Five more blue Harvestore silos loom above the barn to store feed for twice the number of cows. The barn has been expanded to make room for milking 250 cows twice a day, at 4 A.M. and 4 P.M. The outside appearance of Smidle Farms offers no clues to what's happening inside.

"We are over $1 million in debt now at 13½ percent interest," Nancy says hopelessly. "All of us had forgotten the formula the agricultural economists gave us over ten years ago about our debt increasing fivefold in ten years. It seemed ridiculous then. Now it has come true for us and most farmers we know. That's why there are so many farmers filing for bankruptcy. They have no alternative. We can't sell off acreage because there are no buyers. We bought the new land at $1,000 an acre. They reassessed the land in the county and state down to $750 an acre, but we still pay interest on $1,000 an acre. On January 1, 1984, they estimated our net worth at $3½ million. By January, 1985, we were under $2½ million. In January, 1986, we dropped another $900,000. Bear in mind we didn't buy or sell a thing during those years. Our net worth may have gone way down, but our payments are the same. You don't get out of a million-dollar debt. No one wants to buy a farm these days. The only thing that's helping us is that we have all registered cattle and a lot of them can go for export sales to Taiwan and Brazil. We sell all the cows we can. Five years ago we could sell a heifer for $3,600. Now we feel lucky to get $900. Still, dairy farmers are better off than wheat farmers. The bottom has completely dropped out of that market. We're getting about the same price for our milk as we did in the early 1970s, but at least we have some income every month."

Bobbie, Tracy, and their husbands farmed with Dave and Nancy for eight years. Becky married and farmed with them for a short time, too. Dusty lived at home and helped. There came a time when the ailing farm couldn't support all these families. "The kids finally took a good hard look at our debt, and knew they couldn't take it over," Nancy says. "Sometimes the parents get out for the sake of the kids or the kids sacrifice for their parents. We all talked it over. We thought that if they were smart, they should leave. It wasn't a blowup. It was a mutual family decision. We all thought that Dave and I might have a better chance of saving the farm. The girls miss the farm terribly. Bobbie's husband now works for a sheeting and roofing company in Green Bay. They have three children. Tracy has three boys. Her husband is a truck driver. Tracy would come back in a minute if she could, but I don't see any way they can at all. Becky and her husband have bought a small farm near here which they can afford because he's a full-time mechanic. Dusty graduated from high school in June and wants to farm, but we told him positively no. He has to go to school. He's in technical school studying mechanics. When he finishes we'll take another look at our situation and see if he can come in. Some people think that if we can hang on for another three or four years, things will change so we can stay in business. I wouldn't bank on it. We are running the farm with hired help now, all local labor. Dave and I have never worked harder on this farm in our lives."

Nancy tells their story without tears or even the slightest break in her voice. One wonders how long her strength will last under such relentless pressure. "There are days when I really feel drained," she admits. "I have to stay upbeat to keep Dave going. He's so intense, I worry about him sometimes. He can get very depressed. Last fall it was so rainy that we couldn't get the crops in and had to buy feed on top of everything else. We thought 1985 was bad. The winter of 1986 was the worst thing we've ever been through. Dave lost all hope. He doesn't care about the farm anymore. If someone walked in here tomorrow and offered us any fair price, he'd be out in a minute. We've both lost hope, but I still fight. Dave has lost all of his fight. He's still farming intensely and doing his job beautifully. He will still work twenty-four hours a day to get a crop in, but he doesn't have the spirit or love for it anymore. This isn't just happening to us. It's happening to most of the farmers we know.

"I don't think many people realize the emotional impact of this on farm families, especially the men. It has gotten to the point where some farmers are beating their wives. This is not typical of the American farmer, believe me. The suicide rate is terrible. My girlfriend and her husband who live on a farm in North Dakota haven't talked to one another in a year. They live in the same house and never say a thing. Just going into a bank is a humiliating experience. When we were all borrowing money to expand, bankers called us terrific farmers, the best, and welcomed us in. Now if any of us go for a small loan, they make us feel like we are the bottom of the barrel, just dumb

farmers. Men can't cope with that. It kills their pride. They are still the same dedicated farmers they once were, but the situation has changed. They are more than depressed. They are devastated.

"We have been checking into filing Chapter 11 bankruptcy. You just close the door on the farm and walk away from it with nothing. Your creditors figure out what to do with it. We've thought about it more than once because we are at the point where we really can't see how it is going to get better.

"Our one salvation which has gotten us through all this emotionally was having the foresight to buy a cottage up in the north woods three years ago. We can drive up there, stay for a couple of days, and really unwind while the hired men run the farm. It is the only way we get away from the farm and its problems. The cabin brings us back to earth. I sit and read and Dave fishes in the river, plants trees, and hikes in the woods. No one can take that away from us because it is not part of the farm corporation. If we file for bankruptcy, we'll still have the cottage, but that's all we'll have. It keeps us going.

"It would be a miracle if we could sell the farm, but if we could, I think Dave would like to open a greenhouse up near our cottage. He loves landscaping and watching things grow. I can't even keep a houseplant alive. Starting over would be hard for us in our fifties. I don't know if we could do it. Dave has been doing nothing but farming since he was a boy, and I haven't taught in decades. It is possible I could substitute teach up there.

"I don't know what's going to happen to our family farm. We live from day to day. In June I would have said we were going to lose it, but now the crops are all in and the barns and silos are full and we're selling some cows. Things look better. If we made it this far, we'll probably last until spring. Full barns are a good omen. We're hoping. Farmers try to keep hoping. And looking forward to spring."

Nancy Smidle

Margie Cunha Irvin

JUNE, 1976

The scene looked as slapstick as a Charlie Chaplin movie with its main character moving in double time. There was pretty twenty-eight-year-old Margie Cunha running back and forth on a thirty-foot-long course carrying forty-five-pound concrete blocks in her arms while two muscular six-footers timed her with a stopwatch. "I'm not crying, it's the wind!" she hollered to the men as tears streamed down her cheeks on that biting cold, early March day in 1976 in the southern Illinois coal belt. Lifting the heavy blocks off a shoulder-high platform behind Freeman-United Coal Mining Company in West Frankfort, Illinois, she hugged each block as she ran, stacked it at the finish line, then dove for another one, eight in all. She set her jaw with gritty determination as she charged. For Margie, this was serious business.

Margie was the first "victim" of the coal company's new strength test for women based on the kind of work they'd have to do 810 feet below the ground in a coal mine. Freeman was under pressure to hire women miners, but they were choosy. They wanted only a few strong, serious-minded women who had a background of physical labor. No wimps need apply. Coal mining is no glamour job, just hard, dirty, sweaty work. If Margie passed the test and a physical, she'd be one of a handful of Freeman's well-paid women coal miners. "I didn't hesitate," Margie remembers. "I had been waiting for five years for someone to call and give me an opportunity like this. I was excited. I had no idea there was going to be a strength test after the interview. I just put on the man's gloves they handed me and did what they told me to do."

The concrete blocks seemed like child's toys compared with the eight sixty-pound timbers leaning against the wall that she had to lug while running along the same course. They were an ungainly eight feet long. "Go as fast as you can, but don't strain youself," Chuck Holmes and Russ Hays of Freeman's personnel department shouted as they set the stopwatch. They were both amused and concerned at the sight of this eager, panting woman plunging off with a timber like a soldier wielding a battering ram. "Boy, were they heavy," Margie remembers. "I'd pull the timbers away from the wall and let them fall into my arms, then sling them across my hip where I could bear the weight. My gloves were so big, they kept slipping off. I must have looked silly out there, huffing and puffing with tears in my eyes as those two big men watched. When I got back to the office I was tore up and out of breath, but I knew I had done well. They asked me if I could do that kind of work every day. I said, 'Yes, if I don't have to run that fast all eight hours!'"

Though Margie couldn't picture herself as a coal miner, getting the job was important to her. Divorced, with no family or friends to lean on, she was barely surviving, supporting herself and two children on the meager income she earned doing seasonal work for a carnival. She received no alimony payments from her ex-husband, so she would have been entitled to federal aid to dependent children and food stamps, but she refused to apply. "Accepting welfare is admitting failure," she says. "I'm almost thirty years old and have nothing to show for my life. I am determined to do something with myself."

For the strength test it was a real plus that Margie had hammered tent stakes for the Greater American Circus for five

Margie Cunha, twenty-eight, emerges from the Orient 3 coal mine at midnight after her eight-hour shift.

years during its April-to-September season. She's 5'4" and 140 pounds, all muscle. "I hated carnival work from the first day, but it was the only job I could get with my education. It was hard work, noon to midnight, six days a week. We'd take everything down and move once a week to another shopping center in Chicago or one of its suburbs. It was both a small circus with animals and acts and a carnival with a midway full of games and rides. I worked at a game where people had to knock down Coke bottles with a ball. My earnings were 25 percent of what I took in every day. Some days were good, some awful. When it rained, we'd sit there all day and never get a paycheck. I'm shy. I was afraid to talk to strangers before the carnival forced me to meet people. It was good for me to lose my shyness, but working the games embarrassed me and made me feel ashamed. I had to act like a hustler, convincing people they could win. That meant flirting a little with guys, which I didn't like. Some guys practically knock your head off if they spend money and don't win. I've had a few try to whip me. Then there were always characters trying to pick me up.

"Carnival life is fine for some people, especially those who live for the moment, blowing the money they make every day on gambling, drink, and women. It is awfully hard on a working mother. During the carnival season, I was lucky to be able to stay with relatives in Chicago who kept the kids. It was a lot cheaper to pay them rent than to stay in motels, but I often had to drive fifty miles to work, and the long hours didn't give

After a grueling shift in the mine, Margie sits on the floor trying to muster the energy to get up and shower.

me much time with the kids. There were people who were really good to me at the carnival, but I never got used to the hustling or the traveling. Never settling down. That's not what I want out of life.

"The high point in my day was feeding the baby elephants, Paul and Paulina. They could be at the end of the midway, but when they saw me they'd come a-runnin'. I'd bring them special treats like sliced carrots, ice cream, and cotton candy. They'd run their trunks all over me feeling for food. Once Paulina wedged her trunk into the cotton candy machine and got it full of pink sticky stuff. Those crazy little elephants would play in puddles on the lot every time it rained and spray water all over each other. Those were the good times. We were all sick when they died.

"By the end of each season, I only had two thousand dollars or at most three thousand dollars left to take home to Benton [Illinois]. It had to last until the next carnival season because I could never find a job. I had to be tight with the money because my daughter Geni needed things for school. We could never go out to dinner or see a movie. I would have loved an occasional night out, but we couldn't afford anything extra. It was almost impossible to make the money last. Lots of times I had to call my boss at the carnival to borrow a few hundred to get me through until the next season started. He was a good man who never turned me down."

Jobs in Benton for a woman with a ninth-grade education simply didn't exist. "I filed applications in every factory in a fifty-mile radius of here—all the coal mines, Norge, General Tire, a boat factory, a meatpacking plant, and updated the applications every six months. In five long years I never got a nibble. Not one phone call. No one wanted to hire a woman with a grade-school education when men with college degrees were standing in line for jobs."

Margie moved to Benton five years ago. It was the childhood home of a friend at the carnival who thought it would be just the place for Margie. The first time she saw the quaint southern Illinois town of sixty-eight hundred, she felt at home. Benton is pure Americana, a classic midwestern small town with old red brick stores built around a courthouse square and family homes on tree-lined streets with children playing in the yards. "Benton reminded me of the home life I always wanted to have," Margie says. "It's small and country, but it has most of the things I need—good stores, a nice lake, parks. People are friendly here. They welcome you and give you a nice, warm feeling. They make you feel like you belong, that you are part of the town. Clerks in the stores get to know you and talk. They're just acquaintances, but I appreciate them. I miss having an adult person to talk to sometimes, someone I've known for a long time, someone I could just sit down and talk to about things that have happened to me."

Each year when Margie returned from the carnival, she circled the Franklin County courthouse looking for a particular old man who always sat on one of the iron park benches. She hoped he was still alive. "That man symbolizes life as it should be. You should be able to sit out all day on the square with nobody bothering you, if that's what you'd like to do. Seeing him always gives me a big sigh of relief. I know I'm home.

"Chicago is the only big city I've ever lived in. I wanted

desperately to get out to country life. People are constantly on the move in Chicago. Nobody stops long enough to take notice of what's going on around them. I hated getting around in that traffic, hustling through life. You live so close to your neighbors in the city that you can almost reach out and touch their windows. Chicago is just too big, too jammed and crammed for me. Sometimes I thought the city might swallow me up like it did my grandfather. They found him dead on the streets of Skid Row. They tagged him and buried him in a potter's field. None of his children even bothered to claim the body."

Though Benton was a safer haven for Margie, she grew increasingly depressed as the lean winters rolled by. She withdrew, ashamed to let people know the gravity of her situation. In five winters she had not made one good friend. Her entire life centered around her children, Genine, nine, and Kirby, five, and the squirrels, turtles, ducks, and dog who shared their modest home. "I worried myself sick just sitting at home waiting for the phone to ring," Margie remembers. "I thought I could end up having a nervous breakdown and the state would take my kids away from me to be raised in a home like I was. I got to the point of hating to get up in the morning, knowing I'd face another day of worry and uncertainty wondering what would happen to me and the kids. You feel defeated when you never get ahead. I lost all my pride in myself. Everything I touched seemed to go wrong. I was stuck up against the wall and I couldn't make a move. Let's face it, you can't do anything without a little bit of money. I felt like someone had it in for me, like I was being punished for something. I wondered why life always had to be so damn hard. I never wanted to be any-

thing outstanding, just one of the people in town reasonably contented with life. Why couldn't I be lucky enough to get one little break?"

Then the phone rang. It was Freeman. If she passed the routine physical, she'd be a "red-hat" trainee coal miner at the starting salary of $46.66 *per day*. "I couldn't believe it. I was so excited when I climbed up on the doctor's examining table, I realized I had two different color knee socks on. I assured him I wasn't some kind of nut. Last year if someone told me I was going to be a coal miner, I'd have laughed. I thought it was impossible. Nothing is impossible. Absolutely nothing. Determination gets you there. If you work hard enough at something, it will eventually come to you. Sometimes I went to Freeman twice a week to remind them of my application and tell them how much I needed the job. Everyone in the office got to know me. I guess I bothered them to death, but I finally got the job." She was hired that week.

"The job was like a prayer answered. It totally changed my outlook on life. I don't worry anymore. I'm learning how to laugh again. I couldn't laugh before. For the first time I can control my own life rather than sitting around waiting for things to change. Nobody can really understand how I feel. This job is as much of a miracle to me as natural things like trees growing and babies being born. All I ever wanted out of life was a good job so I could settle down in a town like this and call it home. Over the years, I hope I'll make some friends and have them over to my home and go to their homes. I want to share things with them and make plans together. I feel like I'm finally coming home. For me, this is the beginning of a new life.

"Sure, it's only coal mining, but it is the answer to almost every problem I've had. Shoveling coal may be a dirty job most women wouldn't touch, but I think it's terrific. If a woman has to work to support her family, she should take any job that pays well enough. I never dreamed of being a coal miner, but I always thought it would be great to get a man's job like construction or bricklaying because salaries are high. I didn't care if I dug ditches or climbed trees as long as it was a decent, honest living. So coal mining is a man's job. Who cares, if it is an opportunity to finally get on my feet? I'm like a little girl who wondered what she'd grow up to be. I thought I'd be a waitress or a clerk in a store. Suddenly I'm all growed up and find myself a coal miner. It's the craziest thing that ever happened to me, but it's exciting and rewarding. Five years ago I didn't even know what a coal mine looked like. Now it's as natural to me as walking through a cornfield. Although I've been on the job about three months now, I still wake up and feel strange, like this is all a dream. It's almost too wonderful to be true. Now I have a chance to forget all the bad times and look forward to better things."

Margie's coal mine, Orient 3, near Waltonville, is Freeman-United's largest mine and the second largest mine in Illinois. It is an endless maze of rooms with eight-foot-high ceilings eight hundred feet below farmland. Running five miles from east to west and four miles north to south, it's like a city underground, complete with its own "subway" to get miners from place to place. Benton, which is only one and a half by two miles, seems tiny in comparison. Orient 3 opened in 1948, but it still has an estimated fifteen years before it will be worked out. The soft,

Margie and the two other women coal miners on her shift talk and clean up in the trailer locker room that Freeman-United set up for its handful of women miners.

bituminous coal seam runs floor to roof, with its walls or "ribs" eerily powdered with white rock dust to prevent explosions. In this vast track mine, 680 employees on three shifts extract eight thousand tons of coal a day to feed voracious power plants in Illinois and neighboring states.

Margie works the 4 P.M. until midnight shift with two other women and some one hundred men. During her three-month training period she does manual labor, usually the tough and

Margie
Cunha
Irvin
225

dirty jobs that experienced miners reject. Trainees aren't permitted to use electrical equipment or run a machine.

"I was so excited when the cage first carried me down to the floor of the mine," Margie remembers. "It's like an open elevator but it goes down 810 feet. What a thrill! The darkness is really strange. The quiet makes my ears ring. The first time I looked around the mine, I wasn't the least bit scared, just curious. Except for the bare bulbs in the main entries, it's pitch dark down there. It takes a while to get used to the light on your head. I was bobbing, trying to take everything in, wondering if I'd be able to find my way out.

"Once you hit bottom, a battery-powered man-trip, a car that holds as many as sixteen miners, carries you on the tracks to the section you're assigned to work. Sometimes it takes a half hour to get there, the mine is so big. The guys plaster dirty pictures all over the inside walls of our man-trip. Even though I'm the only woman in our section, I don't mind the *Playboy* centerfolds. Yesterday was just too much, though. They glued a vulgar picture of a girl with her legs spread and a cigarette dangling out of her mouth right in front of my face where I sit down. They put so much glue on it that I couldn't get the damn thing off. Finally, I peeled it off with my nails. I had to get rid of that thing. It was horrible."

The pick-and-shovel days of coal mining disappeared decades ago. Now, noisy thirty-three-foot-long coal-gobbling machines called continuous miners rip coal out of the seam with

Margie and a group of male coal miners pack into the "cage," an open elevator, to descend 810 feet to the floor of the coal mine.

a giant rotating cutting head with daggerlike bits. The "miners," operated by two men, cost $250,000 each. Orient 3 has seventeen of them. They use the room-and-pillar method of coal mining. The continuous miner grinds fourteen-foot-wide paths through the coal then cross-cuts through these entries. These cross-cuts intersect with another entry, leaving sixty-foot-square pillars of solid coal which, in addition to five- to ten-foot-long steel roof bolts, keep the roof from caving in. These entries and cross-cuts will often extend for miles until the coal seam runs out. When it ends, the continuous miner backs out, pulling 80 percent of each pillar of coal out until the roof falls in, as intended. That area is then sealed off forever as the miner gobbles away at a new section.

At an amazing rate of speed coal travels by conveyor belt from the cutting head of the continuous miner through its long belly. Agile rubber-tired shuttle cars or "buggies" are poised behind the miner, filling up with as much as six tons of raw coal in thirty seconds to two minutes. When one buggy leaves, an empty one pulls up right behind it. Traffic is as hectic as on any Chicago expressway, complicated by the fact that the buggies run in the dark in swirling coal dust. The buggies dump their loads of coal on a three-foot-wide belt, which eventually carries it to a wider "mother" belt and out of the mine to the preparation plant, where it is cleaned, sorted, and then loaded into railroad cars.

Margie is the belt shoveler at the tail of the belt where the buggies dump. It's a backbreaking, dirty job that is light years away from the pink teddy bears at her old carnival concession stand. "My job may not sound very important, but it

An older miner, Vernon, teases Margie as they wait for their shift to begin at the Orient 3 coal mine. He saved her life when a buggy nearly hit her, almost burying her in coal.

is," she says. "You have to keep the area around the tail of the belt clean because coal dust is highly explosive. Friction in the belt area can cause a fire. Nobody wants my job because it is just plain hard work and very dusty. I could get black lung easily breathing in all that dust, but I've learned to keep water running and hose off the area once in a while so the dust settles. You learn those little tricks.

"One night there were three buggies running continuously in our section. They were dumping on the belt so fast that I barely had time to shovel up one mess before another one would be there dirtying up what I had cleaned. I couldn't seem to get ahead. I jumped out and tried to get a couple of extra shovels. Suddenly my friend Vernon hollered, 'Watch out, Margie!' When I turned around, a buggy was coming right at me. I only had a matter of seconds to dive out of the way. From where he sits the buggy driver couldn't see me. I had my back to him, my light turned away. If Vernon hadn't seen him coming and been watching out for me, I would have been crushed under the buggy and buried in coal. They were working so fast that night that they wouldn't have noticed that I wasn't around until the end of the shift. By that time I would have been dead. All the coal miners call each other "buddy" and they mean it, even though some resent having women in the mines. Everyone looks out for the others. They are concerned. Someone is always there to help you.

"Whenever the coal dumps off the buggies it reminds me of a black waterfall and the Calumet River I used to live by in Cudahy, Indiana. When I was a kid, the river was just a trickle I could jump over. Now it's one of the biggest rivers in the state, so black and nasty you can't get near it because all the steel mills use it for drainage. I don't imagine there were more than a dozen homes in Cudahy and nothing else but a drugstore and a tavern. We had to walk over a mile to catch a city bus into Gary to go to school.

"My father was a welder at Inland Steel for twenty-eight years. My mother sometimes worked at restaurants. There were eight of us, five boys and three girls. I was next to the youngest. Ever since I can remember, Mom and Dad had problems—drinking, fighting, and arguing. They both drank heavily, but Dad was an alcoholic. After Dad got off work, he'd always stop at the tavern and find my mother there already. She might have been sitting there all day. She never spent much time at home with us kids. We didn't have much of a family life as far as sharing things and having a good time together. All we shared were hard times. We kids would sit on the windowsills and look down the alley toward the tavern waiting for Dad's car to zigzag home every night. 'Here comes Daddy,' we'd all say. Then Mom and Dad would scream at each other and fight. I saw a lot of bad things. Sometimes my mom would get beat up pretty bad. It was that kind of home life.

"I think back on the times when I was growing up and wish things could have been different for my family and that Mom and Dad could have got straightened out. That's the way it is for some people. It made a stronger person of me. Whatever happens to me I look at it and think it could have been much worse because I know how bad it can be. Nothing could possibly come up now that would really bother me beyond my ability to take it. Life isn't that easy sometimes, but I've always had the attitude that things would get better for me.

"There were some good times for us kids, too. We played football and baseball and went swimming together. We had big hills by our house, so we got inside old tires and rolled down them. In the winter we'd slide down them. Those are the times I like to remember most.

"Dad built our house. It was nothing, just an old five-room frame place. To most people it was probably just an old shack with two outhouses out back, but to us it was home. It had a great big living room with a coal-burning stove. We used to huddle up there together in the wintertime listening to radio programs like 'Yukon King' and 'The Shadow' because it was the only room that had heat. In the kitchen Dad had one of those old water pumps built right into the sink. I remember crawling up on a bucket and working that pump four or five times to get water. It was hard for us little kids to get it started and keep it going long enough to get our mouths down there for a drink. Finally we got smarter and put a bowl under the pump. It took us a while to figure that out! On bath night my mom would get a big old washtub and set it in the middle of the floor, then fill it with buckets of warm water heated on the stove. We'd all bathe in the same tub, just adding more water occasionally. The water looked pretty grimy by the time the last of the eight of us had finished. It was like taking a bath in mud."

The family left Cudahy when Margie was about seven to move to an old cabin near a small lake in Whiting, Indiana. "All there was were oil refineries and steel mills there. Sometimes the sky was a rusty red from Inland Steel where my dad worked. On damp, breezy days an awful smell from the refineries would knock you down. When I was twelve my dad left home for good. He took a room by the plant. Dad was always a good worker. In spite of everything, he worked. My dad is gone now, and I miss him as much as I did when he left us. I didn't even know he was sick. They told me one Christmas. The company made him retire early. He had cirrhosis of the liver because of the alcoholism, equilibrium problems, hardening of the arteries, permanent brain damage, and tuberculosis—all when he was only sixty-one. He died that year. I think of him often and wish I had spent more time with him. I believe Dad needed us badly. I think he was going through one hell of a time.

"Shortly after Dad left home, Mom got dressed up to go out for the evening as she did every night, promising me she'd be home early. She didn't come back. No word. No calls to let us know where she was. She was gone a month. I was twelve and my brothers at home were ten, thirteen, and sixteen. We just held on, hoping she'd eventually come back. We managed to keep her leaving a secret from the neighbors. We didn't even tell my older brothers and sisters because it would have been a bother for them to look after us. They did so much babysitting when they were at home that when they grew up, married, and moved out, I knew they never intended to take care of us again. I became the head of the house, cooking and caring for the others. We got by on the food we had because we had no money to buy more. My older brother had quit school and had a job, but he didn't contribute to our support. He spent all his money on girls and his own good time. I quit school and started rationing out the food. Some days we had nothing to eat, but I sent my two brothers off to school and took care of them the best I could. When my mom finally did come back a month later, she moved to an apartment over a tavern and took my three brothers with her. The court granted one of my married brothers custody of me. You hear of the hard times pulling members of a family together. In our case it was just

the opposite.

"I stayed with my brother and his family from the winter until the following fall, when it was time to go to school. My sister-in-law decided I was in her way, and there was not enough room for me in their house. She went to Catholic Family Services and told them she couldn't live with me anymore and that I'd have to be placed in a foster home or adopted out. They sent me to Kentucky to a home for girls from broken homes run by a cloistered order of nuns who devoted their lives to us. It wasn't an orphanage because we all had parents, parents who didn't want us. I guess when both of my parents left I realized they didn't really care about us. If I had to go somewhere, I'm glad it was the home because I was treated good. Under the circumstances, I made the best of what I had. I had missed a lot of school after my mother left because I was ashamed to let anybody know all our problems. I stayed at the home until I was seventeen and was able to graduate from ninth grade. I had a job, too. You know those pins and strings you use to keep the stuffing inside a turkey? I used to string those things for seventy-five cents a day. We didn't get to spend the money we made because there was no place to go. I just saved it until they took us on a shopping spree to Cincinnati. I must have spent four hundred dollars on clothes in one day. Was I happy! After I left the home I went to work for a department store."

Margie's voice cracks when she talks about the disintegration of her family. Her eyes have a sad, hollow stare. "I don't see my mother or married brothers and sisters much, maybe about three times in the last seven years. They aren't that far away, but when we all get together, we can't get along. We hardly know each other anymore. I have nieces and nephews I've never seen. I love my brothers and sisters, and I wish they'd come to see me sometime. I'd gladly open my door to them. I keep in touch with my mother and some of my brothers and sisters by letter, even if I don't see them. I want them to have my mailing address and know a little about what I'm doing, even if they don't care. I want them to tell me when one of them is sick so I can help them.

"The thing I think most about in raising my kids is that I want them to have a lot better life than I had. I'm not talking about giving them a lot of material things they don't need, I'm talking about giving them love. Kids got to know they're loved. I know what it's like not to be loved, and I never want any of that in my family. No hatefulness and hostility either. I want to get close to my kids and spend as much time as I can with them and do everything to keep them happy. I worry about raising them without a dad and hope nothing is missing from their lives. I enjoy their company. We always have a lot of fun together, maybe because I never really got much of a chance to be a kid before. That's the way families should be. I want them to come to me with their problems. I could never go to my mom without feeling I was bothering her. She told me I was more trouble than I was worth. Maybe I just had a quick question for her, but one that was important to me. She never answered. She never took the time. Neither my mother nor father ever spent time with any of us kids. We were in their way. They avoided us. It hurts to be left alone and ignored when you are a kid. When one of us got hurt and ran up to Mom or Dad there was never no sympathy, just, 'Get away from me

Margie's job as a coal miner who "digs her work," as her bumper sticker proclaims, allows her to take her kids on outings like this one to a lake near Benton.

and stop crying.'

"I take my kids everywhere I go. They're my babies, and they'll always be my babies no matter how old they are or how old I am. They're all I have."

An Emmett Kelly expression frequently appears on Margie's face. Perhaps it is the "miner's eyes," that band of coal dust under her eyes that looks like drowned and smeared mascara after a good cry. Even five-year-old Kirby notices it, and he's

*Margie
Cunha
Irvin*

231

a roughneck blond with fullback's shoulders, the kind of kid people refer to as "all boy." "Mom," he says sympathetically, "you look like you are going to cry. What's wrong?" It's a dreamy thoughtfulness mistaken for sadness, a life changing faster than the mind can cope with. Geni is even closer to her mother. She is a pretty, dark-haired nine-year-old with a wide range of expressions and seems older and wiser than her age. "I sit and talk to Geni about things as if she was another adult," Margie says. "She listens to her mother's problems. Of course she's just a kid and probably doesn't understand a lot of things I say, but I like to hear how she feels about things. I want to maintain our close relationship as she grows up so she'll never be afraid to come to me with problems or questions as she turns into a teenager and then a woman. I don't think anybody can give her a more honest opinion about life than her own mother."

The one thing Margie always wanted out of life was to be a wife and a mother. "When I was eighteen and just out on my own, I was much too anxious to get married. I dreamed of having kids and giving them the kind of life I never had. I'm a homebody. I never wanted to be anything special, just a mother, a wife, an old wash lady, and a slave to my family. I met Phil through my brother. I had only known him eight or nine months before we married and hadn't even dated him that much. He was a pesky fellow, always bothering me. Although he was ten years older than I was, he was a very immature person. He never really cared about anybody, never

Margie and nine-year-old daughter Geni have an especially close relationship.

took anything to heart. He always ran around with women, even after we married, but I didn't know it at the time. Then he'd come home and ask me point blank who I'd been sleeping with. I knew then it would never work, but I was tired of being shifted from one place to another. I figured being married was the way to stop it. It was a bad, bad mistake. I was dumb and inexperienced. To this day I don't know why I married him. It wasn't love. Hell, I hadn't known him long enough to love him. It makes me sick to think I was so blind and ignorant. Something should have told me he wasn't the right person.

"We were married in May. I got pregnant with Genine right away and in April of the next year Phil was sent to prison in Minnesota. He had stolen some traveler's checks before that, but I didn't think too much more about it. Then two well-dressed guys came to the door and flashed their badges. They were from the FBI. They walked over to Phillip and told him he was under arrest for robbing the Hoosier State Bank in Indiana. Seven other FBI agents came in and started reading him his rights. I was in a state of shock. Geni was in her bed, just a baby. The FBI couldn't believe I had no idea what had been going on. 'Your man robs a bank and you don't know it?' they said. It was true. I had heard about the robbery on the news. There were four fellows involved and they got something like eighty thousand dollars, but I never saw any of it. He bought a new car, but I thought that was from the money he made supposedly going to work every day. You make a man a lunch and send him off to the job . . . you don't expect him to rob a bank. He might have bought our house with some of that money. He was making good money as a truck driver. We re-

ally might have made it if he had stayed straight. All he did was drive the getaway car. He would never have done anything else. He was too much of a coward. He wasn't altogether a person. It didn't take me long to get over him. I felt relieved that he was gone. I had wanted to get out of it, but not in that way."

Out of duty, Margie visited Phil a few times when he was in prison, then disappeared into the inner city of Chicago where she hoped he would never find her. "I went to Chicago to find a job, but I was scared. I didn't know which way to go, who to turn to or where I was going to end up. It seemed like I was taking a big chance, but I did it. I was going nowhere. I had to venture out. I sliced meat in a delicatessen for a while, then worked on the assembly line of a tea company, stuffing tea bags in a box for ninety-eight dollars a week until I got laid off and joined the carnival. Phil got out of prison and caught up with me, but I stood up to him and told him it was over. We stayed married for a long time, but only because I didn't have money for a divorce. I never lived with him again. I have no idea where he is now.

"I don't want everybody to think I was some kind of angel. I was still married to Geni's dad when I got pregnant with Kirby. I met Troy at the carnival where he ran several concessions. Troy lives in Chicago, but his family is from Benton. Our only problem is that he has his hang-ups about marriage. He's thirty-eight and still a bachelor. Kirby's daddy is one of the best people I've ever met. He helped me through a lot of hard times and got me settled in Benton. He's a terrific father to Kirby and Geni, too. He's the only father she remembers. I'm still crazy about him. We see each other often and I think it will work out that we'll eventually be married someday. I should have been a little more careful, but I'm not sorry for Kirby in the least. I never gave abortion a thought. I would never do it. It's not the baby's fault. If I get caught in something, I'm big enough to face it. Troy gave Kirby his name. He's got a daddy."

A few of the other miners tease Margie, insisting that she goes below only to snag a rich coal-miner husband. She just laughs. It infuriated her to learn that a good many people in the area typecast all women coal miners as whores. "There's this man in town who is distantly related to Kirby's father. He's a religious fanatic, Church of God, and has a lot of seniority in the mines. Before I started working, I asked him if he'd speak up for me to help me get a job in one of the mines. He turned around and looked at me so cold he looked like the devil. Then he said to me, 'Any woman who goes to work in the coal mines ain't nothin' but a prostitute, and I ain't gonna get no whore a job.' I was crushed. A lot of women give me the cold shoulder because I'm a miner. They look down on me without knowing anything about me. They've just decided that if you are female working in a coal mine, all you are doing is looking for someone to lay up with."

Nothing could be further from the truth. "Goldilocks," as some of the miners call her, is just plain shy, never really cutting loose. Like the pet turtles Kirby keeps in the bathtub, Margie is still feeling out her new environment, only poking her head out of her shell occasionally. Her life has changed so quickly in the last three months that the protective walls she has built around herself will have to crumble gradually. "When I go to town now I can pass people I know and blow

the horn," she says excitedly. "Three months ago I didn't know a soul. Before I got this job, I never went out and socialized. Around here all social life is centered around taverns. I don't drink. Why would I want to be in a tavern? If a woman goes to a tavern by herself, everybody thinks she's there to be picked up. That's what keeps me away from places like that. I'm hardly a whore. I don't even flirt. I'm not saying I don't want to get married again. I do. Every woman thinks of that sometimes. There must be some wonderful things about marriage. I've never had the opportunity to experience them. If I ever decide to marry again, it will be to the right person, and it will be forever. I want a one-woman man. If it doesn't happen, I'm not going to worry about it, especially now when I know I can take care of the kids on my own. A coal mine is no place to fool around looking for a man. When you go below you take the chance of never seeing daylight again. It's a lot different than crossing the street and working in a restaurant. Anything can happen down there, but I made up my mind I wouldn't be scared. Coal mining means a future for me and the kids.

"I tell Geni she can do anything she wants to if she puts her mind to it and really works at it. There is nothing wrong with a woman doing man's work. It is nonsense to put up with the hard times just because you are a woman. I feel sorry for the women years ago who were led to believe that all they could do was stay home and raise babies.

"I hate women's activities like playing bunco and bingo and going to 'coffee clutches.' What a big waste of time. The only organization I belong to is the United Mine Workers Union. When a group of women get together, they are usually too catty for me. I hate gossip. I find most women hard to get along with. My children are my best friends, my buddies. As long as I have two kids, that's all I need. I'm a family-type person. I don't get involved in anything because I hate to feel obligated. I feel my place is at home whether I have a husband or not. I want all my free time to do spontaneous things with the kids. Maybe I'm just an overgrown kid myself."

Home for Margie and her kids is a neat, box-shaped house of no particular design on a quiet, tree-lined street. Margie rents the home from Troy's mother, Mary Irvin, who lives behind them across a long backyard, which the family treasures. The three bedroom, one-bath home is furnished simply, but comfortably. With pictures on the walls and flowers in vases, it is cheerful. An American flag hangs proudly in the hall, just inside the front door. Margie keeps the house neat and clean and covers the living room sofa and chair with blankets to make them last longer. The focal point of the living room is an antique wooden carousel horse that the owner of the carnival gave to Kirby when he was very young. Troy had it lovingly crafted into a huge family-size rocking horse. It is so well built that Margie, Kirby, and Geni can all climb aboard and rock into the night, which they often do. As in most homes, the hub of activity is the kitchen, especially on payday. Margie cashes her check into small bills, sits at the kitchen table with the serious expression of a banker, curlers in her hair, and divides the money into neat little piles. One stack goes for rent, another for electricity, another for the telephone, and so on. A good portion of it goes straight back to the bank in a savings account, but Margie derives a certain pleasure from see-

Margie and her children Kirby and Geni play Frisbee in the front yard of their rented home in Benton, Illinois. Margie spends almost all of her free time with her children. As she puts it, "I know what it is like to be left alone and ignored as a kid. I don't want it to be that way in my family."

ing it all lying there, however briefly.

"By God, if you don't have a little money, you can't make it," she says, stacking money. "I just made up my mind that the only way I was going to have it is to work for it and earn it. That way no one can take it away from me. Everything looks better to me now. For once I can change my life. I don't

Margie
Cunha
Irvin

235

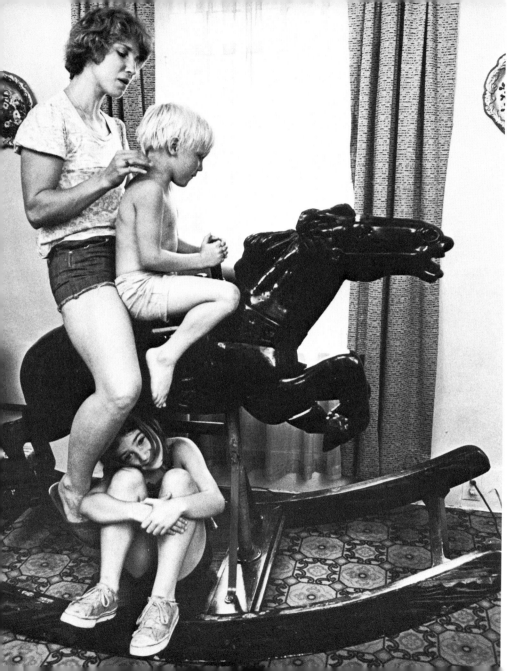

have to worry and wait for it to change by itself. I can sit at the kitchen table and count money for the first time in my life and pile up a little to save. I'd like to take the kids on a trip to see different things. I'd love to travel and look at natural things in life like trees, birds, and flowers. The lean years taught me to get a lot of enjoyment from the smallest things. It may sound old-fashioned, but I like little things like sunshine, squirrels, and baby ducks. There is honestly nothing I'd rather do than be home with the kids. We don't have to blow a lot of money to have fun. I can be perfectly content in my own backyard."

Margie and her children are inseparable. She's usually down on the ground with them, laughing and playing. At times it is hard to distinguish parent from child. When they go to the park, Margie climbs the jungle gyms right along with the kids. She pushes them on the swing, then they push her. Even when they cut the grass, all three push the lawnmower together. "I love the good times with Geni and Kirby, even if we are only in the yard. If I spend time with them now, I think they'll come back to see me when they grow up. I never want anything to change our close relationship. I'd like my kids to always be around me, but wherever their lives take them, I wish them happiness. I don't want them to have hard times like I did."

Margie is a great animal lover. She keeps a pen of ducks in her backyard near the vegetable garden she slaves over. Margie and the kids fill a wading pool with water and give the ducks

When Margie and Troy Irvin's son Kirby was born, their boss at the carnival gave Kirby this antique rocking horse.

a swim nearly every warm day. Margie often picks up one of the ducks and hugs it, rubbing her face against its soft, downy head. At those moments her fragility shows and the tough, muscular coal miner disappears.

Ducks are only one of a variety of animals Margie and the kids raise. "Last year Troy's nephew cut down a tree without realizing there was a squirrel's nest in it. Troy brought me three homeless baby squirrels. I had to get up in the middle of the night to warm canned milk and feed them with an eyedropper. They thought I was their mother. As they grew up, they followed me around the house like baby puppy dogs. I gave them the run of the house because it is only natural that squirrels should run. I'm sorry I didn't bring a tree in. It would have been more natural. I looked like a tree most of the time with those squirrels hanging on me. Their nails were so sharp it really hurt me when they climbed me, but I loved them so. They really got to be good pets, and smart. They figured out that the closet was the best place to store the nuts and sunflower seeds I gave them. They'd 'bury' them in the pockets of my clothes. Only bad thing about it was when they wanted a nut, they'd just bite through the pocket to get it. Whenever I'd get dressed to go somewhere I'd discover a shirt with a big hole in it. We took the squirrels to Chicago with us when we went to the carnival. I gave one away, then another got loose, but we brought Chippy back. She'd wake me up every morning by climbing in my bed and rubbing my nose. One day she went out to play and we never saw her again. I hope she's still playing. When I see a

Margie climbs the playground equipment with her son Kirby.

Margie and her children are so inseparable, they even mow the grass together.

squirrel I stop the car and call, hoping it may be Chippy. I miss her and I wish she'd come back home."

Down 810 feet below there's a tough little belt shoveler who loves squirrels, sunshine, baby ducks, turtles in the bathtub, and Humphrey Bogart movies. Many of the male miners seem to sense something different about Margie. They are more protective of her than they are of the other women. Though they tease her unmercifully, they rarely treat her as a sex object. The resentment they feel toward most women miners for

taking a man's job doesn't seem to extend to Margie. Perhaps it is because she works so hard.

"One night the boss took me to a concrete block wall three cross-cuts down, handed me a sledgehammer, and said, 'Knock that wall down.' I kind of looked at him funny and asked if it was all right if I went back to where I was working and put on my gloves. I picked up that sledgehammer and had to swing it all the way around in a circle to get enough power. They were solid concrete blocks, not the hollow kind, and he gave me the heaviest sledgehammer they had. I knocked down quite a bit of the wall before he and another miner helped me finish the job. I think they were testing me. I heard later that the other girls refused to try. I suppose they figured I'd chicken out, too.

"I made up my mind when I got the job that I'd work like a man if I could, without complaints. If I couldn't do the work, I'd back off and quit. I never want those guys to think they have to carry my load. I think they respect me for trying. As long as you do the work, the guys will treat you as one of them. They won't give you any trouble. Some of the miners feel a woman doesn't belong below, but they don't resent me. They treat me equally. The job is there. It's hard work, but if you are hired, it is what you have to do. I just rub my stiff hands with Mentholatum and go on. Aching muscles and stiff knuckles will never make me quit, not when I have the opportunity to really do something with my life.

"When I first started, I helped build a wall three concrete blocks thick to seal off a worked-out area of the mine. The blocks weigh forty-five pounds apiece and I had to carry them about a quarter of a mile to where I was working. The roof was so low in one area that I had to bend over and hug the block, then cock my head to get low enough. That's sort of uncomfortable! The eighty-pound masonry sacks were four or five cross-cuts down on the other side of a steel door. There was so much air pressure when I bent down and opened the door that my hard hat blew right off my head. I doubted if I could carry an eighty-pound sack fighting all that air pressure, but I didn't want the guys to do all the work. I asked them to lift the sacks onto my shoulder. I probably carried them about a half block through the mud and water before I had to let them down. I was pushing myself and hurting but I managed to get three of those sacks down there, stopping every ten minutes for a break. It's a good thing they didn't need the cement right away because it took me forever."

Margie and the guys work well together. One night a team of ten of them, including Margie, ran 227 buggies of coal on their shift, setting a mine record. "The company is going to take us all out for a steak dinner and all the drinks we can drink. I'm going to have a good time. I don't go out very often."

The coal mine is rapidly giving Margie the family relationship she never had growing up. "I've got a lot of brothers down in the coal mine. They call me 'buddy' like all the others. I'm really a part of them. I've never had so many friends before. Someone is always there to look after you, to help you. We eat together in the dinner hole every night about 8 P.M.

Margie is a real country girl who loves animals and dreams of having a home on an acreage to raise them. Here she hugs one of the ducks she raises in the backyard.

Some miners object to having women below, but most miners, like this one, are like brothers to Margie, always ready to help.

It's like a picnic. Somebody will tell a joke and we'll all laugh. The older guys will tell me what it was like to work in the mines years ago. I swap them hard candy for stories. Our work isn't so serious that it keeps us from communicating. We talk about fishing, gardens, and crops. They've even taught me how to warm biscuits and gravy and soups on the battery of our man-trip as it charges."

The coal mine is full of rats, so the miners hang their aluminum dinner buckets on the roof where the rats can't get them. "Some of the rats are as big as cats, so when I come around the corner to the dinner hole I'm always armed with chunks of coal. When I see a rat, I'll try to hit him, or at least scare them so they'll scatter. Baby rats are so cute, though. They remind me of Chippy. Sometimes I feed one a bite of my sandwich and say, 'Ain't he cute?' The guys think I'm crazy.

"A lot of guys use snuff or chew tobacco down there because you aren't allowed to smoke. I can't see myself doing all that spittin'. They tease me and ask me if I want a chew. I say, 'Yeah, I'll take Doublemint.' That kind of teasing goes on all the time."

Sometimes the camaraderie goes too far. With miners packed into a cage like steers on a livestock trailer, anything can happen. One night on the way down to the mine someone goosed Margie. She turned around quickly, swung her dinner pail in a circle and yelled, "God damn you!" in quiet good taste. "It made an impression. They all backed off with eyes as big as saucers. I guess they expected me to stand there quietly and take it. I don't mind them poking me in the ribs, pulling on my hat, or jerking my light cord, but I won't be manhandled. I think they thought I was going to clobber them all. It didn't happen no more . . . until the next night on the cage. This time there were only a few and I saw which one did it and kicked him with my steel-toed boot just as hard as I could. Then I felt bad because I knew I hurt him. Another one tried it. I grabbed him by the jaw and cussed him I was so mad. Now they all say, 'Stay away from Margie, she'll hit ya, she'll hurt ya.' They never bothered me again."

Shortly Margie will be a "green-hat" miner, classified to

run a buggy or assist in running the power equipment. After a year of work below and passing the state oral exam, she'll be a full-fledged "white-hat" papered miner with the ability to bid on any job that opens up in the mine. "When I get my papers, I don't want to just sit and run a machine. I'm not a sitter. If I'm going to sit, I'd rather do it in my own backyard. I came here to work. I might like to be a roof-bolter, driving shafts every four feet into the roof behind the continuous miner. So the roof cracks and pops a little at the face. So what? I don't mind the dirt and danger because I have a job now. There was a lot more danger to me mentally and physically before, sitting around the house worrying. Sure, the roof might fall in on me. Chances are it won't. Going crazy is worse. I put one up against the other and say the hell with it.

"My dream is to build my own country home and have a little bit of land around it that I can farm. It would be a brick home with a fireplace and a big basement that we can use as a family room. I like to plant things and go out every day and watch them grow. I'd like to wake up in the morning and hear birds singing. It would be a good feeling, really peaceful. I'm not going to be able to do a whole lot with my life, but I'm more content now. I know working in the mine will pay off. Now I have a future. Before it was only a dream.

"When I'm old and sitting in a rocking chair, I won't have to worry. I'll have a miner's pension. I hope not the black lung!"

Margie's job as a coal miner is helping her make friends and feel good about herself again.

As 1976 progressed, Margie's life improved almost on a weekly basis. "My job in the coal mines was a big turnaround for my life, the beginning of the good times," says Margie, now thirty-eight. Her voice is lilting and upbeat now, completely free of the tension and insecurity that once crept into every sentence. She became a full-time "white-hat" miner right on schedule. "Although I was qualified to do many things in the mine, I returned to my first job as belt shoveler, the job nobody else wanted, just to get on the day shift so I could live a more normal life with the kids. Then I went to school so I could be qualified for better jobs in the mine and did real well. I was running all kinds of machinery, even the continuous miner when someone was out sick. I never had a miner of my own, and I'm glad of that. In my section, we were pulling out pillars. It's pretty dangerous up there in front. I ended up in a newer part of the mine where they were replacing old equipment with much better machines. I did a lot of demonstrating that equipment for companies like General Dynamics."

By 1977, Margie was fulfilling her dreams one by one. That was the year she married Troy Irvin, Kirby's father, the only man she ever loved. "We are a very happy, close family, just as I hoped we'd be," Margie says. "In 1977, I also bought my dream home outside Benton in the country. I call it my farm, though it was only three acres. I had a big garden plus goats, chickens, cows, and my own horse."

Even dreams have a few rough spots. Over the years there were times when Margie became impatient with coal mining.

"The coalfields are always troubled, especially at contract time when we always miss a lot of work. I worked every day the mines were open, but we had strikes and walkouts for a lot of dumb reasons. One time two miners were fired for sleeping on the job, so everyone went home in protest. I wish I didn't have to miss work for the things that other people do."

During the early years of their marriage, Margie saw very little of Troy. "He was on the road constantly, trying to launch his own mirror business, hustling his products. It was an idea he had after running concession stands at the carnival for years. He prints pictures of rock stars, popular animals like unicorns and Garfield the cat, and advertising promotions on mirrors that range in size from 2×2 inches to 20×20 inches. When he first started, he printed a simple black silhouette of Elvis Presley on a mirror. Now his work has five or six colors and looks like a photograph or poster printed on the face of a mirror. He sells his mirrors all over the country and Canada, mostly to carnivals, theme parks, and different fairs. Carnivals use various-size mirrors as prizes. It was a seasonal, part-time business that kept growing. People are going crazy over his mirrors. I'm proud of Troy. He started alone and worked hard. Now he's the president of a company with ninety-five employees and two buildings in St. Charles, Illinois. It's still a seasonal business, but that's changing, too. He is making mirrors for Keebler, the huge baking company in Chicago, and Harley-Davidson, the motorcycle company. As more companies like that want him to make mirrors for them to sell or use as promotions, his business will keep growing.

"I'm a lady of leisure now, a fishing lady. I've worked hard, and it is good to know I can do hard work, but it is awfully nice not to have to work anymore. I quit being a coal miner in 1981, after five and a half years in the mines. I enjoyed coal mining, especially in the early years, but it got old. I could feel myself thinking that coal mining can't be all there is for the rest of my life. I didn't want to be down there forever. About that time, the mines near Benton started laying off, then closing down. I guess western coal was too much competition for them. They said they couldn't sell their coal anymore. I held my job up to the end when Orient 3 closed. We had no idea the mine would shut down. We heard rumors, but we never paid much attention to them. It was a shock. Fortunately, Troy's business was going well by then. I feel sorry for my friends who had no other income but coal mining. They are really hurting. With most mines out of business and the farmers in trouble, many businesses in Benton have closed. People had to go elsewhere.

"We sold our farm and moved to the Florida Keys, near Key West. We used to vacation here almost every Christmas holiday when the kids were out of school. We love the warm weather and decided we want to stay here. We sit down here and listen to weather forecasts of cold, snowy midwestern winters and are glad we're not in them. I'll never have to drive icy expressways again. We have a big Boston Whaler fishing boat with twin engines. We all love to fish, explore the islands around here, dive, and snorkel. Troy's business is still seasonal enough that he can spend most of the winter here relaxing with us. He has a very dependable business manager in Illinois. He goes back there in April, and I join him when Kirby gets out of school. I work in Troy's business during the peak season answering the phone and taking orders. We have a small apartment there near the plant. I enjoy being back in Illinois in the summers when the tomatoes are ripe. There's nothing better than a southern Illinois tomato. I made a lot of friends in Benton in those five and a half years I worked in the mines. I enjoy visiting them. I see my brothers and sisters now, too, at least twice during summer. We all get together on the Fourth of July and Labor Day. They've all done pretty well. After they got married and out on their own, their lives started improving. One of my nieces and a couple of my nephews work for Troy in the summer.

"I miss the farm and having a big backyard. We live on a reef. You can't dig a hole and plant a plant like you do in Illinois black dirt. But I love life here on the Keys. It is beautiful. It's the kind of place you visit once and always want to come back. It's great to spend time together being a family again. Somehow, I knew we'd always stay close. Geni is nineteen now and lives right across the street from us. She finished high school and married a local boy, a "conch." They call the natives around here conches after the shell. He's an electrician who works with his contractor father building homes and hotels. They are already building their own home. I don't think she'll have hard times like I had. Kirby is a high-school sophomore and real good in school. He's fifteen and 5'10" and 165 pounds. He's interested in all kinds of things from water sports to Halley's Comet. We all go out on the boat and fish and dive together. Looks like we'll always stay close together as I had hoped. I don't think we'll ever move to the Chicago area.

Margie Cunha Irvin

243

"When I was very young I remember saying that I'd like to grow old on some island and sit in a rocking chair and drink cold Pepsi. About the only difference is that I drink mostly iced tea. It's almost as nice. I'm enjoying it. Coal mining was good to me, but I don't miss it. When I was making good money at the mines, I helped Troy establish his business. Now that he's built himself up to a higher platform in life, I don't have to work and he can take it easier and let other people in his company run some things. I never complain. I have no problems. The kids and I and Troy are together now and I can't see us ever being away from each other for very long. We're just too close a family. We have so much fun working and playing together and enjoying things. When you can see things happening the best for everyone, it's great."

Enduring Women was composed into type on a Compugraphic digital phototypesetter in eleven-point Goudy Old Style with two-point spacing between the lines. Obliqued University Roman was selected for display. The book was designed by Jim Billingsley, typeset by Metricomp, Inc., printed offset by Thomson-Shore, Inc., and bound by John H. Dekker & Sons. The paper on which the book is printed bears acid-free characteristics for an effective life of at least three hundred years.

TEXAS A&M UNIVERSITY PRESS : COLLEGE STATION